THE MORONIC INFERNO
And Other Visits to America

THE MORONIC INFERNO
And Other Visits to America

MARTIN AMIS

VIKING

VIKING
Viking Penguin Inc.
40 West 23rd Street
New York, New York 10010, U.S.A.

First American Edition
Published in 1987

The essays in this collection first appeared, some in different form,
in the *London Review of Books*, *The Observer*, *The Tatler*,
New Statesman, *Vanity Fair*, and *Sunday Telegraph*.

LIBRARY OF CONGRESS CATALOGING IN PUBLICATION DATA
Amis, Martin.
The moronic inferno.
1. United States—Social life and customs—
1971–   . I. Title.
E169.02.A663   1987   973.92   86-40229
ISBN 0-670-81432-6

Printed in the United States of America by
R. R. Donnelley & Sons Company, Harrisonburg, Virginia
Set in Sabon

*To Christopher, Eleni
and Alexander*

Contents

Introduction and Acknowledgments

On a couple of occasions I have been asked to write a book about America; and I must have spent at least four or five minutes contemplating this monstrous enterprise. America is more like a world than a country: you could as well write a book about people, or about life. Then, years later, as I was up-ending my desk drawers to prepare a selection of occasional journalism (and this book is offered with all generic humility), I found that I had already written a book about America – unpremeditated, accidental, and in instalments. Of the hundreds of thousands of words I seem to have written for newspapers and magazines in the last fifteen years, about half of them seem to be about America. I hope these disparate pieces add up to something. I know you can approach America only if you come at her from at least a dozen different directions.

The academic year 1959–60 I spent as a ten-year-old resident of Princeton, New Jersey. I was the only boy in the school – the only male in the entire city – who wore shorts. Soon I had long trousers, a crew cut, and a bike with fat whitewalls and an electric horn. I ate Thanksgiving turkey. I wore a horrible mask on Hallowe'en. America excited and frightened me, and has continued to do so. Since that time I have spent at least another year there, on assignment. My mother lived in America for years, and many of my expatriate friends live in America now. My wife is American. Our infant son is half-American. I feel fractionally American myself.

Oh, no doubt I should have worked harder, made the book more representative, more systematic, et cetera. It remains, however, a collection of peripatetic journalism, and includes pieces where the travel is only mental. I have added links and postscripts; I have wedged pieces together; I have rewritten bits that were too obviously wrong, careless or bad. I should have worked harder, but it was quite hard work getting all this stuff together (photocopying back numbers of journals can be a real struggle, what with the weight of the bound volumes and that Xerox flap tangling you up and getting in the way). And it was hard work writing it all in the first place. Journalists have two ways of expending energy: in preparation and in performance. Some exhaust themselves in securing the right contacts, the intimate audits, the disclosures. I am no good at any of that. I skimp it, and so everything has to happen on the typewriter. I find journalism only marginally easier than fiction, and book-reviewing slightly harder. The thousand-word book review seems to me far more clearly an art form (however minor) than any of the excursions of the New Journalism, some of which are as long as *Middlemarch*.

All these pieces were written left-handed. They were written, that is to say, not for my own satisfaction but for particular editors of particular journals at particular times and at particular lengths. The hack and the whore have much in common: late nights, venal gregariousness, social drinking, a desire to please, simulated live-liness, dissimulated exhaustion – you keep on having to do it when you don't feel like it. (Perhaps this bond accounts for the hypocriti-cal burnish of the vice-entrapment story, where in the end the reporter always makes his excuses and staggers off nobly into the night.) Insidious but necessary is the whorish knack a journalist must develop of suiting his pitch to the particular client. Luckily it all seems to be done subliminally. You write like this for the *London Review of Books*, and you write like that for the *Sunday Telegraph Magazine*. You can swear here but you can't swear there. (I have greatly enjoyed debowdlerising these pieces – and restoring cuts, some of which, as in the Brian De Palma profile, approached about 80 per cent of the whole.) The novelist has a very firm conception of the Ideal Reader. It is himself, though strangely altered – older, perhaps, or younger. With journalism the entire transaction is much woollier: every stage in the experience seems to involve a lot of people.

I got the phrase 'the moronic inferno', and much else, from Saul Bellow, who informs me that *he* got it from Wyndham Lewis. Needless to say, the moronic inferno is not a peculiarly American condition. It is global and perhaps eternal. It is also, of course, primarily a metaphor, a metaphor for human infamy: mass, gross, ever-distracting human infamy. One of the many things I do not understand about Americans is this: what is it like to be a citizen of a superpower, to maintain democratically the means of planetary extinction? I wonder how this contributes to the dreamlife of America, a dreamlife that is so deep and troubled. As I was collating *The Moronic Inferno* (in August 1985, during the Hiroshima remembrances), I was struck by a disquieting thought. Perhaps the title phrase is more resonant, and more prescient, than I imagined. It exactly describes a possible future, one in which the moronic inferno will cease to be a metaphor and will become a reality: the only reality.

I am particularly grateful to the *Observer,* under whose auspices, in effect, this book was written; I am also indebted to the *New Statesman*, the *Sunday Telegraph Magazine*, the *London Review of Books, Tatler* and *Vanity Fair*. Throughout I have been exceptionally lucky in my editors and colleagues, and here salute them, in roughly chronological order: Terence Kilmartin, Arthur Crook, John Gross, Claire Tomalin, Anthony Howard, Julian Barnes, Deirdre Lyndon, Donald Trelford, Miriam Gross, Trevor Grove, Karl Miller and Tina Brown. Special thanks are due also to Ian Hamilton and to Clöe Peploe.

THE MORONIC INFERNO
And Other Visits to America

The Moronic Inferno

Iggy Blaikie, Kayo Obermark, Sam Zincowicz, Kotzie Kreindl, Clara Spohr, Teodoro Valdepenas, Clem Tambow, Rinaldo Cantabile, Tennie Pontritter, Lucas Asphalter, Murphy Verviger, Wharton Horricker ... The way a writer names his characters provides a good index to the way he sees the world — to his reality-level, his responsiveness to the accidental humour and freakish poetry of life. Thomas Pynchon uses names like Oedipa Maas and Pig Bodine (where the effect is slangy, jivey, cartoonish); at the other end of the scale, John Braine offers us Tom Metfield, Jack Royston, Jane Framsby (can these people really exist, in our minds or anywhere else, with such leadenly humdrum, such dead names?). Saul Bellow's inventions are Dickensian in their resonance and relish. But they also have a dialectical point to make.

British critics tend to regard the American predilection for Big Novels as a vulgar neurosis — like the American predilection for big cars or big hamburgers. Oh God, we think: here comes another sweating, free-dreaming maniac with another thousand-pager; here comes another Big Mac. First, Dos Passos produced the Great American Novel; now they all want one. Yet in a sense every ambitious American novelist is genuinely trying to write a novel called USA. Perhaps this isn't just a foible; perhaps it is an inescapable response to America — twentieth-century America, racially mixed and mobile, twenty-four hour, endless, extreme, superabundantly various. American novels are big all right, but partly because America is big too.

You need plenty of nerve, ink and energy to do justice to the place, and no one has made greater efforts than Saul Bellow. His latest novel, *The Dean's December*, has caused some puzzlement in its country of origin, and one can see why. Far more sombre and less exuberant than its major predecessors, it has every appearance of being an 'engaged' novel, a mature novel, a statement, a warning; Bellow himself has gone on record, perhaps incautiously, as stressing the difficulty people will have in 'shrugging this one off'. In 1976 Bellow was awarded the Nobel Prize for Literature, praised by the Swedes 'for human understanding and subtle analysis of contemporary culture'. T.S. Eliot said that the Nobel was like an invitation to one's own funeral: no beneficiary of the prize had ever gone on to write anything good. It may be coincidence (as opposed to an onset of Delphic delusion), but Bellow's first post-Nobel novel transmits all the strenuousness of a juggernaut changing gear. The vision has widened but also become narrower; most noticeably, the fluid musicality of Bellow's epics — the laughter, the didactic generosity, the beguiling switches of register — has disciplined itself, in the interests of literary *form*. This, it seems to me, is what Late Bellow is going to be like. It is all very interesting.

If we take an introductory glance through the dramatis personae of the new book, we see the usual rhythmical clinches but also sense that Bellow is playing in a minor key, and using the mute. There are various judges, shysters and ambulance-chasers with names like Ellis Sorokin, Wolf Quitman and Maxie Detillion (these hardly rival the three divorce lawyers in *Humboldt's Gift*, who are called Tomchek, Pinsker and Srole); there is a rock-hard black whore called Riggie Hines, and a suave black rapist called Spofford Mitchell; there is an ageing athlete called Silky Limpopo, a prison-reformer called Rufus Ridpath, a world-famous journalist called Dewey Spangler . . . That last name looks a bit artful and specific for a Bellow character, and perhaps this provides a more general clue to the novel's intentions. A pivotal figure in the book, Dewey Spangler is somewhere between Walter Lippmann and André Malraux, a flashy trader in geopolitical generalities and global diagnoses. 'Dewey', of course, is America's great philosopher, its star-spangled thinker; and 'Spangler', I suspect, has something to do with the decline of the West.

The Dean's December is spent in Bucharest, 6,000 miles from home. The Dean is Albert Corde, ex-journalist, ex-womaniser, ex-trivialiser (he is also a Gentile — surprising for such an obvious and detailed Bellow surrogate). Home is Chicago. The year is uncertain: there are mentions of Carter, Margaret Thatcher, but also of Entebbe, Cambodia. The Dean has come to Bucharest with his Rumanian wife, Minna, a distinguished astronomer. Minna's mother, Valeria, is dying. 'Corde had come to give support.' He is consciously testing his reserves as a good husband, exhaustively considerate and correct. He is a reformed character, proving his seriousness. In a way, this is what the novel is doing too. It is a necessary connection. 'I was then becoming careless about time,' says Charlie Citrine in *Humboldt's Gift*, 'a symptom of my increasing absorption in larger issues.' Such a crack would be unthinkable in *The Dean's December*. There has been a moral tightening. No more gadabouts like the unpunctual Citrine. You have to get life right before you start going on about its meaning.

Old Valeria, one-time Minister of Health, is in an ambiguous position *vis-à-vis* the Party, and Minna herself is a defector. The powers that be being what they are, Mr and Mrs Corde are given a hard time as they brace themselves for their bereavement. And 'the city was terrible!' says Corde, helplessly, in a bracketed aside. 'Aged women rose at four to stand in line for a few eggs'; the queues have 'an atmosphere of compulsory exercise in the prison yard'. But this is not crudely emphasised. Bucharest is summoned in terms of peeling stucco, bad food and bad light. 'Air-sadness, Corde called this. In the final stages of dusk, a brown sediment seemed to encircle the lamps. Then there was a livid death moment. Night began. Night was very difficult here, thought Albert Corde.'

There is not much Corde can do in Bucharest. He attends to his wife's grief, and to the stiff cousins who glide in their bad clothes through the antique apartment. He sits in his wife's childhood room. He goes to bed after breakfast. 'As he did this, he sometimes felt how long he had lived and how many, many times the naked creature had crept into its bedding.' For the Bellow hero, however, solitude always opens the way to the gregariousness of memory — to the inner riot of the past. In *Herzog*, Herzog relives a marriage while putting on his tie. In *Humboldt*, Citrine reviews a literary career while meditating on his sofa. Albert Corde has his own 'restless ecstasy' to contend with: but the Dean's December, like *The Dean's December*, is caught up in more public matters.

Corde's troubles emerge slowly, piecemeal. *Humboldt*'s Citrine came out of his Chicago apartment block one morning to find that his Mercedes had been beaten up with baseball bats: 'Now the moronic inferno had caught up with me.' The phrase recurs here:

but this time we are closer in, much nearer the first circle. As college dean, Corde is involved in an investigation into the murder of one of his students. It happened during a torrid Chicago night: 'one of those choking, peak-of-summer, urban-nightmare, sexual and obscene, running-bare times, and death panting behind the young man, closing in'. On the night of his murder, the student 'had been out for dirty sex, and it was this dirty sex momentum that had carried him through the window'.

The Dean's involvement with the moronic inferno has another dimension. Recently Corde published two long articles in *Harper's* – articles about Chicago, 'the contempt centre of the USA'. (One reflects that Bellow has been very lucky with his home town: a great city, vast, bloody, hugely mercantile, and not trodden flat by writers.) In these pieces Corde submitted to an atrocious anger: 'he gave up his cover, ran out, swung wild at everyone'. The articles examine Chicago's 'underclass', the disposable populations of the criminal poor. Born into slums, jails and hospitals, the Morlock sub-race is permitted – even expected – to destroy itself with violence, lead-poisoning and junk. In Bucharest, with its 'strict zero-blue and simple ice', 'the trees made their tree gestures, but human beings were faced by the organised prevention of everything that came natural'. Chicago is repeatedly described as a jungle populated exclusively by rats. In Bucharest, the city rodents have been 'rolled flat by trucks and cars'; they are 'as two-dimensional as weather vanes', just like everything else. In Bucharest, a communist dog barks in the street, 'a protest against the limits of dog experience (for God's sake, open the universe a little more!)'. In Chicago, a capitalist Great Dane wallows at his own birthday party, showered with 'ribboned presents' and 'congratulatory telegrams': 'the animal came nudging and sighing. What to do with all this animal nature, seemed to be the burden of the dog's groans.'

The Rumanian ordeal continues. During the frigid Christmas, Corde and Minna preside over Valeria's obsequies. Tottering relatives in fake fur coats join the Cordes at the suburban crematorium. Feeling himself 'crawling between heaven and earth', Corde descends from the fiery crematorium into the deep-frozen crypt, 'the extremes of heat and cold splitting him like an ax'. It is a memorable scene, conspicuously intense, the emotional crisis of the book. And here, the slowly solidifying 'thesis novel' – so carefully and subtly arrived at – is abandoned, rejected, put aside. *The Dean's*

December ceases its inspection of East and West, the vying perversions of humanity, and goes on to bigger things.

The heroes of Saul Bellow's major novels are intellectuals; they are also (if you follow me) heroes, which makes Bellow doubly remarkable. In thumbnail terms, the original protagonists of literature were gods; later, they were demigods; later still, they were kings, generals, fabulous lovers, at once superhuman, human and all too human; eventually they turned into ordinary people. The twentieth century has been called an ironic age, as opposed to a heroic, tragic or romantic one; even realism, rock-bottom realism, is felt to be a bit grand for the twentieth century. Nowadays, our protagonists are a good deal lower down the human scale than their creators: they are anti-heroes, non-heroes, sub-heroes.

Not so with Bellow. His heroes are well tricked out with faults, neuroses, spots of commonness: but not a jot of Bellow's intellectuality is withheld from their meditations. They represent the author at the full pitch of cerebral endeavour, with the simple proviso that they are themselves non-creative − they are thinkers, teachers, *readers*. This careful positioning allows Bellow to write in a style fit for heroes: the High Style. To evolve an exalted voice appropriate to the twentieth century has been the self-imposed challenge of his work. It began with *The Adventures of Augie March* (1953), at times very shakily: for all its marvels, *Augie March*, like *Henderson the Rain King*, often resembles a lecture on destiny fed through a thesaurus of low-life patois. *Herzog* erred on the side of private gloom, *Humboldt* on the side of sunny ebullience (with stupendous but lopsided gains for the reader). *Mr Sammler's Planet* (1970) came nearest to finding the perfect pitch, and it is the Bellow novel which *The Dean's December* most clearly echoes.

The High Style is not a high style just for the hell of it: there are responsibilities involved. The High Style attempts to speak for the whole of mankind, with suasion, to remind us of what we once knew and have since forgotten or stopped trying to regrasp. 'It was especially important', Corde reflects, 'to think what a human being really was. What wise contemporaries had to say about this amounted to very little.' The Bellow hero lays himself open to the world, at considerable psychological cost. Mr Sammler is 'a delicate recording instrument'; Herzog is 'a prisoner of perception, a compulsory witness'. All that can be done with these perceptions, these data, is to transform them into − into what? Humboldt suffered from 'the longing for passionate speech'. Corde, like Sammler, aches to deliver his 'inspired recitation'. It is the desire to speak, to warn – to *move*, above all.

Albert Corde is 'an image man', 'a hungry observer'. He has a 'radar-dish face', for ever picking up signals 'from all over the universe'.

> He looked out, noticing. What a man he was for noticing! Continually attentive to his surroundings. As if he had been sent down to *mind* the outer world, on a mission of observation and notation. The object of which was? To link up? To classify? To penetrate?

Corde has 'the restless ecstasy' common to Bellow's heroes – a global version of Henderson's *I want, I want, I want.* He suffers from 'vividness fits', 'storms of convulsive clear consciousness', 'objectivity intoxicated'. And

> it wasn't just two, three, five chosen deaths being painted thickly, terribly, convulsively inside him, all over his guts, liver, heart . . . but a large picture of cities, crowds, peoples, an apocalypse . . .

Up to now the Bellow hero has always kept these convulsions to himself. They provide the substance of his meditations and, at most, they give the spur to some climactic effort of passionate utterance – to a friend, a girl, anyone who will listen. But Corde, like the book built round him, has gone public. The key to his self-exposure, and self-injury, is his journalistic outpouring on Chicago, which might almost be seen as a pre-emptive strike for the novel itself. Corde's articles are reckless, irresponsible: but their main presumption, as Dewey Spangler gloatingly points out, is that they are full of 'poetry'. They constitute an act of romantic regression and are an embarrassment to everyone, Corde included.

An old childhood pal, Spangler is 'just another VIP' (in his own words) passing through Bucharest in a 'sweep' across Eastern Europe. Like Dr Temkin in *Seize the Day*, or Allbee in *The Victim*, Spangler is a malevolent *alter ego*, a traveller on a parallel path, the wrong path. He lives in 'a kind of event-glamour', unaware that

> the increase of theories and discourse, itself a cause of new strange forms of blindness, the false representations of 'communication', led to horrible distortions of public consciousness. Therefore the

first act of morality was to disinter the reality, retrieve reality, dig it out from the trash, represent it anew as art would represent it.

The alternative to the East is not the West; the alternative to the West is not the East. The alternative to both is the unobtainable world glimpsed through art, the 'pangs of higher intuition' which balance 'the muddy suck of the grave underfoot'.

So matters have long stood in Bellow's topology. According, however, to *The Dean's December* (and the title is not autumnal so much as candidly wintry), a great and uncovenanted unification is at hand. Seeing the first marks of old age on an ex-lover's face, Herzog identified 'death, the artist, very slow'. But if death has always been an artist, he is now an ideas-man too, a formidable illuminator. Mr Sammler, in his lucid ripeness, felt the 'luxury of non-intimidation by doom' and was free to make 'sober, decent terms with death'. With the Dean it is more a case of creative collaboration, of ecstatic symbiosis. In an extraordinary paragraph Corde looks down at the Chicago lakescape through the guardrails of his sixteenth-storey balcony:

> It was like being poured out to the horizon, like a great expansion. What if death should be like this, the soul finding an exit. The porch rail was his figure for the hither side. The rest, beyond it, drew you constantly as the completion of your reality.

La Rochefoucauld said that neither 'the sun nor death can be looked at with a steady eye'. Maybe this is Bellow's last assignment — the eye narrowed, as it must be, by the strictest, the most precise artistry.

Saul Bellow has always been an energetic recycler of his own experience, and *The Dean's December* shows signs of the flattened, chastened, almost puritanical mood which waylays the traveller to a stricken country. 'They set the pain level for you over here,' as Corde remarks. Some readers may regard the result as a top-heavy novel, with too much instruction, and not enough delight. But there are many, many thrilling pages here. Reading Bellow at his most inspired, you are reminded of a scene in *Augie March*, when Augie, down on his luck in a small Mexican town, sees Trotsky alight from his car in the cathedral square:

> what it was about him that stirred me was the instant impression he gave — no matter about the old heap he rode in or the peculiarity of his retinue — of navigation by the great stars, of the

highest considerations, of being fit to speak the most important human words and universal terms. When you are as reduced to a different kind of navigation from this high starry kind as I was and are only sculling on the shallow bay, crawling from one clam-rake to the next, it's stirring to have a glimpse of deep-water greatness. And, even more than an established, an exiled greatness, because the exile was a sign to me of persistence at the highest things.

*   *   *

The Dean's December promised the arrival of a fresh inspiration in Bellow's work, and this stirring collection, *Him With His Foot In His Mouth*, confirms that it is here to stay. Without tempting providence too much, I think we can agree to call the new phase Late Bellow. It has to do with last things, leave-taking, and final lucidities.

Late Bellow expresses itself through the familiar opposition: a rich, generously comic and fanatically detailed record of the human experience and habitat, set against a wayward dreaminess or mooniness, an intoxicated receptivity to ideas – Bellow's own poetry of meditation. None of these delights is withheld, but there are now two changes of emphasis. First, a more formal artistry, with sharper focus, a keener sense of pattern and balance. And secondly a countervailing ferocity in his apprehension of the peculiar disorders and distortions of the modern era. 'I don't know what the world's coming to' may not sound like much of a topic-sentence when you hear it at the bus-stop – yet this is Bellow's subject. Actually it is the central subject, and always has been.

While he concedes that America is now ruled by drunkards, liars and venal illiterates, Bellow decides that the most vivid symptoms of distemper can be found a little closer to home. On the lake-front, shrubs are razed and sentry-box toilets are installed, to thwart rapists. In a snow-bound airport a woman asks an official for directions, and, instead of being merely rude or unhelpful, he stamps her instep with his heel. City cops moonlight for the Mob as hired executioners. Meanwhile, 'We Care' stickers are gummed to the walls of supermarkets and loan corporations. Meanwhile, a woman consults a lawyer to ask whether she should describe herself as a person of 'high integrity' or 'known integrity' as she prepares to swindle a medical school. Meanwhile, 'a good American makes propaganda for whatever existence has forced him to become'.

These are stories about Chicago (new and old Chicago) and about families. They shore up one's impression that Bellow's greatness has always been endorsed by two lucky accidents – and this is to belittle neither the strenuousness of his discipline nor the luck of literary talent itself. First, Chicago. When Chicagoans call their home town 'the city that works' they have more in mind than efficiency and high employment, bustle and brawn. They mean that they have accepted money as the only 'vital substance'; and they regard the ubiquitous corruption that results from this as a sincere definition of maturity: 'If you're so smart, how come you ain't rich?' Such distortions, which include an aggressive, even a disgusted philistinism, provide the writer with a wonderfully graphic reversal of human values. Arriving in Chicago in 1924 (from St Petersburg via Montreal), Bellow was uniquely well placed to witness the formation and summation of the American idea – and to stay outside it, in his writer's capsule.

Bellow's second slice of congenital good fortune lies in his Jewishness, which, along with much else, provides him with an unusual tenderness for the human ties of race and blood: 'Jewish consanguinity – a special phenomenon, an archaism of which the Jews, until the present century stopped them, were in the course of divesting themselves.' In the same story Bellow's narrator asks why the Jews have always been such energetic anthropologists, virtually the founders of the science (Durkheim, Lévy-Bruhl, Mauss, Boas, *et al.*). Was it that they were 'demystifiers', their ultimate aim to 'increase universalism'? The narrator demurs. 'A truer explanation is the nearness of the ghettos to the sphere of Revelation, an easy move for the mind from rotting streets and rancid dishes, a direct ascent into transcendence.'

This describes Bellow's origins as a writer, and perhaps accounts also for the strong vein of (heterodox) transcendentalism in his work. In the middle-period novels the transcendental 'alternative' takes on structural status, affording a radiant backdrop against which the protagonists shuffle and blunder. The primitive princeliness of Africa in *Henderson the Rain King*, the Wellsian dreams of lunar escape in *Mr Sammler's Planet*, the 'invisible sciences' of *Humboldt's Gift*: these are respectively ranged against the nullity of

New England, the hysteria of New York, and the gangsterism — both emotional and actual — of Chicago.

The emphasis on these illusory otherworlds was probably too heavy, laying Bellow open to charges of crankery and self-indulgence. In Late Bellow, however, the transcendentalism has found its true function, which is Yeatsian — a source of metaphor, a system of imagery that gives the reader an enduring mortal pang, a sense of his situation in larger orders of time and space. 'What were we here for, of all strange beings and creatures the strangest?' Bellow has made the real world realer (sharper, harsher), and has confronted its perversities; but human destiny still 'depends on what you think, feel and will about such manifestations or apparitions, on the kabbalistic skill you develop in the interpretation of these contemporary formations'. He keeps a soul's watch upon the world, as passionate as ever and yet disinterested now, with no stake in the outcome.

There aren't any weaklings in the new book: each story has the same consistency of brilliance and vigour. (One of them, 'What Kind of Day Did You Have?', is longer, and better, than *Seize the Day*.) In the title story an old man languishes in British Columbia, facing extradition to Chicago, a fall-guy for various financial crimes committed by his family. *His* only sin has been his spontaneity, whereas the sins of his adversaries were always shrewdly premeditated. The narrator is one of Bellow's lighter, more playful presences, like Charlie Citrine, who suffered from the same difficulty: 'I mean, if I were a true hypocrite I wouldn't forever be putting my foot in my mouth.' Up in Canada, the only company is the landlady, a mad widow who babbles of the Divine Spirit. No one wants to hear all this, but the old boy finds that he is more than ready to listen:

> The Divine Spirit, she tells me, has withdrawn in our time from the outer, visible world. You can see what it once wrought, you are surrounded by its created forms. But although natural processes continue, Divinity has absented itself. The wrought work is brightly divine but Divinity is not now active within it. The world's grandeur is fading. And this is our human setting . . .

Of course, the myth of decline — the elegiac vision, which insists that all the good has gone and only the worst remains — has never looked less like a myth and more like a reality. But perhaps the world always looks that way, especially when you start your preparations for leaving it. At the height of his earthly powers, Bellow makes generous reparations to the credit side of the ledger, helping 'to bring back the light that has gone from these molded likenesses'.

London Review of Books 1982 and *Observer* 1984

The Killings in Atlanta

1. Murder in America

'It looked like a straight verbal mugging. The kid points the gun and says: "Gimme all your money." The guy hands over $90, credit cards, watch, links, everything. Then as the kid walks off he turns around, real casual, and shoots him anyway. These days, man, it's your money *and* your life.'

'Then the handyman flipped and laid into the old lady with an ax ... Then this transvestite took a monkey-wrench out of his handbag ... Buried her body under the ... Sawed his head off with a ... Watch out for the Downtown Slasher ... the Uptown Strangler ... the Midtown Mangler ... '

Conversation about murder in America is as stoical and routine as talk about the weather. A New Yorker will tell you about some lurid atrocity in his own flatblock with no more animation than if he were complaining about the rent. Terrible things happen all the time. This is the terrible thing.

The outsider's view remains hazy, cinematic, exaggerated, formed by cop-operas and a chaos of statistics. To the outsider, American murder seems as vehement and anarchic as American free enterprise, or American neurosis, or American profanity ... But sometimes, and far more worryingly in a way, shapes and bearings do emerge from the turmoil, and portents are suddenly visible among all the blood.

During the week that I was in Atlanta an eighteen-year-old boy cut the throat of an elderly neighbour and stabbed her forty-two times with a butcher's knife (over a trespass dispute); a schizophrenic former jailer and preacher raped and sodomised one woman and then shot both her and her friend in the head; a young crime reporter, having been raped the year before by an escaped convict, was found with thirty-five stab wounds in her chest (the convict was back inside on another rape charge, so it couldn't have been *him*).

These are killings in Atlanta. But they are not the Killings in Atlanta.

2. The Killings in Atlanta

> Piano keys don't lock doors.
> Footballs don't have toes.
> And, of course, cabbage heads
> Don't have a mouth or a nose.
> And kids don't go with strangers.
> They never go with strangers.

But they do. In the last twenty months, twenty black children have been murdered in Atlanta. No one has any idea who is doing this or why. District Attorney Lewis Slaton, in his creaking, leathery office, leaned back in his chair and said, 'Oh, we got a lot of theories. But we're not any nearer than we were when this thing started happening. We got no motive, no witnesses, no murder scenes, no hard clues at all. We ain't got lead one.' Only the compulsive confessors, who monotonously turn themselves in at the station houses, seem convinced of the identity of the culprit: 'Me. I did it,' they say. 'I did them all.'

Kids don't go with strangers ... The jingle comes from a local rockabilly hit. Car-bumper stickers say the same thing. So do children's colouring books. There are curfews for minors, haphazardly enforced. The Atlanta Falcons and the Westside Jaycees print trading cards of their teams, with safety tips as captions. There are teach-ins and pray-ins. There is great fear. But kids still go with strangers, one every month.

The murders began in the summer of 1979. It took a long while for any pattern to surface from the tide of Atlantan crime. Every year five or six black kids meet violent deaths (three, perhaps four, of the current cases are probably unconnected domestic killings: 'the assailant was known to the victim' − this is code talk for murder within the family). A year passed, and a dozen deaths, before anyone sensed the real scope of the disaster, the serial catastrophe, that was overtaking the city.

'Pretty early on I started to get a sick feeling about it,' said Camille Bell, who runs STOP, the Committee to Stop Children's Murders. The walls of her improvised office are covered with maps (coloured pins denote the site of the victims' disappearance and discovery), hand-painted uplift posters ('We are not about *Poverty*. Instead, we are about *Prosperity*. *Prosperity* of the *Heart* and *Soul* ... ') and information sheets from the Department of Public Safety.

Mrs Bell has a holding device on her telephone. She dodged from call to call. 'Officer? There are two kids hanging around outside All Right Parking. Could you get 'em taken home?' 'Venus, you heard the latest? I'm getting $1,000 a lecture. Some joke, huh?' As Mrs Bell talked, I scanned the public safety handout. There he was, number four:

YUSEF BELL, BLACK MALE, 9 YEARS OLD

Yusef Bell was last seen on October 21, 1979, en route to a grocery store on McDaniel Street. His body was found on November 8. The cause of death was strangulation.

Camille Bell is a public figure these days. There is a lot of glare in Atlanta now, and a lot of money, federal and commercial. Mrs Bell has her critics. There is talk of cashing in, of joining the parade. I would be ashamed to question Mrs Bell's motives; but these are poor people, and these things are inevitable in America. Camille Bell finished her call and said, 'The fear just grew, all through last year. I just knew it. Someone is stealing the kids off the streets.'

3. The Time Bomb in the Nursery

Atlanta, Georgia, is one of the model cities of the New South. The scene of many a crucial battle in the desegregation war, Atlanta has since dubbed itself 'the city too busy to hate'. The 600,000 population is predominantly black, as is the city administration. The airport, the world's largest, is designed by black architects, its concourses adorned with the work of black artists. Downtown, among the civic mansions and futuristic hotels, the streets are so clean that you expect to see ashtrays, standard lamps, Hoovers, on every corner.

It was the random nature of the killings which first persuaded Atlanta that the city's crisis was a racial one. Where else do you find any link or motive? This kid was shot, that one bludgeoned, that one stabbed. None of them had any money. There was no obvious sexual factor in the killings, except perhaps in the case of the two girls (Latonya Wilson was found four months after her death, her body partly eaten by dogs; Angel Lanier was found a week after her disappearance, sexually molested, tied to a tree). All the children were dumped, having been killed elsewhere. Some had been hidden, some had been laid out openly, in natural, relaxed postures. The victims have only three things in common: they were black, they were poor, and they were children.

'Sure we thought it was racial,' I was told. 'Or political anyway. Some movement might be doing this to force a situation. Might be extreme right or extreme left. And with us black folks squeezed in the middle.'

Racial disquiet climbed in the city all last year, until October. Then came the bomb in the nursery. An explosion in a day nursery killed three children and a teacher, all of them black. 'Now I am a mild man,' said an elderly negro. 'I don't hold with this vigilante stuff. But after that explosion, I was ready to go. I didn't think it was a bomb. I *knew* it was a bomb. And it was the Klan put it there.'

The day nursery is on a broad street, one marked by an air of colourful poverty, opposite a run-down school. It is not difficult to imagine the scene on that hot autumn day. Hoax calls forced five nearby schools to evacuate. There must have been a lot of fear and anger milling around on the street.

Mayor Maynard Jackson and Commissioner Lee Brown, the two prongs of the black administration, did what they had to do: they acted fast. Within hours black experts were on the scene, pronouncing the cause of the explosion: old boiler, faulty wiring. 'If that thing hadn't been open and shut the same day,' I was told, 'well, it could have been a bloody night in Atlanta.'

No one thinks the killings are primarily racial any more. No one thinks the killings are primarily anything any more. Fear and bafflement are very tiring, and Atlanta is a weary city by now. Twenty have died, but the effects of the trauma are incalculable.

In a sense, the bomb in the nursery is heard and felt every day. Children no longer play in the parks and streets. In the housing projects, council estates which combine urban decay with a tang of authentic suburban dread, children stand and talk in groups, and stare at the cars. There have been alarming increases in all symptoms of juvenile anxiety: bedwetting, refusal to sleep alone, fear of doors and windows. Reports go on about children having 'lost the capacity to trust people'. If the murderer or murderers, the leftist or rightist, the madman or madmen unknown are caught and convicted tomorrow, there won't be a black child in Atlanta whose life has not already been deformed by these killings.

4. Circus of the Supercops

Last November, Dorothy Allison, known as 'the vendetta psychic', came to town at the invitation of the Atlanta police. Dorothy had been fighting crime with her paranormal powers since 1967, when a dream led her to discover the body of a five-year-old boy, stuffed into a drainpipe. She worked on 100 cases, finding 38 bodies and solving 14 murders. But Dorothy drew a blank in Atlanta. Townspeople complain that she spent most of her time here promoting her autobiography on local radio shows. One mother said that the psychic never returned her only photograph of her murdered son.

The FBI were in Atlanta by this stage, and the Missing Persons Bureau (originally with a staff of four) had been belatedly expanded into a thirty-seven-member Task Force, working in the showrooms of the old Leader Lincoln-Mercury dealership in the centre of town. A reward of $100,000 was established. 'That ought to smoke them out' was the general view. 'That'll shake the trees.'

But it didn't. And then the supercops hit town: from Manhattan, Detective Charles Nanton, who worked on 'Son of Sam'; from Los Angeles, Captain Pierce Brooks, the man who caught the cop-killers in the 'Onion Field' case; and several other crack enforcers from all over the States. The supercops left Atlanta a fortnight later, quietly.

Epidemiologists from the Centre for Disease Control set up their computers. Advice was sought from the anti-terrorist training school in Powder Springs. The Guardian Angels from New York are the latest in a long line of fêted hopefuls. Two $10,000-apiece German Shepherd dogs, so high-powered that they respond only to German commands, contributed their hunting skills. Someone with tracking experience in Africa offered to . . .

'It made a lot of people mad,' said one old Atlantan. 'Hell, it was all PR. They all just wanted to *look* good.' Since the Killings in Atlanta are now world news, everyone wants to look good in the glow: George Bush, Burt Reynolds, Frank Sinatra, Ronald Reagan.

The supercop circus didn't find what it was looking for. But it found something else: more crime. Quotidian lawbreaking doesn't stop while massacres take the headlines; and the intense investigations in Atlanta were uncovering whole new layers of transgression and turpitude.

An officer searches an abandoned building for clues: in a stairwell he finds the skeleton of a forty-year-old man. A tracking dog returns to its master — with the skull of an adult female in its jaws. The weekly citizen area-sweeps routinely turn up caches of guns and stolen goods. Peaceable burglars panic at road-blocks.

Late last year three kids in their mid-teens were arrested for robbery. A health-check revealed that they had all contracted syphilis. Soon afterwards a forty-one-year-old man was arrested for sodomy; several other under-age boys were involved. A nine-year-old girl was picked up off the street by the police, for her own protection. She turned out to be an experienced prostitute. She had been giving 'head and hand' since she was five.

There is certainly a childish underworld lying beneath the surface of Atlanta life. But the murder victims did not belong to it. Several of the boys were street-wise; they hustled for work, for tips, for errands, but they were not delinquent. One boy, Aaron Jackson Jnr, aged nine, used to break into houses, but only for food and warmth. A woman woke up to find Aaron asleep on her sofa. The refrigerator had been raided. Little Aaron was last seen on November 1, 1980, at the Moreland Avenue Shopping Center. His body was found the next day, under a bridge. The cause of death was asphyxiation.

5. The 'Invisible Man' Theory

'Theories — that's one thing we've got plenty of,' said the DA. 'Me, I still think it's sex'n'drugs.'

I mentioned that the bodies of the boys showed no sign of sexual interference.

'Don't *have* to be no sign of it. They get the kids, smoke a little marijuana, try some sex stuff. The kid might just be an onlooker . . . Or maybe some of the kids are pushing a little dope, and need teaching a lesson by the Man. Or maybe it's their *parents* who're being warned. Has to be money involved. Bottom line for a whole lotta stuff is money.'

On one of the early clue-sweeps, police entered a recently abandoned house. They found an axe, a hatchet, a shovel, and some children's clothing. They also found two Bibles — nailed to the wall. The Bibles were open, one on Isaiah 1:14 to 3:25, the other on Jeremiah 15:4 to 18:4. Back at the Atlanta America Hotel, I picked up the complimentary Gideon and read through the passages: 'Bring no more vain offerings . . . your hands are full of blood. Wash yourselves . . . /I have brought against the mothers of young men/a destroyer at noonday;/I have made anguish and terror/fall upon them suddenly.'

After the discovery of the nailed Bibles the 'Cult' Theory gained currency for a while. The kids were being killed to satisfy the rituals of some voodoo brotherhood; several of the children had been carefully washed, after all, and laid out in stylised postures. For a short time in 1980, and again in the last three months, the monthly cycle of the killings encouraged the 'Disturbed Female' Theory. Perhaps a failed mother or a childless woman was acting out a complicated revenge on the living world.

Are the killers white or black? To begin with, of course, this was the crucial question. Several of the kids were picked up in areas where a white man would stick out like a pink elephant. The city population splits 60–40, but the street presence is much more one-sided than that. If the murderers and the victims turned out to be the same colour, the Killings in Atlanta would accord with the mainstream of American crime. Blacks make up an eighth of the US citizenry, and a half of its prison population. Most crime is still segregated. To a wildly disproportionate extent, violence in America is black on black.

Atlanta is a scattered city, surrounded by a lot of open and unfrequented country — lakes, wide plains, woodlands. The killers use all this space and are heavily reliant on their mobility. It sometimes seems that only a black could go to work with the unobtrusive speed and freedom that he needs.

In Chesterton's story 'The Invisible Man', the detective Father Brown orders four people, two of them policemen, to keep watch on the only entrance to the flat of a potential murder victim. The murder takes place, the four men claim that 'no one' went through the door. Oh yes he did, says Father Brown — and he walked past you all with the body in his arms. 'The Invisible Man?' someone asks. Correct, in a sense. The murderer was the postman, and he carried the victim in his sack.

A uniform confers facelessness, jurisdiction, and a degree of invisibility. 'Now that could be anyone,' said a local crime reporter, 'delivery man, bus driver, utility worker . . . or a cop.'

The switch from a white to a black administration has happened only over the last few years. A lot of people were edged out in that shift. Many white cops, in particular, got sacked or passed over for promotion (with accompanying scandals: exams were rigged to favour black candidates, and so on). Now, if the motive was to discredit and humiliate the black-run police force, then the 'Rogue Cop' Theory has life in it.

Perhaps, though, motive is the wrong thing, the irrelevant thing, to look for. It is possible that the twenty murders will break down into four or five weird clusters. What strikes you again and again is that the Killings in Atlanta have been so easy to do. Despite the propaganda, the campaigns, the fear, kids still go with strangers. Last month black and white plainclothes-policemen drove in unmarked cars round the housing projects, the vacant lots, the shanty houses with ripped car seats on their patios. There are no adults about, there is no authority, there is not even a memory of the survival instincts of the old ghetto. 'Hey, kid,' the decoys would call to the children they found, 'you want to earn ten bucks? Hop in.' They got a rider *every time*.

6. The View from Peachtree Plaza

The Peachtree Plaza Hotel is the centrepiece of downtown Atlanta. It is a billion-dollar masterpiece of American efficiency, luxury and robotic good manners. 'Mm-hm. Mm-hm,' everyone says five times a minute as they glide across its fountained halls.

Among its other accomplishments, the Peachtree is the tallest hotel in the world. If it's essence of vertigo you want, take the scenic elevator to the seventy-second floor and enjoy a Cloud Buster ('a refreshing blend of coconut milk, pineapple juice and vodka served in a souvenir replica of the Hotel' — $7.95. 'Thank you.' 'Mm-hm') in the revolving Sundial Lounge.

There you will see the scalextric of the city, with its flyovers and chicanes, the dwarfed high-rise car-parks, the windshields blazing in the malls, the elevated trains, EQUITABLE, OMNI, LIFE OF GEORGIA, thruways glistening like canals ... and the acres of toytown prefabs on the criss-crossed suburban streets, where a person or persons unknown is still stealing the kids off the streets.

To the south-east lies Miami. Last May, four white policemen were acquitted there after the fatal beating of a black suspect, Arthur McDuffie. It happened on the street, after a chase. The medical examiner said that McDuffie's injuries were consistent with 'falling four storeys and landing between your eyes'. When the acquittal was announced there were three days of rioting: 16 dead, 400 injured, $100 million worth of damage.

In Buffalo, New York, last September, four random blacks were shot in the head by the same white man. A fortnight later, two black cabbies were found with their hearts ripped out. In Oklahoma City, a black man and a white woman were shot to death in a parking lot. In Fort Wayne, Indiana, black leader Vernon Jordan was shot in the back while climbing out of a white woman's car. In Johnstown, Philadelphia, a mixed couple were murdered as they walked across the street. In Salt Lake City, Utah, two black men were shot while out jogging with white women.

In Birmingham, Alabama, there is a Ku Klux Klan military training camp, called My Lai in honour of the war criminal William Calley. In Greensboro, North Carolina, last November, an all-white jury acquitted six Klansmen and Nazis of the murder of five black and white Communists. In Chattanooga, Tennessee, acquittals and dropped charges have released five Klansmen accused of killing five black women on the streets.

Are these things connected? Are the Killings in Atlanta connected, to these killings or to each other? It is very tempting to see patterns here, or simply a change in the emphasis of murder in America.

Atlanta looks peaceful enough in the mild winter light. Atlanta in August will be a different proposition from Atlanta in January. The killings will not have been solved; and by then, too, President Reagan's passive attitude to pro-black legislation will have begun to hurt. Anyway, the summer is the time for racial anger and despair. In summer, the ghettos always heat up. They will expand and swell in the sun. Some will burst.

Observer 1981

*   *   *

Postscript Early in 1982, an irregularly employed black disc-jockey called Wayne Williams was convicted of two of the Atlanta child murders and, by implication, some or all of the remaining twenty-seven. There was much that was unsatisfactory about the trial. The evidence for the prosecution centred on the (circumstantial but compelling) fact that 'fibres' found on the victims matched the Williams family carpet. Williams's defence was agreed to be feeble verging on incompetent. The trial raised all sorts of questions about the exertion of public — and media — pressure to effect a palliative outcome. It seemed to me weirdly characteristic that the first thing Williams did, on his arrest, was call a press conference. Meanwhile, serving his life sentence, Williams ponders the legal options, his hand occasionally strengthened by such things as Abby Mann's five-hour drama-documentary for CBS, *The Atlanta Child Murders*, which was very partial, very anti-establishment and very pro-Williams (the killer, Mann implies, was probably white). Have the murders come to an end? The violent death of poor American blacks, unless given urgency by politics, has never much exercised the American judiciary; and some observers suggest, most depressingly, that the Atlanta murders continue, as they always have and always will. Perhaps, then, the Killings in Atlanta are over, while the killings in Atlanta go on.

The Case of
Claus von Bulow

There are two sides to every marriage, and two sides to every murder. Husband and wife can regale you with their rival versions of reality; we all know those long-running sanity contests that many marriages turn into. But murderer and victim seldom have equal access to the sympathetic ear.

Look at them now. On a typical summer evening Claus von Bulow might be hosting a dinner party in a fourteen-room Fifth Avenue apartment of scarcely describable opulence. The guests include people like Lady Annabel Goldsmith, Mercedes Kellog, Elizabeth of Yugoslavia. Behind every other chair stands a liveried footman ... Meanwhile, across town on upper Broadway, among the flophouses and retirement hotels, von Bulow's wife, Martha, is being well taken care of by money too, in a sense. She lives in a guarded room. She is visited every morning by the family doctor. Full-time nurses clean her tubes and catheters and adjust her body every two hours to prevent bedsores. Rumour — in the form of the *New York Post* — has it that a hairdresser and manicurist attend her daily. Her limbs twitch. She makes gurgling noises. Her eyes open and stare but she is probably blind.

'What do you give the girl who has everything?' runs the joke, often told – if not actually originated – by von Bulow himself. The answer is 'Insulin'.

Martha von Bulow, known as Sunny to her friends, has been in a coma for two-and-a-half years. Claus has been found guilty of putting her there, at the second attempt, with an insulin injection. Sunny is worth $75 million. Both parties have their advocates. Family, friends, acquaintances — and the whole of tabloid and small-screen America — are split down the middle. Hardly anything in either version is demonstrably false.

1. Sunny's Story

'Claus Bulow — born Claus Borberg and yet to invent the "von" — was a middle-class Danish adventurer. His father was practically the *only* Dane to be prosecuted for collaboration with the Nazis. That'll give you some idea. As far back as his London days Claus was always shady. He stood bail for Stephen Ward during the Profumo scandal. He hung around with Lord Lucan — now there's another man who bungled the murder of his own wife.

'Claus never had any money of his own to speak of but he contrived to live on the edge of the high life. He was an art dealer and businessman, a courier, a fixer. He had languages, presence, a phoney aristocratic aura. In 1966 he met and carefully courted Princess Sunny von Auersperg.

'Sunny was a dream, the classic American heiress. She was the only child of George Crawford, the utilities magnate. She looked like Grace Kelly, a long-legged rose. Between them, she and her mother had about $150 million. At the time she met Claus, Sunny had just been amicably divorced from her first husband, an Austrian prince of great charm but no great wealth. She had two beautiful children, Alexander and Ala. She was a quiet, self-contained woman, perhaps even a little withdrawn. She regretted her lack of education and read widely. She liked to stay in. A private person, not a hostess.

'Claus seemed right for her, at first. They had one of the grandest apartments in New York — it makes the Astors' place look like a pigsty — and a dazzling mansion in Newport, Rhode Island. They poured a lot of time, energy and money into those places. They went on buying trips to Europe, and so on. But their style wasn't ostentatious. It was just family life at the highest pitch of polish. And they had a daughter of their own by now — Cosima. Cosima von Bulow! Named after the woman who started life as a Liszt and ended it as a Wagner. Poor old Hans von Bülow, the most famous cuckold of the nineteenth century.

'But Claus was bored. So was Sunny, in her way. Let's get one thing straight. It's garbage about Sunny being an alcoholic and a pill-popper. We have the testimony of the maid and the butler that she drank far less than the average American. She may have used aspirin, aperients, but not twenty a day of each. As the prosecution lawyer said, anyone who took that many laxatives for twenty-four years would have spent eighteen of them on the toilet. All the rumours about Sunny's addictions go straight back to Claus. She was stable. It was he who was changing.

'For one thing, he was in love – with Alexandra Isles, a socialite and minor TV actress. And he wanted to work again. He was tired of being a kept man, or so he claimed. So he started sounding out a divorce. Sunny was absolutely amenable and he knew her to be generous – the first husband had gotten well over a million. Claus dithers. Alexandra gives him a deadline: "Let's be together for Christmas."

'This was 1979. On the night of December 26, Sunny goes into a coma. Well, what do you know? All the next day Sunny lay unconscious on her bed. Maria, the maid who had been with Sunny for twenty-five years, was incensed, hysterical: "Call a doctor!" she told him. "No," he said, "she's just sleeping." It wasn't until late afternoon, when Sunny's breath started to rattle, that Claus finally gave in. All day he just lay by her side, fully clothed, waiting. He must have been tranquillised to the eyeballs himself. Why didn't he just tell Maria to get lost? It came out in court that Claus was heavily reliant on Valium.

'At the hospital Sunny's blood-sugar count was found to be abnormally low. After several glucose shots it was even lower! Something was eating her blood sugar. Insulin, for instance. But she recovered, and the doctors diagnosed reactive hypoglycemia . . . In February, while tidying a closet of Claus's, Maria found a little black bag. There were drugs in there. She showed it to Ala. From then on they monitored the bag's contents. One day they found a vial marked INSULIN. "Insulin?" said Maria. "What for, insulin?"

'And the following Christmas it all happens again. Another showdown with Alexandra Isles, another morning of stall and bluff at Clarendon Court, another coma. This time Claus had obviously given her the shot the night before, and seen to it that Maria stayed in New York. And this time Sunny did not recover . . . The family – Sunny's mother and stepfather, Alexander and Ala – initiated a private investigation. When they got hold of the black bag the vial was gone but there was a dirty needle, tipped with insulin. Richard

Kuh, a lawyer, an ex-DA, talked to Sunny's doctor, who said simply, "Either you go to the police or I will."

'At the trial everyone was amazed at the strength of the prosecution's case. Maria's testimony was devastating. So was Alexander's. (He and Ala had no financial motive, by the way — a few million here or there, in their forties.) Even Alexandra Isles, when asked if she still believed in Claus's innocence, said, "I don't know." All that can save the defence is a rescue-job from Claus himself. He refuses to take the stand. Why? Because the prosecution would have murdered him. It's open and shut. The mystery is *not* that such a clever man could commit such a dumb crime. The mystery is that he came so close to getting away with it.'

2. Claus's Side

'Let's be clear on one thing. Of *course* Claus is a bastard. Of *course* he's a snob and a money-worshipper. But he's not a murderer. And he isn't dumb. And this was such a dumb murder.

'Claus never made any secret of his origins. He always said, "My mother's Bulows are middle-class Danes. They have nothing to do with the German family." His father was no Lord Haw-Haw, just a fuddled playwright who neglected to resign from the Danish-German Literary Society. The "von" was Sunny's idea. Claus was legitimate. He wasn't the kind of bogus Eurocrat who gets a dukedom on the transatlantic Jumbo.

'In London Claus lived well. He worked for Getty, who doted on him. "What would I do without Claus?" he used to say. Claus would regularly have 200 people to dinner in his vast flat in Belgravia. He would take sixty people out to lunch at Wiltons. He was in the dead centre of the money world. He could have had any number of rich women.

'Claus always wanted the best. He waited — and he got Sunny. Incredibly beautiful, incredibly rich and, it seemed, incredibly easy to dominate. But Sunny proved to be surprisingly stubborn. Claus wanted to entertain, to splash money around. Sunny was reclusive. She never wanted to go anywhere or do anything — and she wanted Claus with her at all times. The marriage soon developed into a kind of Faustian contract for Claus. He could do what he liked all day, while she was flower-arranging or at her exercise class. But at six o'clock he went home, had a TV dinner and watched *Bonanza* with his wife.

'Now Sunny. She might not have been a chronic drinker but she was always high on something. Often it was just nerves. She was the most discombobulated woman you ever met. At parties she would be dead silent, then catastrophically indiscreet. Someone might say, "There's nothing more boring than married sex." And Sunny would say, "Yes, but you're queer." Half the time you couldn't tell whether she knew you were in the room. The first husband, that titled ski-instructor or tennis-pro — he couldn't take it. She winked at his infidelities. But *he* left *her*.

'You probably don't understand about these rich American ladies. They have nothing else to worry about except their looks and figure. When money lets you live at such a pitch of perfection, ageing is intolerably ugly. A hint of flab is an abomination. These women are arrested anorexics. They doctor themselves with diet pills, laxatives, emetics. They eat a sundae and stick a finger down their throats . . . Sunny had a face-lift long before she needed one. Maria, the maid, she wouldn't discuss that at the trial, on principle. Her oath to Sunny superseded her oath to the court. Who knows what else she wouldn't discuss, on principle?

'Clearly Sunny and Claus used to mess around with drugs. Syringes were so much a part of the furniture that the kids used to use them as water-pistols. And here we have Truman Capote piping up, saying that now he comes to think of it Sunny von Bulow once told him that insulin jabs were a great way to lose weight! Truman's affidavit is included in the submission for a retrial. It'll all come out then.

'As for the two comas, I agree it looks pretty bad for Claus, particularly the first one. It's certainly possible that he was guilty of a degree of negligence here. Maybe he thought, "She's bombed herself out again. If that's what she wants, let her get on with it." Maybe he was bombed himself. No one said Claus was Captain Nice. But he isn't stupid. If he was going to kill his wife — there are dozens of more effective poisons.

'From then on you just have to look at the family set-up. With Sunny still technically alive, Claus controls her fortune. In league with the kids, Sunny's mother, who loathed Claus, hires this whole army of private dicks. They had the black bag in their possession for weeks. The insulin-tipped needle could easily have been a plant.

Anyway, why didn't Claus destroy the evidence? As he says, he has the Atlantic Ocean at the back of his garden.

'Two more points. It's been said that Claus murdered for love. Claus wouldn't cross the street for love, let alone kill his wife for it. She had already settled an allowance on him: the income from a million-dollar investment. Now, if Claus were the sort of man who wanted really spectacular wealth, why didn't he wait a couple of years? Sunny's mother was past eighty and in poor health. With her gone, he'd have come into some serious money – $150 million.'

3. The Life of Pure Money

What's the difference between $75 million and $150 million? Hardly any difference, surely, in our terms. But in the life of pure money, $75 million and $150 million are chalk and cheese. What's the difference? The difference is $75 million.

Look around at your life. Look at your flat, house, your car, the sort of holidays you take, restaurants you eat at, clothes you wear. Not bad, eh? All right for now, at any rate. But in the world of pure money, your life is no kind of life, a nothing life. Your life is too poor to be lived.

'That house is owned by the top Mafia man in Providence,' said my contact, as our tour of Newport began. 'He burnt the place down for the insurance. His wife was in it at the time . . . That's the drive where the heiress ran over her Italian lover. He kept her locked in the attic . . . Alcoholic . . . Get rid of the mother . . . Suicide attempt . . . Disinherited . . . He controls all the money.'

We were driving down Bellevue Avenue. Huddled together on either side of the road are Gothic and Palladian mansions – laughingly known as 'summer cottages'. As von Bulow once said, houses of this size in Europe would be surrounded by 30,000 acres. Here, they are practically terraced. Clarendon Court had comparatively extensive grounds: eleven acres. Clarendon Court had eleven gardeners. You cannot see the house from the road. The tall gate wears a buttoned bib; it looks as anomalous as the vest of a Scottie dog. A few mansions away stands Sunny's mother's place, also screened from the street.

Many of these grand follies are now wholly or partly deserted. Some eccentrics live on in the wings of mansions which are either abandoned or open to the public. The evening Atlantic mist enfolds the ocean lawns (the scenes of legendary parties), watched by the spectres of lost Bouviers, aged Oelrichs and vanished Vanderbilts.

You cannot get into Clarendon Court – few people ever did during Sunny's custodianship. Under an earlier reign, *High Society* was filmed there. I settled for Rosecliff, where they made *The Great Gatsby* and Harold Robbins's *The Betsy*. The blazered young guide led us up the heart-shaped marble staircase, through the silk and brocade of the bedroom, under the coffered ceilings of the salon, into the great ballroom ('the scene of many brilliant entertainments'), and into the baronial dining-room, where the table was set for thirty guests. 'Excuse me, sir,' a tourist asked the guide, 'but would they like eat *lunch* here?'

I slipped past the imported tapestries and pre-faded panelling – out into the Court of Love, designed by Augustus Saint-Gaudens on the model of Marie Antoinette's sanctuary at Versailles. Gum-chewing, super-coiffed young housewives pointed out features to their sleepy, plump-bellied men. Children in *ET* T-shirts skidded in the gravel. Plastic urns, filled with sand, now silted up with bubblegum and triple-band, extra-low-tar filters. Von Bulow gossip suffused the Court of Love. These people like to see how the other half lives. These people want to know how the other half dies.

4. The Clausettes

During the von Bulow trial, the longest in Newport's history, Claus dwelt at the Sheraton Islander Hotel, hard by the innocuous courthouse. The hotel staff loved him. 'So gracious. And every morning, always $10 for the maid.' Every morning, too, The Clausettes – informal cheerleaders in von Bulow T-shirts – would jolly him along to his daily ordeal. Each night, as von Bulow sorted wearily through his fan mail, there would be incessant long-distance calls from assorted vampish lonelyhearts. 'It was extraordinary,' said a friend who did a lot of hand-holding during the trial. 'You know: "It's Suki from Hong Kong" . . . "It's Merouka from Tangiers . . . "'

Claus von Bulow is, to put it mildly, an unlikely folk-hero, yet he has a great deal of solid public support, particularly among the ladies. This can partly be attributed to the uncontrollable nature of fame in America — where, for instance, multiple rapists and winners of ugly-contests are promptly bombarded with love-tokens, marriage-offers, and so on. Von Bulow, the stylish Eurocrat, the man of façades, is particularly strong on such appeal. But it goes a little deeper than that.

William Wright, in his solid, thorough, very pro-Sunny *The Von Bulow Affair*, has an excellent point to make on the subject of Bulowmania. It transpired that the jurors, in their six-day meditations, had one crucial difficulty in reaching a guilty verdict. It had nothing to do with the medical evidence, the permissibility of the black bag, the family 'vendetta'. The jurors were unable to accept that *anyone* could commit such a crime.

Now there is a subtext here. By 'anyone' the jurors meant anyone human, anyone familiar, anyone they knew. They had seen von Bulow every day for several months; however cold and remote, Claus was palpably human. The von Bulow trial was televised in its entirety. The whole of America 'knew' von Bulow. And nobody one knows injects his wife with insulin for money, and then reclines at her side watching her begin to die.

5. The Art of Manipulation

'Martin!' said *my* New York hostess in a hoarse whisper, on the day of my return from Newport: 'It's *Claus von Bulow* on the telephone!' Murders don't travel well, so it is necessary to account for my friend's scandalised awe. The British equivalent of such an exchange would have gone as follows: 'Who shall I say is calling?' 'Oh, it's the Yorkshire Ripper here.'

'Mr Von Bulow,' I said. 'How do you do. How kind of you to call.'

'Well, I heard you were in town', he said in his Wildean drawl, 'and that you were interested in my case. I don't think we'd better meet, but I thought it only right to respond to that interest. I admire your writing. It seems a little obvious to say that I admire your father's writing too.'

Well, well. I asked my new friend Claus if I could prepare some questions and call him back. He nonchalantly agreed. We then talked for fifteen or twenty minutes. In terms of content, von Bulow said very little that he hadn't already said in published interviews.

But the style was markedly different — more droll, more florid, more literary. Here are some gobbets.

'I am innocent of this cowardly and despicable act. After all, it's hardly a *crime passionnel*. It would have required a great deal of premeditation, a great deal of malice.' When asked if his demeanour at the trial had told against him: 'Unquestionably. I am very tall, I look extremely arrogant. A Kraut general who happens to talk like Professor Higgins.' When asked why he didn't use some of his more eloquent sympathisers (Alan Pryce-Jones, for instance) as character witnesses: 'Well of course I absolutely adore Alan, but in Newport they'd need a *translator*.'

Expatiating on his love for Cosima, von Bulow offered an ambitious quotation from Chesterton. When he ruled out the possibility that he might jump bail and flee to his native land, I bounced back with 'Denmark's a prison'. He guffawed obligingly. It is a pleasant laugh; the laugh takes off, takes over . . . 'Why didn't you take the stand?' I asked. 'I can't answer that,' said von Bulow.

I confess that, as we talked, I hoped for von Bulow's innocence. I also confess that I failed to ask the overwhelming question, the question to which there is no answer unless there was indeed a vendetta, an elaborate conspiracy. Experts agree that the coma was caused by an injection of insulin. Either Sunny did it, or Claus did. When von Bulow was first questioned by the investigators — the first suspicion of suspicion — he was asked: 'Would your wife have any reason to inject herself with insulin?' Von Bulow didn't say, 'Why should she?' or 'Yes, she took it to lose weight' or 'You mean it was the *insulin*.' He said, 'My God. That's the last thing she should have!'

Everything about von Bulow points to an obvious character type: the Manipulator. In my experience, Manipulators are always incompetent or transparent manipulators: the true manipulator never has a reputation for manipulating. Everyone harbours their theory about the night of December 19, 1980. Here, for what it's worth, is mine.

The theory rests on the inscrutability of marriage. I don't think von Bulow covertly administered a fatal injection. He must have prepared some mitigation for his conscience; there must have been collusion, however innocent, on Sunny's part. In the ritual, the intimate theatre of the marriage bed, Sunny might have injected herself, sleepily half-deceived about the contents of the syringe. Or perhaps it was an offer of painless death to the tranquillised woman.'Here, you do it. You press.' Then, the next day, the stalling, the play-acting, the vigil.

Von Bulow's appeal is imminent. A squad of lawyers is beavering away at the Harvard Law School, orchestrated by the famous loophole-specialist Alan Dershowitz. The crux of the defence's submission has to do with the large-scale use of private investigators: a private army of gumshoes (answerable not to the public, not to justice, but to the client) which then empties its confiscation cupboard into the lap of the police. As revealed in court, the cost of the operation was $100,000.

Dershowitz is on record with the boast that few of his clients are innocent. His services will take von Bulow's legal expenses far beyond the million-dollar mark. But then this has always been a story about the very rich. At a cost of $1,500 a day, Sunny lives on, incapable of thought, helplessly reliant on the vigorous organism and its separate will to live.

Observer 1983

*   *   *

Postscript Von Bulow and Professor Dershowitz won their appeal. But in 1985 the new attorney-general of Rhode Island, an ex-nun called Arlene Violet, ordered a retrial. Again the prosecution's case was dismissed on technical grounds: the inadmissability of the black bag; the use of private investigators.

An intriguing, and representative, character in this drama is a 'flamboyant' young man called David Marriott. During preparations for the appeal he worked closely with the Claus camp; he was to testify that he had often supplied drugs and needles to Sunny and her son Alexander (Sunny's interest in dope of all kinds is no longer seriously denied). Later, Marriott said that the drugs 'didn't go to Sunny or Alex, they went to Claus'. While working with Claus and Dershowitz, Marriott was paid between $10,000 and $100,000 (claims vary) for expenses and 'lost wages'. Marriott has also signed up with a New York literary agent.

Climbing from his limousine, Marriott answered questions put to him by *The New York Times.* How did he support himself? 'It's nobody's business,' he said. 'Since 1976, I've had the use of a limousine. I've never really worked. And I don't work now.'

So much for 'lost wages'. So much for the strange life of pure money. Von Bulow has challenged — so far unsuccessfully — the estate's control of Sunny's fortune. He lunches most days at Mortimer's, on the Upper East Side. He has not spent a day in jail (indeed, there isn't an embarrassment of millionaires in what America likes to call its 'correctional facilities'). At the time of writing, Sunny is still alive — or, more accurately, not yet dead.

Truman Capote: Knowing Everybody

It was, I hope and trust, a radically below-par Truman Capote who received me at his UN Plaza apartment on an equatorial New York afternoon.

'Truman's sort of sick,' said the lady from Random House who answered the door.

'Oh dear. Would you rather I . . . ?'

'No, he can talk. So long as he can rest at the same time.'

I was led past a couple of reception rooms, beyond whose jungly curios and foliage you could glimpse the burnished leagues of the East River. Then, from the gloom at the end of the passage, emerged the helpless, tottering figure of Mr Capote, who let out a soft wail of greeting and extended a tiny hand.

For pity's sake, I wanted to say — never mind the interview. Let's call an ambulance. Or I can take him there in my briefcase, I thought, as I contemplated the childish, barefoot, night-shirted figure, sixty-three inches tall and barely a hundred pounds. But Truman clutched me dramatically by the hand and urged me towards the bedside chair. The lady from Random House then took her leave with a calming smile.

At once Truman disappeared for a long and complicated session in one of the nearby bathrooms (the first of several noisy visits during my two-hour stay). Shrugging, I looked round the room. Saul Bellow has a thousand ways of describing the human face; Truman Capote, in his fiction and journalism, is the litanist of habitats, furniture, surfaces, clothes, scents.

The room was plain, almost functional. The curtains were three-quarters drawn behind the wickerwork headboard of the bed. The white bedside tables were stacked with medicines, magazines and books – Di-Gel, *Vogue, Interview*, Kenneth Tynan's *Show People, The Great Houses of Paris*. Next to the glass-fronted bookcase lay three pairs of sorrily crumpled shoes. The half-darkness held the authentic, sleepy tang of the convalescent room.

Following a final, convulsive series of nose-blowings and bark-like sneezes, Truman tiptoed back into the room and lowered himself gingerly on to his cot. Poor Truman. In his long-nailed fingers he furled a pink silk handkerchief.

With the great man at such an obvious disadvantage, I naturally felt that I needn't mind much what I said to him. Although Capote is doubtless as touchy as the next Great American Novelist, he gives off very little *amour propre*. He generates vulnerability and candour, and has none of the regality of, say, his old friend Tennessee Williams or his old enemy Gore Vidal. As Capote points out in his new book, *Music for Chameleons*: 'I'm an alcoholic. I'm a drug addict. I'm homosexual. I'm a genius.' As casually as I could, I asked the recumbent Truman about his current relationship with pills and drink.

'No, I'm just . . . exhausted . . . Did four *hours* of TV interviews about the new book . . . No, you know, I uh never drank that much! I mean . . . I just developed a kind of . . . suddenly an *allergy*. It would make me, not exactly . . . oh, well, very, very sick, like someone who's drunk a quart and a *half* or something. Norman Mailer must drink . . . twenty times as much as I ever did. In one *day*, you know, and it doesn't seem to affect him. Irwin Shaw! . . . drinks a *tremendous* amount. Practically everyone I *know* does. Tennessee! Edward Albee!'

I had read somewhere that Capote's voice was thin and high. But nothing had prepared me for this quavering, asthmatic singsong, a mixture of Noël Coward and Lillian Carter. *Turds, ee-bait, inner-stain* and *wide-ass*, for instance, are his renderings of 'towards', 'about', 'understand' and 'White House'. Capote was born in New Orleans, and was then farmed out to rural relations; much of his childhood was spent as a resident of Monroeville, Alabama. There is still something of the erudite hillbilly about him, and this perhaps explains how his obsession with the *beau monde* co-exists so peacefully with an interest in the underworld of murder and madness. He gives new scope to the cliché about 'knowing everyone'.

Capote knew Bob Kennedy, but he also knew Sirhan Sirhan.

Capote knew Jack Kennedy, but he also knew Lee Harvey Oswald – whom he met in Moscow in 1959, at which point Oswald was a gibbering paranoid considering defection to the East ... When I mentioned early on in our talk that I also worked for the *Observer*, we discussed the paper's relationship with its current owners, Bob Anderson's Atlantic Richfield Company. Capote then added reliably: 'I know Bob Anderson very well. He's one of my closest friends. He's a very cultivated man, you know – a charming man, a shy man. We went to Iran together once, had the most fantastic day with the poor old Shah.' (Laughter and coughing.) 'You know, this oil business, this ARCO thing – that's just a sideline for Bob. He's the world's largest single property-owner. Brazil, Arizona, New Mexico, hundreds and hundreds and hundreds of miles of ranches. As a matter of fact it was me who told him to buy the *Observer*.'

'Well, could you tell him not to sell it,' I said.

'Oh all right. If you want.'

Fame and its mysteries have always been intimately bound up with what Truman Capote does and is. 'I knew damn well I was going to be rich and famous,' he has often said. He appears to have sensed early on that celebrity, particularly in America, can be self-generated.

His first novel, *Other Voices, Other Rooms*, published in 1948 when Truman was 23, received as much attention for the pretty-boy photograph on the book's jacket as for the precocity of its contents. 'I didn't even *choose* that photograph!' protests Capote. Ironically, he is the scandalised one these days. 'It was not even *posed*! I was just lying on the couch after lunch! I didn't even choose it, I said just take any old photograph from the *drawer*!'

Capote's early novels and stories, with their cloying Southern settings and high incidence of snaggled grotesques, would have seemed to place him in the Gothic tradition of Carson McCullers and Eudora Welty. But in mid-career his work became squibbish and metropolitan. Above all, his novelistic ear proved adaptable: the novella *Breakfast at Tiffany's* (1958) showed that he could listen to New York as sharply as he had listened to New Orleans. At this time Capote was also turning out some exceptionally acute and original journalism – a cruelly finessing portrait of Marlon Brando, an hilarious account of a trip to Russia with a company of black Americans playing *Porgy and Bess*. During these years Capote became convinced that an unnoticed art form lay concealed within the conventions of journalism: the idea was that a true story could be told, faithfully, but so arranged as to suggest the amplitude of poetic fiction.

That idea eventually became *In Cold Blood* (1966), the story of the apparently pointless murder of the Clutter family in Garden City, Kansas. Capote spent six years 'on and off — and mostly on' following the trail in 'this fantastically depressing Mid-West town, where, you know, there was *nothing*'. The shaken townsfolk never took to Capote, and he had to withstand a good deal of local hostility. One day he sauntered into the courtroom and was confronted by a squad of glowering sheriffs. 'Oh, you don't look so tough to me,' said Capote in his highest voice. One of the men stood up and punched his fist through the courthouse wall. 'I'm beside myself, I'm beside myself!' cried Capote in a sarcastic wail. 'Those years were nerve-shattering,' says Capote now. 'I mean, I never knew whether I had a *book* or not.'

Capote's 'non-fiction novel' earned him several million dollars — and a highly ambivalent critical reception. The most serious attack came from the late Kenneth Tynan, who accused Capote of hastening the execution of the two murderers in order to safeguard the profitability of his book. 'The opposite was true,' says Capote. 'I was just . . . so shocked. Right up to that moment I thought Tynan was my friend . . . What did he die of, anyway?' Although Capote seems to have behaved pretty well irreproachably throughout, the controversy surrounding *In Cold Blood* could be seen as the start of our present permissiveness about turning tragedy into entertainment. 'It was an interest in the *form* that made me write that book, nothing else.' In terms of technique, *In Cold Blood* was seminal, and much-imitated. Capote himself is still following up its implications.

Meanwhile, of course, the stylish Mr Capote had ensconced himself as the ubiquitous lap-dog of high society. I imagine he cut a reassuring and innocuous figure, spryly perched on the edges of sofas and beds, with his crooning, questioning voice, no threat to the menfolk — no threat to anyone, it would seem. Capote's presence immediately induces a mood of sympathetic intimacy — why, I myself nearly poured out my fears and hopes to him. 'But I'm a writer,' says Capote with a thin-lipped smile. 'What did they expect?'

Capote is referring here to the elaborate scandals created by

Answered Prayers, his unfinished autobiographical novel 'about the Very Rich'. Four sections of this labyrinthine *roman à clef* appeared in *Esquire* in 1975, precipitating many a broken friendship, ostracism and snub — as well as Truman's brief bout of pill and drink cross-addiction. Nowadays he tends to pooh-pooh the extent of his own distress at the time; you feel that what bewildered him most was the fact that he had miscalculated, and so gravely. 'I thought they'd all think it was funny. *I'd* have thought it was funny . . . '

Acrimony on this scale has a habit of feeding off itself. Soon afterwards, Capote found himself engaged in litigation with his one-time friend Gore Vidal. In a 1975 interview with *Playgirl* Truman claimed that Gore had been 'thrown out' of the White House after drunkenly insulting Jackie Kennedy (Gore and Jackie, after all, had a step-father in common).

'It's been printed about *nine times*,' says Capote, his eyes bulging indignantly.

The spat spread to include Jackie's little sister, Princess Lee Radziwill. Lee was Truman's source for the anecdote; she then 'betrayed' him by signing an affidavit for Vidal and telling a New York gossip columnist: 'They are two fags. It is just the most disgusting thing.' An infuriated Capote went on a local TV chat show to poormouth the Princess. 'I know that Lee wouldn't want me tellin' none of this,' he simpered, 'but you know us Southern fags. We just can't keep our mouths shut.' The litigation with Vidal continues. So does the book. 'Just wait till they see the rest of it,' broods Capote.

Music for Chameleons was published in New York during the week of my visit. Capote had already made $4 million from this stop-gap collection of stories, journalism and non-fiction fiction, and, as I talked to him that afternoon, he lay swaddled in reams of laudatory press clippings. Not bad going, you think. For all his fragility, Capote is an operator, and a shrewd and confident one. Evidently he spends months planning the promotion of each book. Up there in the UN Plaza, I was simply a minor puppet in Capote's vast dream. 'The thing about people like me', he says firmly, 'is that we have *always* known what we were going to do. Some people never really find out.'

At this point I nerved myself to ask Capote about his love life — an exiguous topic these days, it would seem. It has been Truman's complex affliction always to be attracted to upright heterosexuals, rather as E.M. Forster was (Forster is, coincidentally, the English writer whom Capote most admires). Such men seem to relish all the difficult ramifications – consternated wives to placate, and so on. Again like Forster, Capote has also been known to hanker for representatives of the less privileged orders. He once squired an ex-prison guard to a dinner-party thrown by Princess Grace at her palace in Monaco. 'At dinner a man sitting next to him said, "Is this your first time in Europe?" And he said, "Yes it is, except for that time in Vietnam."'

'I don't *have* a love life any more,' says a stoical Capote. 'You see, I'm attracted to practically *no*body. It's just . . . sad. I just don't find many people – I really have to *like* them, you know? No, I don't have a love life. It's too exhausting,' he said with a yawn.

Capote had seemed to be on the point of fitful sleep at several stages in the course of the interview; so I now thought it prudent to take my leave.

'Would you be kind enough,' I asked reflexively, 'to sign my copy of your book?'

'Oh, certainly,' he said warmly. Rousing himself, Capote sat up in bed and began to fuss with his pen. He opened *Music for Chameleons*, and stared for several seconds at its blank first page. To my alarm, I realised that he had forgotten my name – if indeed he had ever known it. He sniffed, and looked up cautiously.

'The name's Tony, isn't it?' he croaked.

'No. Martin,' I said, trying to make Martin sound quite like Tony.

'Oh, Martin. Yes, of course.' He wrote on the blank page for a very long time.

Ten minutes later I stood smoking a cigarette on fiery First Avenue. I got the book out of my bag and turned to the first page, where it said, in an exemplarily rickety hand:

> *for Martin*
> *I tried!*
> *and you were so patient*
> *Truman Capote*
> *198*

That '198' wasn't his apartment number: it was a shot at the date. I walked on, hoping that little Truman would get well soon.

*   *   *

Postscript Truman never did. He died six years later, to the month. I liked him, and with hindsight I now find my bedside manner somewhat callous — but there it is. Appropriately doctored, the piece was used elsewhere as an obituary. However, I should like to add, in belated tribute, a brief review of the posthumous *Conversations with Capote* 'by' Lawrence Grobel, which follows.

Two unrelated points. Why do American writers tend to hate each other — hatreds which often extend to litigation (Vidal v. Capote; Lillian Hellman v. Mary McCarthy, an especially vicious attempt at financial persecution)? Perhaps one of the answers relates, as so much relates, to the *size* of America. In England writers mix pretty well: they have a generally middle-class, generally liberal unanimity. In America writers are naturally far flung (Alabama, Washington, Chicago, New England); to come together, they have to traverse great distances; it isn't surprising, when they meet, that they seem so strange to one another.

The second point concerns *In Cold Blood* and the business of the 'non-fiction fiction'. In the *Conversations*, while incidentally rubbishing Mailer's *The Executioner's Song*, Capote repeats his contention that the non-fiction fiction is, or can be, at least as 'imaginative' as the non non-fiction fiction: i.e., the novel. Now it is true that Capote (and Mailer) expends a good deal of imagination and artistry in the non-fiction form. What is missing, though, is moral imagination, moral artistry. The facts cannot be arranged to give them moral point. When the reading experience is over, you are left, simply, with murder — and with the human messiness and futility that attends all death.

*   *   *

Jackie Kennedy? 'I hate her.' John Updike? 'I hate him.' Jane Fonda: 'ucch, she's a throw-up number.' Joyce Carol Oates: 'she's the most loathsome creature in America. She's so . . . oo000gh!' As for Georgia O'Keeffe, 'I wouldn't pay twenty-five cents to spit on a painting [of hers]. And I think she's a horrible person, too.' While gentle, twinkly old Robert Frost is 'an evil, selfish bastard, an egomaniacal, double-crossing sadist'. In such a *galère*, literary comrades are doing pretty well if they are merely 'ghastly' (Thomas Pynchon), 'unreadable'

(Bernard Malamud), 'boring' and 'fraudulent' (Donald Barthelme), or 'unbelievably bad' (Gore Vidal).

Truman Capote lived the life of the American novelist in condensed and accelerated form. By the age of eight he was a writer, by the age of twelve he was a drunk, by the age of sixteen he was a celebrity, by the age of forty he was a multimillionaire, and by the age of fifty-nine he was dead. All the excess, solipsism, enmity, paranoia and ambition of American letters was crammed into those years – and, glancingly, into these pages. One would expect *Conversations with Capote* to provide some scandalous entertainment; but the book, semi-accidentally, goes one further and gives us an endearing portrait of the man.

Called 'the Interviewer's Interviewer' by *Playboy* magazine (his frequent employer), Lawrence Grobel is disciplined, persistent, thorough, and stupid. He is not quite as stupid as James A. Michener, who contributes a wonderfully galumphing foreword, but he is not nearly as smart as Truman Capote. Thus Grobel is thoroughly insensitive to Capote's standard interviewing persona, which is that of the Tease. Frowning now at his tape-recorder, now at his list of questions, Grobel unsmilingly processes the wanton bitchiness and boastfulness that Capote tosses out at him.

There is hidden comedy here, in the narrative links. Grobel is always telephoning, pestering, suddenly flying in from Los Angeles; with some awe and cautious affection, yet quite without self-consciousness or *pudeur*, he repeatedly nags Capote into yet another session with the Sony. And there is pathos too, for by now Capote often has to drag himself from the sickbed to cope with the Californian wretch.

Actually the whole book glows with the pale fire of illness, and one suspects that not a day of Capote's life was uncoloured by it. 'This small brilliant man', as Grobel dubs him, had everything in the American package – everything except brutish good health. His medical chart is dotted with seizures, addictions, dryouts; and yet the malaise sounds habitual and pervasive, as if Capote drank and drugged chiefly to assuage pain. Towards the end, his life appeared to be a bleak alternation between major surgery and Lawrence Grobel. One admires Capote the more for giving such a spirited account of himself.

Serious literary questions are raised, by Capote, and left hanging there by Grobel. This isn't surprising, because the *Playboy* interviewer shows no differentiation of interest, whether the subject is John Updike or Jackie Kennedy. Presumably a fuller treatment of the life and work is on the way. Let us leave Capote, for now, in one of his more triumphant moments, displaying a characteristic mix of fearlessness, spite, and, no doubt, self-flattering embellishment:

> I was sitting there with Tennessee. And this woman came over to [our] table ... and she pulled up her shirt and handed me an eyebrow pencil. And she said, 'I want you to autograph my navel' ... So I wrote my name: T-R-U-M-A-N C-A-P-O-T-E. Right round her navel, like a clock ... Her husband was in a rage. He was drunk as all get-out ... He looked at me with this infinite hatred, handed me the eyebrow pencil, unzipped his fly, and hauled out his equipment ... Everybody was looking. And he said, 'Since you're autographing everything, how'd you like to autograph *this*?' There was a pause ... and I said, 'Well, I don't know if I can autograph it, but perhaps I could initial it.'
>
> *Tatler* 1978 and *Observer* 1985

Philip Roth: No Satisfaction

Philip Roth has just completed a trilogy — the Zuckerman books — and we will come to that in due course. Looking back, though, we see that Roth's previous nine novels arrange themselves in trilogies too — or they do if you nudge them. To begin with we have the three apprentice works: *Goodbye, Columbus* and *Letting Go*, which survey the waking novelist's immediate experience, and *When She Was Good*, which steps self-consciously outside it. Next we have that lip-smacking threesome of frisky Menippean satires, *Our Gang, The Breast* and *The Great American Novel*, where Roth took a manic holiday from his normally sober preoccupations — namely Jewish family life, heartbreak in the Humanities, and the impossibility of getting on with women. Flanking the satires are *Portnoy's Complaint* (1969) and *My Life as a Man* (1974), obsessively personal accounts of emotional failure and collapse, followed by *The Professor of Desire*, which rounds off the trio. Like its weepy, ball-broken hero, David Kepesh, *Desire* is an oddly helpless, melancholy and apathetic continuation of Roth's protracted self-scrutiny; having long been adept at turning his life into literature, Roth here lets life just wash all over him. The new persona is the prostrate man, limping from psychiatrist's couch to psychiatrist's couch, from bed to bed, and from bad to worse.

Roth's women. There are three kinds of them, too, and each novel in the trilogy gives emphasis to a different type (I think we had better call it the 'My Life' trilogy. But stay, gentile reader: mere Jewishness is seen as ever less central to the Roth predicament, and is given only incidental treatment here). The first kind of girl is the Girl Who Will Do Anything. And not many girls, it seems, will Do that. *Portnoy's Complaint* inspected this type most closely, in the person of The

Monkey, the hero's reckless companion, and also, even more enjoyably, through comic fantasy — the world of swinish, gloating sexuality opened up by Thereal McCoy, Portnoy's dirty-talking, cupcake-nippled phantasm. She reappears as Sharon Shatsky in *My Life as a Man* and, one book later, as Birgitta, a daring and predatory Scandinavian with whom Kepesh has a tremulous European jaunt. The good thing about these girls is that you can do whatever the hell you like to them in bed. The bad thing is that you wish they wouldn't let you. While the girls are unfrightened by their own waywardness, the Roth man always is — in the end, anyway. There is something deeply unladylike, also, in the ease with which they get on with their own desires.

The Roth man is not as frightened of the first type of Roth woman as he is of the second type of Roth woman, whom he nonetheless tends to marry. This type is the Ball-Breaker, and her starkest representative in the trilogy is Maureen in *My Life as a Man* (her prototype, though one brilliantly transposed in social context, was Lucy in *When She Was Good*). The Ball-Breaker's mission is to ensnare, flatten and stomp on the Roth man; when she has got him impotent, enervated and wondering if he is a homosexual, she has got him where she wants him. The Ball-Breaker makes a cleverly varied guest-appearance in *The Professor of Desire* as Helen Kepesh, where added stress is given to her vanity, aimlessness, alcoholism, her grandiose fantasies and her wasted intelligence and beauty. You have to look rather harder for the Ball-Breaker in *Portnoy*. The Monkey is a handful all right, but she lacks the Ball-Breaker's destructive energy and deluded self-belief. Who is it, then, who stands over the hero with a knife, who lets him glimpse her menstrual blood, who in some sense 'marries' him with ineluctably horrendous results? Why, Sophie Portnoy, the Jewish Mother — whose hips, Portnoy can't help noticing, even towards the end of the novel, 'aren't bad . . . '

The third type of Roth woman does not scare the Roth man. Instead, she is scared by him. She is the tender realist, methodical, protective, self-abnegating. She is not a Dickensian Little Woman; on the contrary, she is a Big Woman, with a determined if precarious working relationship with reality. Despite her past bruises and hurts, she sees things the way things really are, and longs to rescue the Roth man for the sane world: she is, above all, *unpsychotic*. The Pumpkin and The Pilgrim shared the role of the Big Woman in

Portnoy, Susan played her in *My Life*, and in *Desire* she edges into centre-stage as Claire, with whom the crippled Roth man, at the end of his tether, played out by all that sex and spite, tries to rebuild his life. The great hitch about the Big Woman, though — and now we see Roth's anxieties turning full circle — is that they will not *quite* do Anything. And this tiny omission is enough to allow sexual boredom to nip giggling through the bedroom door; suddenly, a lifetime of depleted possibilities is on view. 'Anything', as usual, is symbolised by enthusiastic fellatio (or perhaps it just *is* enthusiastic fellatio). Claire will do fellatio, but she won't ... you know, do it enthusiastically. This is all it takes. Some people are never satisfied.

Well, never being satisfied is Roth's great theme. I wish I had 50p for every time the phrase 'on good terms with pleasure' is wistfully summoned in the 'My Life' trilogy. For pleasure and the Roth man are incompatible: they just do not get along, they just cannot work it out, they just get on each other's nerves. In *Portnoy* the condition was seen as a subject for black satire (the hero's desires harshly ridiculing his highmindedness), in *My Life* as a subject for tragic farce (the hero's highmindedness proscribing his desires); in the last book, however, the condition is seen as too disabling to be a subject for anything but itself. This is not only no joke, Roth seems to be saying, it is no novel either, nor anything else that has a shape: it is simply how it is. One feels both relieved and surprised when Roth expresses it so poignantly (in a projected introduction to a course of lectures which Claire calls 'Desire 341'):

> I am devoted to fiction, and I assure you that in time I will tell you whatever I may know about it, but in truth nothing lives in me like my life.

Paradoxically, too, Roth seems in this novel to have moved *beyond* autobiography. He no longer looks at life with the selective eye of the novelist: he looks at his own past with the fastidious frown of the literary critic, grading, evaluating, trying to separate the serious from the unserious. (I have always wondered why Roth's 'bookishness' relies on translated works — Chekhov, Gogol, Kafka, Dostoevsky — for its points of reference. I suspect that Roth now regards novels as how-to books about life, and he prefers to get their tips on living without the distractions and evasions of a responsive verbal surface.)

And what a sorrily half-tone world seeps through the self-immersion. *The Professor of Desire* is by far the most exotic in its locations of all Roth's novels — the East and West coasts, London, France, Italy, Prague, Hong Kong — and yet the changing landscapes remain blissfully unobserved (a derisory 'Sorry, Yank, 'e seems a bit sleepy tonight', for instance, is the extent to which Roth captures the texture of life in our own country). 'The whole damn thing could have taken place in Cincinnati!' says Kepesh after his Far East débâcle — and indeed it could have done. *My Life as a Man* contains a good, sharp section in which the narrator focuses his eyes on the year of 1968 and realises just how much has happened while he's been asleep inside himself. Not even this release — or injection of balance — is available to Kepesh: he is lost in a truly lugubrious solipsism, a mere patball of the neuroses which stride unchallenged through his psyche. Accordingly, all ironic distance has gone; nothing separates author and narrator; Roth sees no more than Kepesh sees.

How else has the world changed? It is quieter and flatter than it used to be, and there is no delight in it. Roth's novelistic ear, arguably his greatest gift as a writer, has evidently been well cauliflowered by recent events: only the Jewish-American characters retain their own voices, while everyone else joins the stilted and lachrymose debate on the hero's despair. Even the expository prose has lost its relish, settling for a droll, automatic elegance: it is full of ugly chimes ('my father intends, by the very intensity . . . ', 'ending the term's work with three masterworks', etc.) and back-to-the-drawing-board formulations ('my year as a visiting fellow in erotic daredevilry', 'she is not only stunning-looking, she is also real', etc.). Some of the book's aridities may be an attempt to create a reflection of despair, but the zestlessness does sometimes read like a failure of professional sincerity, or nerve.

Now what? Will the vision re-expand, as it seems to yearn to do, or will it squirm deeper into the tunnel of the self? Is Roth's subject the situation of the American writer (something that could do with a little analysis)? Or is Roth's subject identical to — entirely contiguous with — his life as a man?

*   *   *

It is an awkward and recent truth that most contemporary novelists are deeply influenced by their own lives, and not least by the amount of praise, fame and money their work attracts. A few unpierceable geniuses may smile at the thousandth rejection-slip, may yawn at that staggering cheque, but such things tend to affect the confidence − and the writing. This doesn't matter so much in England, where the boundaries between success and its opposite are often hard to establish. (J. Cowper Powys is the obvious example, a monument of neglect far more renowned for his obscurity than many of his rivals were famed for their fame.) Over in America, though, you can't help knowing where you stand.

In his inimitably wholehearted way, Roth has let success go to his head. Success arrived there in 1980, with a big suitcase, and hasn't moved out. *The Anatomy Lesson* may be the third and final instalment of the Zuckerman trilogy, but it is also Roth's second consecutive novel about what success is like. Such fixity! Though they all want it, in a way, writers tend to be mistrustful of the ridiculous accident of bestsellerdom. Trust Roth, then, to embrace it as his subject. Completing the self-beleaguerment, he has now written two autobiographical novels about the consequences of writing autobiographical novels. I may be wrong (perhaps I'm *very* old-fashioned), but the question appears to me to be: do we *need* this new kind of autobiographical novel? I mean, we seemed to be getting on pretty well without it.

Whereas a British work on literary success would be rather low on incident (do radio interview; have lunch with publisher; get boiler mended), it is true that the American version provides considerable drama . . . You become a millionaire. You are mobbed in the street. Pale 'loners' have your picture tacked to the dartboard. Gossip columnists pair you off with Liza Minelli. Your sexual confessions increase the sale of pantihose, nationwide. PR firms want your mother to star in their rollmop commercials. Bestsellerdom rips the hard covers off life, because 'everyone has read that book'. In Roth's quasi-fictional world, that book is called 'Carnovsky'. We know it as *Portnoy's Complaint*, and we've all read it too.

Starting with the premonitory novella *The Ghost Writer*, moving on through the fame-flurry of *Zuckerman Unbound*, Roth now confronts the aftermath of literary success. Despite the 'trilogy' tag, you often wonder whether they aren't simply three books running with the same hero: Roth's post-*Portnoy* alter egos are so uniform that you could argue for a full pentathlon, roping in *The Professor of Desire* and *My Life as a Man*. The Zuckerman novels, at any rate, have no plot and little patterning. The Anne Frank motif from *The Ghost Writer*, for instance, is briefly taken up in *Zuckerman Unbound*, yet nothing of the first book survives into the third — nothing, that is to say, of artistic centrality.

Zuckerman is there, Aunt Essie is there, but structure is not there. You get joists, braces, buttresses (a skipful of teachabilities): you don't get a house. The books have a shape, that of the case history. Although the author may feign weary contempt for any Roth-Zuckerman equations, it must be said that the novels read like *experience*. Experience reworked, displaced, mordantly heightened — but not distanced, and not transformed.

The Roth themes, or reiterations, are compelling enough, and they are intricately deployed. Nathan Zuckerman's disaffection with the writer's calling has now reached the point where he is blocked, drugged, drunk and practically bedridden, assailed by 'untreatable pain of unknown origin' which makes writing physically as well as mentally unendurable. His persecution at the hands of the Jewish establishment continues, though in more highbrow form. Rabbi Wapter from *The Ghost Writer* has evolved into Professor Milton Appel (a nasty *Commentary* type), whose more sophisticated disapproval takes the same basic line: the charge of self-loathing anti-Semitism, as evinced in that 'mocking, hate-filled bestseller' with its lewd satire on Jewish ideals, sentiments and terrors. This is particularly hard on Zuck, whose pre-'Carnovsky' image was one of crew-necked maturity and high seriousness. But his most stinging excruciations come from guilt, and from a transgression that lies much closer to home.

The guilt theme appeared to have peaked out at the end of *Zuckerman Unbound*, when the hero's father died with the word 'Bastard' on his lips after reading 'Carnovsky' in hospital. 'You killed him,' confirmed Zuckerman's brother. 'With that book.' In *The Anatomy Lesson*, Zuckerman pins his mother's death on 'Carnovsky' too. The loved son inflicted a fatal wound on his mother: 'literature is literature, but still, there were things that were real that Nathan has used' — *used*, with the additional sense of violation and betrayal. Interestingly, his guilt is never for a moment identified as *literary*. There are literary reasons, after all, for not 'using' real things, including oneself, without some countervailing

broadness of vision or design. Zuckerman never blames himself as a
writer. He blames himself, and he blames writing, but never both at
once.

And here he is, doing it all over again. Is the present book a way of
compounding the sin or of absolving it? As if to propitiate the ghosts
of his parents, Zuckerman decides (like Bellow's Eugene Henderson) to make a late bid for medical school, to become, however
tardily, the good boy in the *Portnoy* joke. 'Help!' cries the Jewish
mother on the beach. 'My son the doctor is drowning!' He flies out
to Chicago, spurning his New York celebrity, his four mistresses, his
inertness, abandoning above all and for ever those three hated words
that have stared him in the face for twenty years: 'qwertyuiop,
asdfghkl and zxcvbnm.'

High on booze and pain-killers, on despair and mother-grief,
Zuckerman undergoes his elaborate crack-up. He passes himself off
as a gross, blaspheming pornographer (called Milton Appel: the
intention is clear, as usual, though the humour here is way off
beam); at a snowbound cemetery he attacks a pious and elderly
Jewish mourner (Mr Freytag, one of several superb cameos): he falls
(or is he pushed by his Nazi-ish chauffeuse?) and splits his face open
on a headstone. Hospitalised, and silenced by his wired jaw,
Zuckerman finally submits to the only real anatomy lesson. He finds
out what pain can do — 'he'd had no idea' — and what it does to
others. And he learns the impossibility, so the last sentence promises,
of escaping 'the corpus that was his'.

Well. Roth's corpus certainly has a funny shape to it by now,
entirely transformed as it has been by that 'hate-filled bestseller',
Portnoy's Complaint. No modern writer, perhaps no writer, has
taken self-examination so far and so literally. What would Roth's
oeuvre look like now, if *Portnoy* had simply sunk without trace? He
recognises that 'the size of the success' was largely fortuitous, and
yet he has written three whole novels about what that success did to
him. Where next? A novel about *this* novel? A tetralogy about the
trilogy?

'It wasn't literary fame,' says Zuckerman, 'it was sexual fame, and
sexual fame stinks.' This may be true, but *Portnoy* remains the only
novel in which Roth's contorted genius managed to shed its inhi-
bitions. With the case of Nathan Zuckerman, the self-revelation
exhausts its power to titillate or scandalise, and the reader starts
looking for the artistic content of the work, not the symbols, the

décor, so much as the phrasing, the responsiveness. Roth's prose is usually elegant and sprucely ironic, but it has lost the capacity to surprise. There is not enough laughter or lyricism, there is not enough weather, there is not enough happening on the page. The Zuckerman novels look like life looks before art has properly finished with it. And Roth's corpus still gives the impression of a turbulent talent searching for a decorous way to explode.

New Statesman 1978 and *Observer* 1984

Elvis: He Did It His Way

At this stage in the obsequies, a genuinely 'shocking' book about Elvis Presley would disclose that the King secretly gave away vast sums to charity, that he was actually very slim and healthy, and spent much of his free time working with handicapped children. But it is not to be. Following the slanderous testimonies of every hanger-on in the entourage, we are now offered a definitive summation of the grossness, egomania and barbaric vulgarity that was, apparently, Elvis.

Albert Goldman's *Elvis*, which one is obliged to call an investigative biography, begins and ends with an eerie evocation of the mature Presley. First, the house — Graceland. It looks like a brothel or a gangster's triplex: red velour, gilded tassels, simulated waterfalls, polyurethane finish. Elvis always insisted that everything around him had to be *new*. 'When I wuz growin' up in Tupelo,' he is quoted as saying, 'I lived with enough fuckin' antiques to do me for a lifetime.'

On to the master bedroom — black suede walls, crimson carpets and curtains, 81 square feet of bed with mortuary headboard and speckled armrests. To one side is an easel supporting a large photograph of Elvis's mother, Gladys; to the other is a sepia-toned portrait of Jesus Christ in his pink nightie. On the bed lies Elvis himself — 'propped up', in Goldman's gallant formulation, 'like a big fat woman recovering from some operation on her reproductive organs.'

Before going to work, Elvis rings his valet and junk-food guru, Hamburger James. After a midnight snack — $100 worth of Fudgesicles — Elvis consumes a pound of Dixie Cotton bacon, four orders of mash with gravy, plus lots of sauerkraut and crowder peas.

He sleeps in diapers these days, thick towels pinned round his middle. He weighs over 18 stone.

This is a modern biography, so we now follow Elvis from the bedroom to the bathroom. Not that Elvis can get there under his own steam: a bodyguard has to carry him. The bulb-studded sanctum is full of devotional literature, high-powered laxatives, and the King's special 'medication' − i.e., his drugs. Elvis hates drug-addicts; he would like to see them herded into concentration camps. He once had an audience with Nixon, offering himself as a figurehead in the battle against dope. He was stoned at the time. In fact, he is a drug-addict. His doctor must delve between his toes for an unpopped vein.

In his six-door Batmobile Elvis leads the motorcade to Memphis Airport. His private plane, like his house, is a kitsch nightmare of velvet and plastic. At dawn the *Lisa Marie* (named after Elvis's daughter) lands at Las Vegas. Waiting limos ferry the party to the Imperial Suite of the Hilton International. Elvis is cranked down into sleep. 'Mommy, I have to go to the bathroom!' he tells his girl-friend. 'Mommy will take you.' He sleeps. He is cranked awake. He eats, with a handgun beside his plate.

Bandaged and 'braced' − i.e., corseted − Elvis dons an outfit embroidered with the crowned head of King Tutankhamun and buckles his $10,000 gladiator's belt. He stumbles and mumbles through his act, climaxing with his 'American Trilogy': 'Dixie', 'The Battle Hymn of the Republic', 'All My Trials'. He comes off stage pouring with sweat and screaming for his medication. Soon he is back in his tomb, vowing that never again will he play 'this fuck'n' Vegas'.

Elvis: What Happened?, published just before Presley's death, was the first exposé, cobbled together by a couple of sacked goons. Since then, everyone has blabbed. Well, what *did* happen? How did Elvis's life, like his voice, turn from energy and innocence into canting, parodic ruin? Goldman's answer is that the whole phenomenon was corrupt and farcical from the beginning. 'There is', he warns, 'absolutely no poignance in this history.'

Elvis's family were hillbillies, 'a deracinated and restless race'. Elvis's father, Vernon, 'greedy and stupid', 'a dullard and a donkey', was clearly a fine representative of the breed. Elvis was 'a silly little country boy' who just happened to be able 'to sing like a nigger', the 'acne-spotted self-pity' of his early songs making a strong appeal to 'the hysterically self-pitying mood of millions of teen-agers'.

Nursing dreams of becoming a new Valentino, Elvis's real ambition was to become a movie star. Soon 'the biggest putz in the history of film-making' was well established as 'one of the ugliest and most repulsive presences on the American screen'. When this bubble burst, he settled for the Vegas routine. The audience was ideal, consisting of 'a couple thousand middle-aged people sated with food and drink'.

Personally Elvis was always 'a momma's boy', a bully, a coward and a fool. His career as 'pervert', 'voyeur', 'masturbator' and so forth, was predictable as early as 1956, when Goldman pictures him 'thrusting his fat tongue into the mouth of a backstage groupie'. Finally, the 'freak', the 'pig junkie', completes his 'deterioration into homicidal madness'.

It quickly becomes clear — does it not? — that Goldman isn't to be trusted. In his palpable eagerness to explode the Presley Myth, he has erected an anti-myth to replace it — which, in turn, is already being whittled away at by transatlantic commentators. It may indeed be the case that Elvis was no more than a horrible, and horribly uncomplicated, embodiment of American Success; but *Elvis* leaves us none the wiser.

In biography, displays of such inordinate aggression leave one wondering about the personal problems of the author rather than the subject. I read *Elvis* under the impression that Goldman was a surly young iconoclast of the *Rolling Stone* school of New Journalism. On the back flap I am confronted by a middle-aged chipmunk who used to be Professor of English and Comparative Literature at Columbia. As should by now be evident, the book is a prodigy of bad writing, excitable, sarcastic and barely literate. It is also as exploitative as the exploiters whom Goldman reviles, and no more tasteful than a Presley pants-suit.

Observer 1981

Diana Trilling at Claremont Avenue

In New York, Diana Trilling is regarded with the suspicious awe customarily reserved for the city's senior literary ladies. Whenever I announced my intention of going along to interview her, people looked at me with trepidation, a new respect, a certain holy dread. I felt I was about to enter the lion's den — or the den of the literary lioness, which is often just as dangerous.

I had tangled with Mrs Trilling before, more than ten years ago, and had my own reasons for fearing her well-known asperity. Mr and Mrs Lionel Trilling were on a visit to London at the time, and, knowing of my admiration for Mr Trilling's work, a common friend had arranged a meeting: tea at the Connaught, the London hotel where all distinguished Americans seem to put up. I remember Lionel as milky-haired, laconic and serene; I remember Diana as dark, foxy and fierce. At one point I made an incautious remark, illiberal in tendency — an undergraduate remark. Mrs Trilling cracked her teacup into its saucer and said: 'Do you really mean that? Then what are we doing here? Why are we sitting here having tea with this person?'

Diana Trilling lives in Claremont Avenue, near Columbia University, where her husband taught: he was the first Jew to gain tenure there, incredible as that now seems. American cities appear to have a habit of surrounding their seats of learning with slums. In the foreword to her first collection of articles, *Claremont Essays* (1964), Mrs Trilling wrote about the exact sense of urban positioning that Columbia affords. The community is perched on its grassy hill, a fortress of intellection, with boiling Harlem just down the slope.

On the telephone Mrs Trilling had given me carefully, indeed grimly detailed instructions for the subway. One false move, I gathered, and I would find myself clambering out of a manhole on Duke Ellington Boulevard. In the end I took a cab — through the Upper West Side, along bending Broadway for the lawless Nineties, and up into the beleaguered castle of the University, and Claremont Avenue, a wide clean street with the solid, civic feel of old New York. Punctual to the second, I warily pressed the bell. Now, perhaps, the real perils would begin.

Mrs Trilling received me in her ground-floor apartment. I liked her immediately — actually, I had liked her the first time — and knew that I was going to enjoy the afternoon. However, I quickly re-identified the kind of unease that a woman like Diana Trilling is always liable to provoke. You have to *watch what you say* when she's around. I mean this in the best sense. Mrs Trilling is not touchy or snobbish or over-sensitive; she is just intellectually vigilant, snake-eyed. In her company you are obliged to move up a gear — you must weed out your lazier, sloppier thoughts (like the one that had briefly incensed her in the Connaught). No, she isn't the most soothing of companions; but you end up chastened and braced, and there is much laughter and enlightenment to be had on the way.

The life of the American intellectual is qualitatively different from its British equivalent. In America, intellectuals are public figures (whereas over here they are taken rather less seriously than ordinary citizens — at most, they are licensed loudmouths). The intellectual life therefore has a dimension of political responsibility; the crises of modern liberalism — the race question, McCarthyism, feminism, Vietnam, Israel — are magnified but also taken personally, vitally. Spats between writers are transformed, willy-nilly, into unshirkable crusades. The Trillings lived this life together and experienced all its triumphs and wounds. Lillian Hellman, Martha's Vineyard, 1952, 1968, Little Brown, UnAmerican Activities, the *New York Review* . . . it is a ceaseless, swirling litany. These hatchets may look pretty rusty to the outsider, but they will never be buried. And maybe the positions are more fiercely held now that they are held alone.

It is all the more unexpected, then, that Diana Trilling suddenly finds herself the author of a bestselling book about a tabloid homicide. The murder of Herman Tarnower and the trial of his mistress Jean Harris electrified America in a way that (I suspect) will never be fully comprehensible to the British public. It is hard work trying to dream up a home-grown equivalent of the crime — as if, say, the headmistress of Roedean had done away with Jimmy

Saville. Diana Trilling's original title, vetoed for legal reasons, was 'A Respectable Murder', which is doubly appropriate. To the public, the murder was all about class, and in America class tends to shade into race: Mrs Harris was a high-class Wasp, 'Hi' Tarnower a vulgar diet doc, a Jewish counter-jumper. And, as a rejected mistress, one spurned for a younger replacement, Mrs Harris's case seemed to dramatise the universal female fear. It wasn't just a respectable murder; it seemed, at first, almost to be a justifiable one.

But the most extraordinary thing about *Mrs Harris* is its energy. Not until later did I discover Mrs Trilling's true age: I had thought she was ten years younger, and even then I was astonished by the stamina that had gone into the book. Every day Mrs Trilling would drive out to the court-house (before the trial, also, she did a little investigative work in the Westchester suburbs, hampered by bad weather, lack of co-operation, and by her own reluctance to pry into other people's lives). After a day of scandal and/or back-breaking boredom in court, she would drive back to Claremont Avenue, and start to write. 'I was working fifteen hours a day for three-and-a-half months,' says Diana Trilling, who, it transpires, is now in her mid-seventies.

The energy of the book, however, is not only a matter of endurance. After its slowish start, *Mrs Harris* builds into an intricate compendium of wit, social grasp, clarity of thought and novelistic brio. Diana Trilling's essays and articles were never dull, but here she is revealed as a writer with an infallible eye for the interesting. And now it seems that we can look forward to an extended period of productivity – facilitated, perhaps, by the condition of widowhood. 'When Lionel was alive, we tended to do what he wanted to do. Now there's nothing else to do but work.' Literary widowhood often means a long spell of literary executorship, and Mrs Trilling has duly completed her editing of the twelve-volume *Uniform Edition of the Works of Lionel Trilling*. She is now engaged on a book about her early life. It is possible, too, that she has in some sense emerged from her husband's shadow, and feels a new freedom and confidence.

'Growing old is hard. Growing old alone is harder,' she said. 'You become more sensitive with your friends. You wonder whether you are being asked out because of pity. There is an increased dependence on routine. I won't leave the bed unmade in the morning. I won't stand by the refrigerator and eat a boiled egg. I *want* to, but I don't.' She talks of her husband without self-drama but with palpable regret. 'I feel the usual things . . . I wish now that I had worshipped him a bit more.'

The apartment in Claremont Avenue is as elegant and well-preserved as its owner. Everywhere there are books, framed photographs, mementoes. 'The individual is best defined by his social geography,' wrote Diana Trilling in *We Must March My Darlings* (1977). Lionel Trilling wrote about society but normally only in relation to literature, or culture: he was also a critic with certain bold mythologising tendencies, with a love for the exciting idea, the daring construct. 'Yes,' said Diana Trilling, with some self-deprecation, 'I was always the one more interested in the social side, in the here and now.' 'But there aren't many people like you,' I said cautiously. 'You're a clear thinker.' 'That's right. Too clear, perhaps,' said Mrs Trilling.

Observer 1982

Mailer: The Avenger
and the Bitch

The year was 1955. At thirty-two, Norman Mailer was the celebrated and reviled author of three novels, and a notorious brawler, sage and drunk. By his own admission, he was at this point arrogant, terrified, greedy, spoilt – and galvanised on marijuana.

> Q. Do you feel that age will mould you into a high-priced please-the-public author?
> A. I doubt it, but I also know that exhaustion of the will can come to anyone.

It would be tempting, here in 1981, to pounce on the young Mailer's stoned foreboding. His latest money-spinner, *Of Women and Their Elegance*, has taken a pummelling from the American press and is due for a torrid time of it over here. With its terrible title (that 'Of' somehow guaranteeing the vulgarity of the enterprise), its irrelevant photographs and coffee-table packaging, the volume seems to boast its own vulnerability to attack. As you flap through its slippery pages, you find that it is Mailer's second book about Marilyn Monroe, and his third book running about the recently dead and their sex lives (its immediate predecessor was *The Executioner's Song*, the story of the murderer Gary Gilmore, who demanded death by firing squad in 1977). What happened to the man who has said – loud and often – that he hoped 'to dare a new art of the brave'? Clearly it is time for some revision of Mailer's American dream.

Now, at fifty-seven, Mailer has accumulated six wives and eight (or maybe nine) children. He is obliged to earn over $400,000 a year to stay abreast of alimony and tuition fees. Last year his summer house was confiscated by the taxmen. He has received, and spent, a $635,000 advance on an unwritten novel. And he is still half a million dollars in debt.

In his three-storey brownstone apartment in Brooklyn Heights, overlooking New York Harbor and the Dunhill lighters of Manhattan, Mailer perched on a stiff-backed chair, and told me to sit on the old velvet sofa. 'I can't sit on a soft chair. I writhe around a lot. Hurts my back,' he said with an apologetic wince.

The battered but comfortable apartment feels like a ship. A pulley system leads to the upper floors. Mailer used to have a crow's-nest office at the top; the once-vigorous author would clamber up a rope to begin the day's work. Now he goes to a rented office down the street, trudging back for lunch. Children of alarmingly various ages had gathered for their supper in the dining area. Mailer's sixth wife, the dark-eyed model and actress Norris Church ('she's half my age and twice my height'), sat imposingly near by, reading a buxom magazine.

His face is more delicate and less pugnacious than you would expect, the body more rounded, dapper and diminutive. The tangled hair is white but plentiful, the frequent smile knowing but unreserved. Despite his long history of exhibitionism, he no longer enjoys giving interviews. You can sense him wondering how much of his charm he will need to disclose.

Mailer watched wistfully as I feasted on my drink. 'It's the terrible price you have to pay,' he said, referring to his own eight-month abstinence. 'The day just wasn't long enough, and I have to work so hard now, to make the money. My nerves have been pretty well encrusted by booze, thank God. It's okay. It just means there's nothing to look forward to at the end of the day.'

'Thanks a lot,' said Norris. 'What about me?'

'No, the sex is great. The fucking's great. I just miss it, that's all.'

This reminded me of another sacrifice Mailer has been forced to make. He has always argued that any act of sex is invalid, corrupt, soul-endangering, etc., if the chance of conception has been ruled out. 'I've got eight kids,' said Mailer. 'I can't *afford* to believe that any more ... My hopes and expectations have changed. I no longer feel prepared to go to the wall for any big ideas.'

'Have you mellowed', I asked cautiously, '— or what?'

'Not really. Let's say I've adjusted to circumstances. At last.'

Well, it has been a long haul. This is the man — and here headlines and half-impressions flash past — who stabbed his wife, who ran for mayor, who butted Gore Vidal, who 'won the election for Kennedy', who went on TV in his boxing trunks, who told novelist Alan Lelchuck that when he got through with him 'there'd be nothing left but a hank of hair and some fillings'.

This is the Existential Hero, the Philosopher of Hip, the Chauvinist Pig, the Psychic Investigator, the Prisoner of Sex. For thirty years Mailer has been the cosseted superbrat of American letters. It has taken him quite a while to grow up. But the process has made for a fascinating spectacle.

'Early success — that was the worst damn thing that could have happened to me.' A bright Jewish boy from Brooklyn, a Harvard graduate, Norman went off to fight as a rifleman in the Philippines. Showing that mixture of recklessness and calculation which marks his entire career, Mailer had the express intention of gathering material for the Great American Novel of the Second World War. A brave but clumsy soldier, he survived his few skirmishes, came back to Brooklyn, and wrote *The Naked and the Dead*. He was twenty-four.

Before publication Mailer left for France with his first wife, Beatrice. Calling in at the American Express office in Nice, Mailer was handed what amounted to a swag bag of money and fame. American express! Number-one bestseller, sobbing reviews, forty translation rights sold, Norman, get back here! That 'meant farewell', Mailer would write in *Advertisements for Myself* (1959), 'to an average man's experience'.

Early acclaim won't harm a writer if he has the strength, or the cynicism, not to believe in that acclaim. But Norman lapped it up, and is perhaps only now recovering from the deception. True, he was very young, the success was very great — and the book was very good. Reading *The Naked and the Dead* today, one is astounded by Mailer's precocious sense of human variety, by the way he goes a step further into the extremities of exhaustion, yearning and terror, and, above all, by his ability to listen intensely to the ordinary voices of America. The novel was impossibly adult: the immaturity was all to come.

It is hard to imagine the kind of freedom that was suddenly Mailer's. After an equivalent success, an English writer might warily give up his job as a schoolmaster, or buy a couple of filing cabinets.

But Mailer had the whole of America to play with. Flattered and lionised, he bummed around Hollywood failing to write a screenplay, lived it up a good deal and discovered a further perk of literary fame: 'getting girls I would never otherwise have gotten'. 'I was a node in a new electronic landscape of celebrity, personality and status.' The only trouble was that he had nothing left to write about.

The reception of Mailer's second novel, *Barbary Shore* (1951), was hysterical too, but the nature of the hysteria had changed. 'It is relatively rare to discover a novel', wrote one of the more temperate reviewers, 'whose obvious intention is to debauch as many readers as possible, mentally, morally, physically and politically.' A murky, paceless tale of spies and subversives, predators and impotents, the new novel had little of the style and control of *The Naked and the Dead*. The prose gurgles with clichés, tautologies and uneasy mandarinisms. What offended the critics, of course, was the book's supposedly socialist message. What offends the present-day reader is the book's message, period.

The truth is that in the vacuum of success Mailer had fallen prey to the novelist's fatal disease: ideas. His naïveté about 'answers', 'the big illumination', 'the secret of everything' persists to this day. An admirer of Malraux and the equally humourless Jean Malaquais, Mailer dubbed *Barbary Shore* the 'first of the existentialist novels in America' and himself 'a Marxian anarchist' — 'a contradiction in terms, but a not unprofitable contradiction for trying to do some original thinking'. It is all too easy, though not very profitable, to imagine Mailer at this time, sitting around doing lots of original thinking. His thraldom to catchpenny shamanism had begun. Oh well, existentialism (so far as I can gather from Mailer's writing on the topic) means never having to say you're sorry.

Over the next few years Mailer underwent a kind of aesthetic nervous breakdown. The reverse he suffered over *Barbary Shore* released a primal scream of rage and hurt; it also wrecked his artistic confidence. The resulting combination of Big Ideas and naked desperation proved crucial to Mailer's psychology. In a deep haze of illness, depression and drink, Mailer gouged out *The Deer Park* (1955). It was turned down by seven publishers.

Against the grain as always, Mailer had this time fallen foul of the obscenity laws. Or so the publishers feared — or so they claimed they feared. Mailer raged against the 'snobs, snots and fools' of the literary establishment but refused — at first — to tone down his mannered portrait of Hollywood amorality. When the novel was finally accepted Mailer took another look at the page proofs, intending no lawyer's deletions but 'just a few touches for style'.

By this stage Mailer was 'bombed and sapped and charged and stoned with lush, with benny, saggy, Milltown, coffee, and two packs a day'. His artistic nerve began to jangle with his commercial sense. 'I needed a success and I needed it badly ... *The Deer Park* had damn well better make it,' wrote Mailer in a startlingly candid passage in *Advertisements for Myself*. Shamefacedly, he started cleaning up some doubtful scenes. He wanted 'a powerful bestseller' but also wanted 'to save the book from being minor'.

Having rendered the book major (whew!), and even more powerful, Mailer waited anxiously for publication. On a mescaline trip, he rewrote the last six lines. Confident for a while, he lost his nerve again and sent out copies of the book to various bigwigs with fawning inscriptions ('if you do not answer,' he wrote to Hemingway, ' ... then fuck you, and I will never attempt to communicate with you again.' Hemingway didn't answer). *The Deer Park* was a 'half success', as indeed was its due, and not the 'breakthrough' for which Norman had pined. As a last gesture, he put together a full-page advertisement with choice quotes from the reviews: 'Disgusting. Nasty. Sordid and crummy. Junk.'

'Norman,' a friend said to him at the time. 'You're a writer. You shouldn't be doing all this.' 'You're wrong,' said Mailer. 'This is *exactly* what I should be doing.'

American success has been doubly unkind to him. Never timid, Mailer accepted his fate — and proceeded to do his growing up in public. 'I was on the edge of many things', he wrote later, 'and I had more than a bit of violence in me.'

Earlier that winter I had gone to see Mailer on the 1-million-dollar set of *Ragtime*, Miloš Forman's rambling film version of the Doctorow novel. Turn-of-the-century New York had been re-created on an acre of Shepperton mud. Nattily dressed, his wig prinked, Mailer was playing the role of the architect Stanford White, and Norris, appropriately, was playing his wife. In the scene they were shooting that morning, White was to make his entrance into Madison Square Garden (whose facade had been reconstructed for the occasion), there to be shot in the head by an enraged cuckold.

The interior murder scene had already been filmed. In the car on the way back to the studios that day, and later over lunch, Mailer elaborated on his existential anxieties about his 'symbolic death' on the screen. 'They put wires, charges and blood packs in my hair. Unpleasant, but that didn't bother me so much as the idea of enacting my death. Then John Lennon was shot, two days before we did the scene. After that I knew which death was for real.'

'Okay, Norman!' the megaphone had bawled on the set that morning. 'Let's do it again!' For the seventh time the jalopy pulled up at the steps of Madison Square Garden. Mr and Mrs White pushed through the waiting newsmen while antique cameras flared and fizzed. Norman got to say his lines. It was the Mailers' last scene on the film, and the mood was genial. When the final take was finished, Forman shouted out: 'Okay! Let's hear it for Norman!' Norman smiled and nodded at the applause of the crew, pleased, braced, unembarrassable to the last.

During the sixties Mailer directed and starred in three films of his own, *Wild 90*, *Outside the Law* and *Maidstone*, in which he pretends to be, respectively, a mafioso, a cop and a film director. All three were disasters, and much of the money lost was Mailer's own. But still, he hardly needed the big screen by this point: he was doing most of his acting in real life.

So began the years of the Performing Self. Why write it when you can live it? The author was no longer a craven figure hunched over his desk: the Author was a Hero, an Event, a Spectacle.

In the autumn of 1960 Mailer threw a party with his second wife, Adele Morales, a Peruvian painter. 'She's an Indian, primitive and elemental,' he liked to boast. Things got a little too elemental that night on the Upper West Side. After several fistfights, and in a frenzy of alcoholic paranoia, Mailer forcibly divided his guests into two opposing groups, those for and against him. Towards dawn he stabbed Adele, nearly fatally. In a subsequent poem which I have been unable to trace, Mailer wrote that 'So long as you use a knife/There's some love left,' or words to that effect. Cheering for Adele, who anyway didn't press charges.

'Fuck you! Fuck you all!' was how Mailer opened his speeches when he campaigned for Mayor of New York in 1969. 'No more traffic! No more bullshit!' It was Mailer's dream to make New York

City the fifty-first State in the Union; he wanted the city divided into autonomous units, 'some based on free love'. In *The Presidential Papers* (1963) Mailer had proposed the following 'existential legislation': states wishing to retain capital punishment should do so by means of public gladiatorial games; cancer researchers should be executed in this way 'if they failed to make progress after two years'. Today Mailer will look you in the eye and say, 'I was *sure* I was going to win.' John Lindsay won. Mailer came nowhere.

'It seems that people want my ideas,' Mailer had said bewilderedly in mid-campaign. Mailer's ideas: they were coming in a torrent by now. The essays 'Reflections on Hip', 'The White Negro' and 'The Existential Hero' are the keys to how Mailer was regarding himself in those days. Attracted by Hemingway's idea of 'the Good' ('what makes me feel good is the Good') and Lawrence's idea of 'blood' (ditto), Mailer cobbled together a philosophy grounded on drugs and jazz, mighty orgasms, frequent fistfights, and doing what he liked all the time. This credo resembles the usual rag-bag of Sixties sophistries, but it was imbued with Mailer's own kind of extremism.

The effect of these musings on his fiction became apparent in *An American Dream* (1964), a novel which Mailer composed in eight monthly instalments for *Esquire*. The unprepossessing hero, Rojack, is prefigured in the early fragment 'The Time of Her Time', in which the stud hero, who refers to his organ as 'the avenger', finally brings his girl to her first orgasm by whispering in her ear (after sodomy) the words, 'You dirty little Jew.' 'That whipped her over' all right.

An American Dream takes this kind of thing a stage further. In brutal summary, Rojack murders his wife, sodomises the German maid, outwits the police, and impregnates the Wasp princess, having beaten up her super-hip black boyfriend. This is the novel's critical redemptive moment, as Rojack feasts on his blonde:

> ... and I said sure to the voice in me, and felt love fly in like some great winged bird, some beating of wings at my back, and felt her will dissolve into tears, and some great sorrow like roses drowned in the salt of the sea came flooding from her womb and ...

In the Evelyn Waugh *Letters* Mailer is briefly described as 'an American pornographer'. For this book, the description holds. It is the prose of a man in a transport, not of sexual excitement so much as the tizzy of false artistry.

Nothing that Mailer writes is without interest, or without a good deal of negligent brilliance, but *Why Are We in Vietnam?* (1967) walks pretty close to the line. Heavily influenced by William Burroughs, the book consists of 200 pages of disc-jockey jive-talk, loosely recounting a hunting expedition and a *macho* initiation test. A failure at the time, the novel now seems no more than a marooned topicality. Mailer reached the end of something here. And he has written no fiction for fifteen years.

Like President Carter's favourite poet, James Dickie, who is reputed to go around the place muttering 'Oh I'm so big. I'm so damned *big*', Mailer has always seen the novel as a challenge to his masculinity. He refers constantly to the author's 'size', 'vastness', 'stature'. When he writes of writing, his metaphors are always competitive, sexual or military. In *Cannibals and Christians* (1966) Mailer salutes the novel as 'the Great Bitch in one's life'. Assessing the work of some contemporaries 'who have slept with the Bitch', Mailer accuses them all of toadyism, timidity and insufficient 'breadth' or 'weight' — or 'size'. 'You don't catch the Bitch that way, buster,' he tells William Styron, 'you got to bring more than a trombone to her boudoir.' The piece ends: 'Can those infantrymen of the arts, the novelists, take us . . . into the palace of the Bitch where the real secrets are stored?' In other words: can Norman?

For the last fifteen years Mailer has been the most sought-after journalist in America. Following his masterpieces of superheated reportage, *The Armies of the Night* (1968) and *Of a Fire on the Moon* (1969), he has played fast and loose with his reputation, and the quality of his work has declined. In 1973 he wrote the notorious *Marilyn*, surviving a plagiarism suit (settled out of court) and the stink emanating from his claim that Monroe was bumped off by Jack and Bobbie Kennedy. In 1975 he wrote *The Fight*, an extended waffle on the Ali–Frazier match. Then came *The Executioner's Song*.

A matter of weeks before the book appeared, Mailer persuaded his publishers to package the Gilmore story as a novel, or rather a 'true-life novel', along the lines of Truman Capote's 'non-fiction novel', *In Cold Blood*. After the 'factoid' squabble over *Marilyn*, the fictoid squabble over *The Executioner's Song* seemed like opportunism disguised as impatience with genre. In fact, the first 300 pages of the book show irreproachable artistry in their re-creation of the locales and loners of middle America; but then Mailer lets the story run away with him, and his reliance on transcripts, tapes and reports finally dishes its artistic claims. Once again, the fatal yearning for monumentality: Norman keeps overplaying his hand with the Great Bitch.

'I don't know, maybe it was too long,' he now admits. 'Since I started needing all this money,' he says, and in such a way that you know he has said it before, 'I've written twice as many books as I should have done, and maybe they've only been half as good as they should have been.'

Mailer is a well-liked figure among the New York literati: there is much protective affection for the loud-mouth and tantrum-specialist whom they have indulged for so long. 'Oh, I like Norman,' was the typical response of one Madison Avenue publisher. 'I mean, I wouldn't want to room with him next year ... but he's good to have around.' It seems that every MA in Manhattan has his Mailer story: 'Then he smashed this window ... Then he loafed this guy ... Then he grabbed this bottle ... ' But he is spoken of with the reverence customarily accorded to people who live harder than most of us do.

It is always possible that Mailer's best work is yet to come. Age is currently doing a good job on his infinite variety. Although his writing in the Fifties seemed prescient, Mailer's ideas solidified in the Sixties, despite his attempts to get interested in ecology, graffiti, the Yippies, and what not. He seems well-poised to make some sort of reconciliation with his own limits. Money worries constrain him now; but eventually the wives will remarry, and the kids will all grow up. Then the Avenger might get his piece of the Great American Bitch − or, in language more appropriate to his years, Mailer might write the novels that are in him.

*   *   *

In the Belly of the Beast, the book that sprang Jack Henry Abbott from jail, played a key part in putting him back inside. All last week, the State Supreme Court had the carnival atmosphere which New York reserves for its celebrity murder trials. Through a gauntlet of

camera lights and superfat security guards strolled writers Jean
Malaquais and Norman Mailer. Among the intent voyeurs of the
public gallery sat filmstars Susan Sarandon and Christopher
Walken. Already there was speculation about the film of the book of
the trial of the life.

'"It's like cutting hot butter, no resistance at all,"' quoted the
prosecutor. '"They always whisper one thing at the end: 'Please'.
You leave him in the blood, staring with dead eyes." Did you write
that?' Abbott – a jittery figure, terribly thin, a man clearly in a state
of intense and permanent confusion about what the world is making
of him – gave one of his rare, murky grins. 'It's good, isn't it?' he
said.

At the end of the day's hearing, a turbulent press conference was
held by Mr Mailer. He said that he hoped Abbott wouldn't get too
long a sentence for his latest murder. 'Culture is worth a little risk,'
he said. 'Otherwise you have a Fascistic society. I am willing to
gamble with certain elements in society to save this man's talent.'
Mailer is willing. But does society feel the same way?

One thing seems clear: the Jack Abbott story will run and run. 'It
is a tragedy all around,' Mailer had said. But it is a farce too, an
American rodeo of inverted callousness and pretension. Could this
happen anywhere else? The world looks on fascinated, rubbing its
eyes.

Now thirty-eight, Abbott has been in prison since he was twelve.
He was released at eighteen and promptly readmitted for theft.
Three years later he murdered a fellow inmate – 'in combat',
according to his book. At one point he escaped, robbed a few banks
and was recaptured within a month. Abbott is what they call 'State
raised'. Eight years ago Abbott started writing letters to Jerzy
Kozinski, a correspondence that ended, for the novelist, in alarm
and repulsion. 'So stay away, Abbott,' read Kozinski's last
letter. 'You have killed a man already – you won't kill a man in
me.'

In 1977 Abbott tried his luck with Norman Mailer, then at work
on *The Executioner's Song*. Instantly Mailer felt 'all the awe one
knows before a phenomenon'. Extracts from Abbott's letters
appeared in the *New York Review of Books*. Mailer was joined by
other literary figures in championing Abbott's cause in submissions
to the Utah Board of Correction. Abbott's letters were edited down
and Random House made plans to publish. Abbott was duly paroled

and established in a halfway house in the Bowery, where he braced himself for literary fame.

It could be argued that literary fame, in New York, has been more than a match for the equilibrium of Norman Mailer. So God knows what it did to Jack Abbott, a man who had spent half his adult life in solitary confinement. With Mailer, Abbott preceded Dudley Moore on the TV show 'Good Morning, America'. He was photographed by Jill Krementz (Mrs Kurt Vonnegut). He was toasted and praised at literary dinner parties. Then the reviews started to appear: 'One of the most important books of our age . . . a stunning and original writer . . . Conrad-like lyrical beauty . . . awesome, brilliant, perversely ingenuous; its impact is indelible'.

That last gobbet is from *The New York Times Book Review*. Twelve hours before the paper hit the stands, however, Abbott had allegedly stabbed a man to death and was on the run. It has emerged at the trial that throughout his few weeks of freedom Abbott was in a highly volatile state – failing, in other words, to adjust to society. Asked to extinguish a cigarette in a museum, he reportedly flicked his butt in the guard's face. Told in a department store that it would take ten days to complete an alteration, Abbott started upending clothes displays, looking for scissors to do the job himself. Everyday vexations: but it was a routine spat of this kind that led Abbott to stab a waiter at an all-night café.

As Abbott went on the run, his sponsors grew silent. Some suggested that they had wanted simply to encourage a writer rather than unleash a con – as if, wrote one commentator, 'the most they hoped for in writing to the parole board was to provide Abbott with an electric pencil sharpener'. The 'Right', in fact, had a field day. Radical chic, in hiding for over a decade, had taken a peep out of its burrow and been stomped on all over again. Abbott was recaptured, in Louisiana, and the circus resumed. Last Thursday, on his thirty-eighth birthday, Abbott was found guilty of first-degree manslaughter, not murder, a verdict which the family of the deceased regard as 'an outrage'. 'Happy birthday, Jack,' said one of the jurors.

So what is one to make of this mess? First, the book, *Belly*, represents only a fraction of the original 300-odd letters. Even in its reduced form the book is grotesquely uneven, as well as aggressive and deluded, full of giveaways and triple-thinks.

'I have read all but a very few of the world's classics, from prehistoric times up to this day.' Nourished by these bronto-texts, Abbott develops a primitive canvas of the outside world, entirely notional, tendentious and self-reflecting. It is a world-view based on nothing but books and (it must be said) psychosis. Reading Abbott, with his categorical stridency, his hollering italics, is like being drunkenly buttonholed by Colin Wilson's Outsider — all night, and with his finger jabbing at your chest. In a way the book is a precise and miserable testimony to the effects of lifelong isolation and terror. The real mystery is how it got confused with meaningful polemic, let alone with literature.

It was Mailer, initially, who did the confusing. His introduction to the book (not to mention his other cavortings) would be shameful and ridiculous even if Abbott were now a well-established poet and humanitarian. In his introduction Mailer reaffirms that society should seek to cultivate the potential of its violent citizens. We shouldn't bother, he says, about the threat they pose 'to the suburbs'. What are the 'suburbs' doing in this argument? Abbott, anyway, posed his threat on Second Avenue and Fifth, and perhaps will again if Mailer's priorities are honoured.

There are several wishful misapprehensions on offer here: that a 'creative individual' can't be evil; that writers, too, are outsiders, unheeded prophets; that life is a prison in the first place, and that the incorrigible criminal is forged only by contact with the criminal system, a system which gives distress to all well-informed Americans. Which comes first: the Beast, or the man in its Belly?

There have been rumours that it wasn't Mailer and Co. who sprang Abbott from jail: it was the Feds. After a violent strike-beating operation in Marion Penitentiary in April 1980, a beaten Abbott co-operated with the prison authorities. Informers don't live long in the Pen, so it may have been a handy coincidence when Mailer's letters testified that the snitch happened to be a genius too.

In an article commissioned and rejected by *The New York Times* Abbott claimed that 'the Press has helped the Government to make it finally impossible for me to survive in prison'. In the piece, Abbott presents himself as the classic Kierkegaardian poet-martyr, transforming pain into music. To Mailer he is a victim, an existential hero. The sympathies of the public, of tabloid America, are rightly with the murdered boy — who was also, apparently (as if this case needs any more irony), a writer of promise.

Up there on the stand Abbott seemed tremulous, distracted,

half-way between laughter and tears. His reactions to the prosecutor's questions fizzed with indignation, with terrible impatience. It is said that the State-raised convict fears society as intensely as the ordinary man fears prison. Jack Abbott looks as if he has never seen much difference between the two.

*   *   *

Postscript It is absolutely consistent that Mailer should have presided over the publication, in 1985, of the most exhaustive character assassination in the history of letters: *Mailer: His Life and Times*, by Peter Manso. And it is ironical that the only episode in which Mailer fails to gratify rock-bottom expectation is the episode involving Jack Henry Abbott.

The first thing to be said about *In the Belly of the Beast* is that it isn't any good. It isn't any good. One can then add that it is also the work of a thoroughly, obviously and understandably psychotic mind: as such, it is a manifesto for recidivism. Its author, plainly, could never hope to abjure violence. Abbott is quoted in *Mailer*, from his prison cell, and it is pitiable to read the confused and terrified ramblings of the man Mailer called 'an intellectual, a radical, a potential leader'. You can hear paranoia snickering and wincing behind every word.

During the trial Mailer admitted that he had 'blood on his hands'. Yet he never expressed sympathy for the murdered boy or his family. Why not? Why not? The omission was conspicuous, and was meant to be; it is thus doubly inexpiable. But however this may be, the Abbott episode is clearly full of misery for Mailer; and it was, at least, a human folly as much as an ideological one. There is no echo here of the sinister idiocies to be found in Mailer's introduction to *In the Belly of the Beast*. He should have listened to his wife Norris (who, after the release, had the time and will to give Abbott a fraction of the human contact he needed). This is Norris Mailer:

> I hadn't wanted any part of it. My attitude to Norman's involvement all along had been, 'You wrote the book about Gilmore — didn't you learn anything? It's not gonna work, these guys don't change.' Norman is the eternal optimist and said, 'It'll be fine, this guy's different, blah blah blah' . . .

*   *   *

Anthony Powell stabs Lady Violet — near-fatally. William Golding risks a trigamy scandal by divorcing his fourth wife, marrying and divorcing his fifth, and then marrying his sixth in the space of a week. Arrested for drunkenness, Malcolm Bradbury 'takes out' one policeman but is blackjacked by a second, earning himself fifteen stitches. A.N. Wilson goes five rounds with drinking-buddy Frank Bruno.

None of this sounds terribly likely, does it? In British literary circles, what one might loosely call 'bad behaviour' is normally the preserve of Celtic micrometeorites like Dylan Thomas and Brendan Behan, who burn brightly and briefly, and very soon rejoin the cosmic dust. But in the United States, provided you are Norman Mailer, it seems that you can act like a maniac for forty years — and survive, prosper and multiply, and write the books. The work is what it is: sublime, ridiculous, always interesting. But the deeds — the human works — are a monotonous disgrace.

This 700-pager is an oral biography, or better say a verbal one. Peter Manso provides no links, no introduction; after his epic marshallings of the tapes and transcriptions, he was presumably hard pressed to manage the acknowledgments and the dedication. Even in America the book has been sniffed at as a by-blow of the new barbarism, but I think there is an appropriate madness in Manso's method. What's so great about the literary biography anyway? *Mailer* intercuts about 150 voices: family, friends, peers, onlookers, enemies. It is deeply discordant, naggingly graphic and atrociously indiscreet. No living writer, you'd have thought, could have more to lose by such an exposure. But then, programmatic self-destruction has always been the keynote of Mailer's life and times.

'Do things that frighten you' is one of Norman's pet maxims. Needless to say, in real life, doing things that frighten you tends to involve doing things that frighten other people. For some reason or other, Mailer spent the years between 1950 and 1980 in a tireless quest for a fistfight. He liked his dirty-talking, hell-cat women to have fights too, teaching them how and egging them on. 'Drinking runs through this whole story,' as one of his wives remarks, 'drinking, drinking, drinking.' 'I am an American *dissident*,' Mailer has been claiming for more than thirty years. But 'I am an American *drunk*' sounds nearer the mark.

Half-way through most evenings, Mailer would be 'snorting and weaving', insulting his friends, goading strangers. He picked his pals with care, and so there were usually a few ex-boxers, criminals and aspiring tough-guys or psychopaths on hand to engage with him in ritual arm-wrestling, elbow-digging and head-banging bouts. Having walked his two poodles one night in New York, Mailer returned home 'on cloud nine', 'in ecstasy', with his left eye 'almost out of his head'. He had got into a fight, he told his wife, because a couple of sailors 'accused my dog of being queer'. According to the doctor, it was 'a hell of a beating he took'. But 'Stormin' Norman' was unrepentant. 'Nobody's going to call my dog a queer,' he growled.

Irving Howe once said that Mailer risked becoming 'a hostage to the temper of his times'. But he was a willing hostage, and in fact he normally behaved more like a terrorist. 'For I wish to attempt an entrance', wrote Mailer in 1959, with typical pomp, 'into the mysteries of murder, suicide, incest, orgy, orgasm and Time.' He was referring to his work rather than his life, but the two activities (like bar-room brawlers) were hard to keep apart.

The book is strewn with vicious confrontations, drunken couplings, ostentatious suicide bids, cruel human manipulations, incessant violence − and incessant cant. It is like a distillation of every Sixties hysteria, every radical-chic inanity. A girl's drink is spiked with LSD. On a brief homoeopathic fad, Mailer refuses to let his baby daughter have her shots. While Mailer was directing his third cinematic 'happening' (and flop), *Maidstone*, there were 'people by the dozens, running around, chasing each other, fighting, fucking, acting insane'; 'the violence . . . was so thick you could feel it'. Sure enough, 'all of a sudden there's kids screeching, Beverly [wife 4] screaming, and blood.' This is a common background noise in *Mailer*: screaming children.

Of course, everyone was at it, in that convulsive bad-behaviour festival that beset America after the war. Often the urge to scandalise a non-existent bourgeoisie took a more benevolent form. One of the funniest passages in the book describes a cocktail party on Cape Cod given by the distinguished belles-lettrist Dwight Macdonald. 'We got out of the car,' says Mailer's second wife, Adele,

> and there was everyone standing around nude. All these intellectuals, the whole bunch. It was just so cute. Norman and I

71

looked at each other and shrugged and took off our clothes. No, I think Norman left his shorts on.

Let's be thankful for small mercies. If I go to a literary party this summer, I shall certainly pause to count my blessings.

The knifing of Adele – known as The Trouble – stands as the pivotal incident of the book: as Mailer's sociopathic epiphany. In 1960 Mailer threw a party in New York as 'an unofficial kick-off' for his mayoralty campaign (the campaign was perforce abandoned thereafter; and it was a decade later that Mailer made a slightly more serious attempt to become the Ken Livingstone of New York). Intending a creative confrontation between the city's haves and have-nots, Mailer invited the local bigwigs and machine politicians together with a rabble of punks and pimps – the disenfranchised whom Mailer hoped to represent. Predictably, none of the haves showed up. The have-nots, however, had no prior engagements.

Mailer had already got a few fights under his belt by the time the party collapsed and he staggered, bloody-lipped, into the kitchen and reached for the knife. Adele had apparently been baiting him all night; she had been fooling around with a woman 'in the john'; she was 'definitely' heard to remark that Mailer 'wasn't as good a writer as Dostoevsky'. Or perhaps she simply called his poodle a queer. Later, friends were considering whether to go in 'with a baseball bat' to rescue Mailer's daughter. 'He had this marvellous rationale', muses a friend,

> about art and life – and he actually did it, he lived it. And it wasn't just something he did half-ass. It almost killed him – or actually Adele . . .

There is a fair bit to be said on the credit side. And, after all, better writers have behaved worse. There is manifest charm, strong loyalty, an absence of snobbery, the novelist's gift of finding interest everywhere (even in bores and boredom), the enviable – if not admirable – shamelessness, and above all the selective but delightfully strident honesty. In a letter:

> I've decided that at bottom I'm just a sadist, and no damn good for any woman. The reason – I can beat them up. Only with men do I act decently cause I'm scared they'll whop me. Isn't human nature depressing?

One of the most formidable and endearing voices running through this book is that of Fanny ('my kids are tops') Mailer, Norman's 86-year-old-mother. 'I couldn't understand why he hadn't gotten the Nobel Prize.' 'Why he picked Adele I never could understand.' 'If Norman would stop marrying these women who make him do these terrible things.' Fanny named her 'really lovely baby' Nachum Malech Mailer, 'Nachum' becoming Norman, while 'Malech' ('king' in Hebrew) became Kingsley. 'He was our king', 'a little god'. '"He's going to be a great man." I knew that. Absolutely.' Fanny never waivered, and all his life Norman had plenty of collaborators in building the mansion of his self-esteem.

His name is Norman Mailer, king of kings: look on his works, ye Mighty, and — what? Despair? Burst out laughing? In secure retrospect, Mailer's life and times seem mostly ridiculous: incorrigibly ridiculous. Some observers talk of his 'great huge ambition', his 'great grace and correctitude'; others just lick their wounds. A devout immoralist, he always veered between the superhuman and the subhuman, between Menenhetet I and Gary Gilmore. Like America, he went too far in all directions, and only towards the end, perhaps — with no more drink and 'no more stunts', dedicated to his work and to a non-combatant sixth wife — has he struck a human balance. As for the past, nothing beside remains. Round the decay of that colossal wreck, boundless and bare the lone and level sands stretch far away.

Observer 1981, 1982 and 1985

Palm Beach: Don't You Love It?

The only road-accidents in Palm Beach take place between pedestrians. And you can see them happening a mile off. The mottled, golf-trousered oldsters square up to each other on pavement and zebra, and head forward, inexorably, like slow-motion stock-cars or distressed supertankers. (Everyone is pretty sleek and rounded in Palm Beach — unlike New York, where people's faces are as thin as credit cards.) Then it happens. Oof! . . . The old-timers rebound and stagger on. 'Hey!' 'This is a sidewalk, honey.' 'Oh yeah? How'd you like that!'

Meanwhile the tamed gas-guzzlers toil in line along the seafront strip, hearse-like limousines, roadsters with their haunches and biceps — Toronadoes, Thunderbirds, Cutlasses. But these gas-guzzlers are on the wagon. The limit is between 25 and 35 m.p.h., and people drive even slower than that. There are never any accidents, no alarms of any kind. A flat tire on a Mercedes will bring out the squad cars, helicopters, state troopers. The only people who need to get anywhere fast are behind the wheels of the Emergency Service Units, which specialise in heart attacks and are the most efficient and advanced in the world. Everyone else cruises in meandering, Sunday-sightseeing style. The speedometer on my gurgling 1981 Mustang stopped at 85, like a Mini. Energy is being conserved. But for what?

Your psychic clock needs time to adjust to Palm Beach, to the sun, the wealth, the safety and the pool fatigue. For the first forty-eight hours I felt I was going to be spontaneously arrested by the police for having such a relaxing time. ' . . . But Officer — what's the charge?'

'You're too relaxed. Way too relaxed.' The truth was, of course, that I wasn't nearly relaxed enough. I sprawled nervously by my personal swimming-pool, dozed jumpily on my baronial bed, idled edgily into town at the wheel of my sparkling car . . .

There is no sign of any work going on here. There is no sign of anyone who hasn't got lots of money. The only black faces you see, you see through glass: trimming the borders, washing the dishes, or licking your windscreen. There is no litter, there is no crime; a snatched purse in the shopping mall would cause headlines, state-wide man-hunts. There is only one kind of activity in Palm Beach: leisure.

Palm Beach proper, the strip of land between Lake Worth and the Atlantic Ocean, is the most expensive piece of real estate in America, out-tabbing Martha's Vineyard or Beverly Hills. People talk obsess-ively about real estate − partly, I suppose, because it is an informal way of talking obsessively about money. 'And I mean those are top prices. And I mean top. Top. Top.' 'Then I raised the money at 140 per cent of the asking price. Don't you love it?' In one of the main shopping streets in Palm Beach there is a plush-looking office called Creative Realtors. Perhaps there is even a course at Miami Univer-sity in creative realting.

I visited an average middle-income Palm Beach home and was shown round by its droll and hospitable owner. From the point of view of ostentation − well, the house had a monogrammed marble driveway, and went on from there. Additional features included a telephonic computer system (if you dial a certain number in the study, the drapes draw shut in the bedroom), weather control in the jungly courtyard, visual and aural monitoring of the sculpture-infested grounds. In the garage is a custom-built $90,000 Clenet ('I have some Rollses out there too, and they ain't bad'). In the Mae-West bathroom are jereboams of Madame Rochas and Paco Rabanne. The lawn is like astroturf, the carpets like bubble-baths. Never in my life have I seen such clogged, stifling luxury.

My host was a businessman from the North who had settled in Palm Beach. On arrival, he did not attempt to join the 'most exclusive' club in town. There would have been no point: he is a Jew. He did try to join the club next door. He was willing to pay his dues ($20,000 a year), and could prove, as all hopefuls must, that he had given over a million dollars to charity. He couldn't get in there either. His wife hired a press secretary, and the couple began to appear in the *Palm Beach Daily News*, or 'The Shiny Sheet' as it is known. Eventually they were accepted by Palm Beach café society.

Like all provincial élites, the Palm Beach *beau monde* is both baffling and uninteresting, an enigma that you don't particularly want to solve. Names are mentioned with reverence, irony or contempt. Some have an old-style Confederate ring; others sound ersatz European. Appropriately for America, the only monikers with an aristocratic tang are brand-names — perfumes, cars, domestic appliances. There are occasional scandals. The loo-paper heiress has run off with the bra-strap boss! The deodorant queen has divorced the bath-salt giant! Large parties are thrown under the cover of charity. You buy your own drinks and the money goes to a disadvantaged minority group, or to combat a fashionable disease. I formed the impression that most of the entertaining consists of small but opulent pool-side dinner-parties, in which each hosting couple tries to out-Gatsby the other with the vintage of their wines, the poundage of their steaks, the antiquity of their tableware, the multitudinousness of their servants. But there are other big dates on the calendar too.

'The drama of diamonds! . . . Yes, diamonds *are* a girl's best friend . . . This exquisite necklace! A unison of noble gems. Yours for a mere — $250,000!'

This was the seasonal Gucci party, given at the Gucci arcade and fronted by Gucci himself (or, rather, by 'Doctor Aldo Gucci' himself. 'Doctor': don't you love it?). Gucci himself is a resplendently handsome maniac with operatic manners and impossible English. 'Let us give thanks that God has forgiven this evening,' and so on. Swanky girls and jinking pretty-boys modelled the Doc's latest creations. Gucci then repaired to the minstrels' gallery and, with a tambourine in one hand and a microphone in the other, actually *mimed* to the songs being played by the sedative pop group behind him.

Meanwhile I mingled with the clotted cream of Palm Beach. The old men — these tuxed gods and molten robots, with silver-studded dress shirts and metallic hair, all doing fine, all in *great shape*. 'How are you, Buck?' 'Good, Dale. You?' 'I'm good, Buck. I'm good.' And the women, still going strong, prinked, snipped, tucked, capped, patched, pinched, rinsed, lopped, pruned, pared, but still going strong, and intending to be around for a very long time.

The average age in Palm Beach is fifty-seven. According to popular belief — i.e. according to the famous Alan Whicker documentary a few years ago — the Beach is peopled entirely by widows with faces like snake-skin handbags, the menfolk having checked out with the lifelong effort of establishing themselves on this golden mile. 'That Alvin Whicker there. You're not going to write something like that,' I was told on several occasions. No, I said, I wasn't. I saw little of this — or rather I saw other things also.

'Do you do coke?' someone asked me at a cattle-baron's hoedown (dress: Western) at the Palm Beach Polo and Country Club. (How *do* you *do* coke? At Miami airport I happened to notice a flustered-looking Bruce Forsyth, standing in front of an ad that read: 'Do A Daquiri'. As I write this sentence, I am doing a cigarette.) There were plenty of young things at the hoedown, lots of little Bo Dereks and Farrah Fawcetts bobbing to the Okey band, and squired by many a six-gunned young dude. You hear tell of the usual hang-gliding, water-skiing, scuba-diving, Cessna-flying, polo-playing, drug-and-discoing young rabble that traditionally adorn such pleasure spots, their activities indulged by their parents and winked at by the police. The rich have children, just like everybody else.

Driving inland from Palm Beach, you are immediately confronted by the booming chaos of middle America. On the bridge into West Palm (a community founded for the servants and amenity operators of the Beach itself), there are morose old black men fishing for scrod over the rails. Within seconds you are in drive-in, shopping-mall land. Beef'n'Booze, Seven Eleven, X-Rated Movies, Totally Nude Encounter Sessions, Jack's Bike World, Eats — 24 Hrs. Developments are rearing up everywhere, condominiums, conurbations, the bleak toytowns formed by mobile homes. Drive a little further and you are in the redneck swampland of Wellington and Loxahatchee. Anything, you feel, could happen here — crocodiles slithering across the dirt roads, good ole boys staring and snickering at your out-of-county plates ...

Drop me down anywhere in America and I'll tell you where I am: in America. I soon turned round and headed back to the Beach, where you feel old and safe. I longed to be on the patio of my villa, and to hear my maid calling out protectively to ask if I wanted my tea. She deals with everything, with the tradesmen and delivery boys

77

who zoom round to cater to my whims and to fix all the labour-saving appliances. She does all the washing-up and laundry. My shirts never had it so good. Out in the sun I read a little poem by Von Humboldt Fleischer which perfectly answered my mood:

> Mice hide when hawks are high;
> Hawks shy from airplanes;
> Planes dread the ack-ack-ack;
> Each one fears somebody.
> Only the heedless lions
> Under the Booloo tree
> Snooze in each other's arms
> After their lunch of blood —
> I call that living good!

By now my psychic clock was attuned to Palm Beach. I felt completely at home among the old American lions.

Tatler 1979

Brian De Palma:
The Movie Brute

Burbank Studios, Sound Stage 16. In silent hommage *to Hitchcock, perhaps, Brian De Palma's belly swells formidably over the waistband of his safari suit* ... So, at any rate, I had thought of beginning this profile of the light-fingered, flash-trash movie brute, director of *Carrie, Dressed to Kill, Scarface* – and *Body Double*. But that was before I had been exposed to De Palma's obscure though unmistakable charm: three weeks, twenty telephone calls and a few thousand miles later. 'I know you've come all the way from London, and I know Brian promised to see you while you were in LA,' his PA told me at the entrance to the lot. 'Well, he's *rescinded* on that,' she said, and laughed with musical significance. This significant laughter told me three things: one, that she was scandalised by his behaviour; two, that he did it all the time; and three, that I wasn't to take him seriously, because no one else did. I laughed too. I had never met a real-life moody genius before; and they *are* very funny.

So let's start again. Brian De Palma sits slumped on his director's chair, down at Burbank, in boiling Los Angeles. It is 'wrap' day on *Body Double*, his pornographic new thriller: only two climactic scenes remain to be shot. 'Put the chest back on,' De Palma tells the villain, played by Gregg Henry. 'Okay. New chest! New belly!' This means another forty-minute delay. De Palma gets to his feet and wanders heavily round the set. He is indeed rather tubby now, the back resting burdensomely on the buttocks, and he walks with an effortful, cross-footed gait. 'Hitchcock was sixty when he made *Psycho*,' De Palma would later tell me. 'I don't know if I'll be able to *walk* when I'm sixty.' A curious remark – but then Brian is not a good walker, even now, at forty-four; he is not a talented walker.

He walks as if he is concentrating very hard on what he has in his pockets.

I approached the sinister Gregg Henry and asked him about the scene they were shooting. It sounded like standard De Palma: 'I throttle Craig Wasson to the ground or whatever. I jump out of the grave. I rip off my false belly.' The false belly is part of Gregg's disguise, along with the rug, the redskin facial pancake, and the Meccano dentures. As in *Dressed to Kill*, a goody turns out to be a baddy, in disguise. It takes a headlining make-up veteran three-and-a-half hours to get Gregg looking as sinister as this. Presumably it takes the baddy in the film even longer — but this is a De Palma picture, where gross insults to plausibility are routine. The second shot involves an elaborate false-perspective prop (to dramatise the hero's claustrophobia as he is buried alive), like the staircase scene in *Vertigo*. The camera will wobble. 'With luck, you'll feel sick,' says the amiable first assistant. *Body Double* has gone pretty smoothly, within schedule and under budget. The only real hitch was a 'hair problem' with Melanie Griffith. She spent two weeks under the drier and over the sink. 'We tried brown, red, platinum — until we got what Brian wanted.'

Suddenly — that is to say, after a fifteen-minute yelling relay — the shot is ready to go again. De Palma talks to no one but the camera operator. 'Why don't you pull back a bit? Why don't you try to hold him from head to foot?' All his instructions are in this dogged rhetorical style. Action. Gregg Henry and Craig Wasson perform creditably ('Oh *man*,' says Gregg, peeling off his false belly, 'you ruined my whole surprise ending'), but De Palma is unhappy about the camera's swooning back-track. He should have been unhappy about his surprise ending, which doesn't work. 'New belly,' says Brian, and the delay resumes. A series of delays interrupted by repetitions: that's motion pictures.

De Palma went trudge-about. 'I think this would be a good time for you to be introduced to Brian,' said Rob, the unit publicist — also likeable. 'He's in a receptive mood.'

'Are you sure?'

'Yes. Very receptive.'

We walked over. I was introduced. De Palma wearily offered his hand. Rob explained who I was. 'Uh,' said De Palma, and turned away.

'Is that as good as it gets?' I asked as we walked off.

'See him in New York,' said Rob. 'He'll be better, when he's wrapped.'

And so an hour or two later I left him in the lot, which was still doing its imitation of Hell. Gaunt ladies lurk near the catering caravan. Fat minders or shifters or teamsters called Buck and Flip and Heck move stoically about. The place is big and dark and hot, swathed in black drapes, vulcanic, loud with vile engines, horrid buzzers, expert noise-makers. Nearly all the time absolutely nothing is happening. Eight hours later, at midnight, De Palma wrapped.

As a film-maker, Brian De Palma knows exactly what he wants. Unlike his peers and pals, Spielberg, Lucas, Coppola and Scorsese (they all teamed up at Warner Brothers in the early Seventies), De Palma doesn't shoot miles of footage and then redesign the movie in the editing room. His rough cuts are usually shorter than the finished film. Every scene is meticulously story-boarded, every pan and zoom, every camera angle. Here's a sample on-set interview:

> *So, Brian, before you make a movie, do you see the whole thing in your head?*
> Yes.
> *Do you have problems re-creating the movie you see?*
> No.
> *How does the actual movie measure up to what you originally imagined?*
> It measures up.

He seldom advises or encourages his actors. Michael Caine has said that the highest praise you'll hear from De Palma is 'Print'. As a film-maker, Brian De Palma knows exactly what he wants. The only question is: why does he want it?

Always an ungainly cultural phenomenon, De Palma's reputation has never been more oddly poised. He likes to think of himself as over the top and beyond the pale, an iconoclast and controversialist, someone that people love to hate or hate to love — someone, above all, who cannot be *ignored*. In moments of excitement he will grandly refer to 'whole schools of De Palma criticism' which say this, that and the other about his work. Well, too many people have failed to ignore De Palma for us to start ignoring him now. But it may be that the only serious school of De Palma criticism is the one where all the classrooms are empty. Everyone is off playing hookey. They're all busy ignoring him.

De Palma's history forms a promising confection, full of quirkiness and mild exoticism. His parents were both Italian Catholics yet little Brian was reared as a Presbyterian. The Catholic imagery was naturally the more tenacious for the young artist ('that is one spooky religion') and its themes and forms linger in his work: the diabolism, the ritualised but arbitrary moral schemes, the guilt. De Palma Senior was a surgeon — orthopaedics, the correction of deformity. Brian used to sit in on operations, often catching a skin graft or a bone transplant, and would later do vacation jobs in medical laboratories. 'I have a high tolerance for blood,' he says. The cast of *The Fury* (1978) nicknamed him Brian De Plasma. On the set his most frequent remarks are 'Action', 'Print' and 'More blood!' De Palma was tempted by medicine but rejected the discipline as 'not precise enough'.

He used to be keen on precision, and still sees his work in terms of 'precise visual story-telling', streamlined and dynamic, all pincer grips and rapier thrusts. In fact, 'precision' in De Palma is entirely a matter of sharp surfaces and smooth assembly; within, all is smudge and fudge, woolliness, approximation. The young Brian was also something of a physics prodigy and computer whiz. At a National Science Fair competition he took second prize for his critical study of hydrogen quantum mechanics through cybernetics. (This is impressive all right. *You* try it.) One imagines the teenage De Palma as owlish, bespectacled and solitary, like the kid in *Dressed to Kill*. That solitude is still with him, I would say. Then at university the brainy loner changed tack, selling his home-made computers for a Bolex film camera, 'trading one obsession for another'.

Born in Newark, raised in Philadelphia, a student of physics at Columbia and of drama at Sarah Lawrence College, Bronxville, De Palma is solidly East Coast in his origins, urban, radical, anti-establishment, anti-Hollywood. He admired Godard, Polanski and of course Hitchcock, but he entered the industry from left field: via the TV-dominated world of documentary and vérité, low-budget satire and chaotic improvisation, war protest and sexual daring — a product of the Sixties, that golden age of high energy and low art. It must be said that of all De Palma's early work, from *Greetings* in 1968 to *Phantom of the Paradise* in 1974, nothing survives. These films are now no more than memories of art-house late nights, student screenings, left-wing laughter and radical applause. De Palma's first visit to Hollywood, for *Get to Know Your Rabbit*, was a disaster movie in itself. His authority attacked, his star out of control, De Palma 'quit' the picture two weeks before its completion — as he would later quit *Prince of the City* and *Flashdance*. The film was shelved for two years. On his own admission De Palma was suddenly 'dead' in Los Angeles, where the locals are superstitious about failure; they quarantine you, in case failure is catching. No one returned his calls. They crossed the street to avoid him. 'People think — what has he *got* in that can?' In any event, *Rabbit* was a dog. Furtively released in 1974 as a B-feature, it interred itself within a week.

Then two years later along came *Carrie*, far and away De Palma's most successful film, in all senses. By now Brian's contemporaries, his Warner brothers, were all drowning in riches and esteem, and he was 'more than ready' for a smash of his own. 'I pleaded, *pleaded* to do *Carrie*.' And so began De Palma's assimilation into the Hollywood machine, his extended stay in 'the land of the devil'. The Sixties radical package was merely the set of values that got to him first, and he had wearied of a 'revolution' he found ever more commercialised. De Palma now wanted the other kind of independence, the 'dignity' that comes from power and success within the establishment. He is honest — or at any rate brazen — about the reversal. 'I too became a capitalist,' he has said. 'By even dealing with the devil you become devilish. There's no clean money. There I was, worrying about *Carrie* not doing forty million. That's how deranged your perspectives get.' Nowadays his politics are cautious and pragmatic: 'capitalism tempered by compassion, do unto others — stuff like that'. The liberal minimum. His later films do sometimes deal in political questions of the Watergate-buff variety, but the slant is personal, prankish, paranoid — De Palmaesque. All that remains of the Sixties guerrilla is an unquenchable taste for anarchy: moral anarchy, artistic anarchy.

What use has he made of his freedom? What exactly are we looking at here? 'Mature' De Palma consists of *Dressed to Kill*, *Blowout* and now *Body Double*. These are the medium-budget films which De Palma conceived, wrote, directed and cut. (*The Fury* and *Scarface* we can set aside as fancy-priced hackwork, while *Home Movies*, a shoe-string project put together at Sarah Lawrence and released in 1980, is already a vanished curiosity.) De Palma's three main credits, or debits, reveal his cinematic vision, unfettered by any constraints other than those imposed by the censors. They also show how blinkered, intransigent and marginal that vision really is. Such unedifying fixity has no equivalent in mainstream cinema, and none in literature, except perhaps Céline, or William Burroughs – or Kathy Acker.

Each instalment in the De Palma trilogy concerns itself with a man who goes about the place cutting up women: straight razor, chisel, power drill. The women are either prostitutes, sexual adventuresses or adult-movie queens. There is no conventional sex whatever in De Palma's movies: it is always a function of money, violence or defilement, glimpsed at a voyeuristic remove or through a pornographic sheen (and this interest in flash and peep goes right back to *Greetings*). The heroes are childish or ineffectual figures, helpless in the face of the villain's superior human energies. There are no plots: the narratives themselves submit to a psychopathic rationale, and are littered with coincidence, blind spots, black holes. Like its predecessors, *Body Double* could be exploded by a telephone call, by a pertinent question, by five minutes' thought. Most candidly of all, De Palma dispenses with the humanistic ensemble of character, motive, development and resolution. He tries his best, but people bore him, and that's that.

Brian has something, though. Without it, he would be indistinguishable from the gory hucksters of the exploitation circuit, the slashers and manglers, the Movie Morons who gave us *The Evil Dead*, *Prom Night* and *I Spit on Your Grave*. Brian has style – a rare and volatile commodity. Style will always convince cinematic purists that the surfaces they admire contain depth, and that clear shortcomings are really subtle virtues in disguise. De Palma isn't logical, so he must be impressionistic. He isn't realistic, so he must be surrealistic. He isn't scrupulous, so he must be audacious. He isn't earnest, so he must be ironical. He isn't funny, so he must be *serious*.

And so I hung around in damp New York, waiting on the man. Every now and then De Palma's 'people' at Columbia would apologetically pass on the odd message: 'Brian's probably going to decide tomorrow whether he'll let you have this interview ...' I had urgent reasons for returning to London. A week passed. Now, there is no reason why celebrities should submit to journalistic inspection, and in fact they are increasingly reluctant to do so — except in the trash press, where publicity is always tilted towards celebration. But having agreed to an interview, they should play by the rules, which are rules of ordinary etiquette: do unto others — stuff like that. A week passed. And then Brian came down from the mountain.

'Mr De Palma? He's right over there,' said the porter down in lower Fifth Avenue. Brian sat ponderously on a bench by the lift with a newspaper under his arm. Always keen to stay in touch with 'street reality', De Palma had just staggered out for a *New York Times*. 'Hi,' I said, and reintroduced myself. De Palma nodded at the floor. 'It's kind of you to give me your time.' De Palma shrugged helplessly — yes, what a bountiful old softie he was. In eerie silence we rode the swaying lift.

'Coffee?' he sighed. With studied gracelessness he shuffled around his four-room office — televisions, hi-fis, a pinball machine, De Palma film posters, curved white tables, orderly work-surfaces. This was where Brian did all his writing and conceiving. Wordlessly he gave me my coffee mug and sloped off to take a few telephone calls. At last he levered himself in behind the desk, his nostrils flaring with a suppressed yawn, and waved a limp hand at me. The interview began. *Great*, I thought, after ten minutes. *He really is bananas. This is going like a dream.*

'My films are so filmically astute that people think I'm not good with actors. Actors trust me and my judgment because I'm so up front about what I feel ... I don't make "aggressive" use of the camera. I make the *right* use. I go with my instinct ... I use Hitchcock's grammar but I have a romantic vision that's more sweeping and Wagnerian ... I have a tremendous amount of experience. I'm not afraid to try new things ... Financially in Hollywood I'm a sound economic given. Three-quarters of my films have made money. Anybody who can make *one* film that makes money is a genius!'

'Casting all modesty aside,' I said, fondling my biro, 'where would you place yourself among your contemporaries — Coppola, Scorsese?'

'Oh, I don't know. I'm up there, I guess. Time ... ' he said, and paused. De Palma is generally tentative about time — aware, perhaps, of what time has already done to much of his *oeuvre*. 'Let's face up to it! I'm never going to get a lifetime-achievement

award. I never bought those values anyway. In ten years hence they
... I don't know. Time will find a place for me.'

On this note of caution, Brian unwound. His mood of frenzied
self-advertisement receded, alas, and I have to report that he then
talked pretty soberly and fluently for well over an hour – bearish,
grinning, gesturing, his laughter frayed by hidden wildness. Of
course, the time to catch De Palma in full manic babble is when he is
writhing under the tethers of a collaborative project, as on *Scarface*,
or tangling with the censors, as he did on *Dressed to Kill*, which
barely escaped an X. But he was relatively calm during our meeting,
with *Body Double* in the can and another project nicely brewing:
Carpool, in which he intends to indulge his fascination with
rearview mirrors. 'Steven will produce,' says Brian snugly. In
January he had told *Esquire*: 'As soon as I get this dignity from
Scarface I am going to go out and make an X-rated suspense porn
picture.' Later he added, 'If *Body Double* doesn't get an X, nothing I
ever do is going to. I'm going to give them everything they hate, and
more of it than they've ever seen.' What major company, you
wonder, would finance and distribute an X? I asked Brian about
this. He grew sheepish. 'No major company would finance or
distribute it,' he said. So it's an R. 'Most frustrating,' De Palma
muses. 'I mean, look at cable TV. Kids can watch anything these
days.'

Despite such checks and balances De Palma is quick to claim full
responsibility for his projects. 'It *is* an *auteur* situation out there.
You guys, you writers, you got to stop thinking of directors as still
living in the Fifties. It's not an entrenched power system. There's a
lot of free will. No one wants to confront you. No one wants to take
responsibility. That's why directors are emergent figures. If the
executives lean on you, you just have to say, "Okay, guys, *you* do
it." Either they let you alone, or its "Goodbye, Bri! Well, De Palma
fucked up!"'

After a little coaxing, however, Brian confessed to moments of
self-doubt. 'It's an intolerable kind of regime. You wake up at four
in the morning, thinking – Who *wants* it! Who *needs* it! It's all so
com*plex*. It's like *Waiting for Godot* [this last word stressed oddly
too, like *Gdansk*]. Then the rushes, the final mix – that's pleasure. I
like to write. My own pace. I basically like to work by myself.'

At this point I recalled the morose and taciturn figure at Burbank
Studios, in LA. Among all the clamour and clatter, the compulsive

wisecracking and bovine bonhomie, there was De Palma, doing as good an impersonation of a man alone as the circumstances could well permit. Occasionally, too, I thought I glimpsed the obsessive and abstracted kid in him, the bristle of a more rarefied talent. Human relations are always difficult for this kind of artist — messy, confusing, 'not precise enough'. De Palma has been married once, and briefly, to Nancy Allen, whom he had cast as a monosyllabic hooker in three movies running. Informed Hollywood gossip maintains that Nancy wanted a family, and Brian didn't. Well, he's batching it now. Asked why he always equates sex with terror, De Palma says equably, 'Casual sex *is* terrifying. It's one of the few areas of terror still left to us.' And this is why pornography interests him. It is casual, but safe. And it is solitary: nobody else need come in on the act.

The time had come for the crucial question, made more ticklish by the fact that De Palma's manner had softened — was bordering, indeed, on outright civility. One could now see traces of his man-management skills, his knack with actors, how he calms and charms them into a confident partisanship. Despite De Palma's indifference to characterisation, there are remarkably few bad performances in his films. 'I always felt that Brian adored me,' John Travolta has said. 'He seemed to get pure joy out of watching me work.' But perhaps Travolta feels that way about everybody. De Palma is best with the stock types of lowbrow fiction, as in *Carrie*. Elsewhere, he is about as penetrating as the studio make-up girl. Even with an award-winning writer (Oliver Stone), an award-winning star (Al Pacino) and an unlimited canvas ($22 million and three hours plus of screen time), De Palma showed no inkling of human complexity: *Scarface* might as well have been called *Shitface* for all the subtlety he applied to the monotonous turpitude of Tony Montana.

Girding myself, I asked De Palma why his films made no sense. He bounced back with some eagerness, explaining that Hitchcock was illogical too and that, besides, *life* didn't make any sense either. 'Hitchcock did it all the time! Didn't anyone look at the corpse in *Vertigo*? In *Blowout* the illogic was immense — but it was in Watergate too! I'm not interested in being Agatha Christie! Life is *not* like a crossword puzzle! I trust my instinct and emotion! I go with *that*!'

*

87

Brian De Palma once described, with typical recklessness, his notion of an ideal viewership: 'I like a real street audience — people who talk during and *at* a movie, a very unsophisticated Forty-Second Street crowd.' He is right to think that he has an affinity with these cineasts, who have trouble distinguishing filmic life from the real thing. De Palma movies depend, not on a suspension of disbelief, but on a suspension of intelligence such as the Forty-Second Street crowd have already made before they come jabbering into the stalls. Quite simply, you cannot watch his films twice. Reinspect them on video (on the small screen with the lights up, with the sharply reduced *affect*) and they disintegrate into strident chaos. Niggling doubts become farcical certainties. Where? When? How? Why? There's hardly a *sequitur* in sight.

The illogicality, the reality-blurring, the media-borne cretini-sation of modern life is indeed a great theme, and all De Palma's major contemporaries are on to it. De Palma is on to it too, but in a different way. He abets and exemplifies it, passively. In the concep-tion of his films De Palma has half-a-dozen big scenes that he knows how to shoot. How he gets from one to the other is a matter of indifference. On some level he realises that the ignorant will not care or notice, and that the over-informed will mistake his wantonness for something else.

De Palma is regarded as an intellectual. Now it clearly isn't hard to come by such a reputation in the film world, particularly among the present generation of movie-makers. Spielberg, the most popular, is bright and articulate; but his idea of intellection is to skip an hour's TV. And Scorsese, the most brilliant (and the most prescient), is a giggling mute. De Palma isn't an intellectual, though his films, like his conversation, have a patina of smartness. He isn't a cynic either, nor is he the cheerful charlatan I had geared myself to expect. Is he a 'master' (as critics on both sides of the Atlantic claim), or is he a moron? He has no middlebrow following: his fans are to be found either in the street or in the screening-room. Occupying an area rich in double-think, De Palma is simply the innocent bene-ficiary of a cultural joke. It *is* an achievement of a kind, to fashion an art that appeals to the purist, the hooligan, and nobody else.

Vanity Fair 1984

Here's Ronnie: On the Road with Reagan

Ronald Reagan's personal jet, which goes by the name of Free Enterprise II, flew in late for a Reagan Rally at the Transient Terminal of El Paso Airport, Texas. Practically everyone in the waiting crowd was either a journalist, a secret-serviceman or a delegate, one of Reagan's local 'people'. We were all wearing prominent name-tags, something that Americans especially like doing. I strolled among the Skips and Dexters, the Lavernes and Francines, admiring all the bulging Wranglers and stretched stretch-slacks. This felt like Reagan Country all right, where everything is big and fat and fine. This is where you feel slightly homosexual and left-wing if you don't weigh twenty-five stone.

The blue-jodhpurred Tijuana band fell silent as Reagan climbed up on to the podium. 'Doesn't move like an old man,' I thought to myself; and his hair can't be a day over forty-five. Pretty Nancy Reagan sat down beside her husband. As I was soon to learn, her adoring, damp-eyed expression never changes when she is in public. Bathed in Ronnie's aura, she always looks like Bambi being reunited with her parents. Reagan sat in modest silence as a local Republican bigwig presented him with a pair of El Paso cowboy spurs to go with his 1976 El Paso cowboy boots. Then it happened: 'Ladies and gentlemen! The next President of the United States!' And with a bashful shrug ex-Governor Ronald Reagan stepped up to the lectern.

'You know, some funny things happen to you on the campaign trail,' Reagan mused into the mike. 'Not so long back a little boy came up to me — he must have been, why, no more than eleven or twelve years of age. He looked up at me and he said, "Mister, you're pretty old." (*Forgiving laughter as Reagan cleverly defuses the age*

89

issue.) "What was it like when you were a boy?" (*Long, wry pause.*) And I said ... "Well, son. When I was a little boy, America was the strongest country in the world. (*Applause and cheers.*) When I was a little boy, every working American could expect to buy his own home. (*Applause.*) When I was a little boy, gasoline was twenty-eight cents a gallon." (*Cheers.*) ... The little boy looked up at me and he said, "Hey, mister. You ain't so old. Things were like that when I was a little boy too."' (*Laughter, applause, cheers and whoops.*)

Ronald Reagan is quite right. Some funny things *do* happen to you on the campaign trail.

Lined up with forty swearing pressmen over the chaotic trench of a hotel reception desk in Fort Worth, Texas, I noticed that the two-faced illuminated sign in the courtyard said, on one side, HOLIDAY INN – WELCOME GOV MRS REAGAN, and, on the other, STEAK AND SHRIMP SPECIAL $6.95.

In the Chattanooga Room of the Opryland Hotel (2800 Opryland Drive, Nashville, Tennessee), Governor and Mrs Reagan hosted a $250-a-plate fund-raising dinner. Ronnie, Nancy and half-a-dozen local dignitaries sat on a raised dais in front of metallic blue drapes. Over cocktails, the entire company swore allegiance to the flag, then listened with heads bowed to the pre-prandial prayer: 'Help us, God, to resolve our economic difficulties', and so on.

In the foyer restroom of the Holiday Inn, Midland, Texas, the Muzak was playing 'My Way'. As I came out into the hall, where Reagan would soon delight an expectant crowd, the Robert E. Lee High School Brass Band was playing 'Hot Stuff'. When the applause died after Reagan's speech, the band played 'I Wish I Was in Dixie'.

As the campaign Braniff jet took off from El Paso, Nancy Reagan rolled an orange down the aisle from the first-class section (where, I imagined, Ronnie was either asleep or completing a course of vitamin injections) to the back of the plane, where the news-cameramen shouted and laughed. Their laughter, like so much American laughter, did not express high spirits or amusement but a willed raucousness. As the plane landed in Dallas, the news-cameramen rolled the orange back to Nancy in the nose. It was a ritual. Half-way through the flight, Nancy came by with some chocolates, including one for your reporter. She still looked moist and trusting, even though a violent lightning storm coruscated the evening sky, and Ronnie was at least thirty feet from her side.

Reagan's stump speech is by now as pat and unvarying as his story about the twelve-year-old boy — an intro which alternates with the tale of how Ronald and Nancy were once mistaken for Roy Rogers and Dale Evans. Both anecdotes serve to mellow the audience for the honest sagacities to come.

Make America strong again. We don't want our soldiers on food stamps. 'Carter wants to preserve the *status quo* — that's Latin for the mess we're in.' Tackle inflation by 30 per cent tax cuts over three years (an idea which, incidentally, alarms even the most reactionary economists). Cut federal spending. Less government! We are not energy-profligate: we are an energy-rich nation. Scrap the Department of Energy. Nukes are good. Abortion-on-demand is bad (REAGAN IS PRO-LIFE, say several hand-held posters). 'Just because you can't keep guns from criminals, why keep them from honest people?' Able-bodied people on welfare should be put to work on 'useful' community projects. He did it in California — he can do it here. No more Taiwans! No more Vietnams! Carter is afraid that nobody will like us. Reagan doesn't *care* whether people will like us. He just wants people to *respect* us!

It is all delivered with mechanical verve, and with only a few stumbles and slips of the tongue — 'welfare', for instance, has a habit of getting mixed up with 'windfall'. You watch and listen to Ronald Reagan much as you do to Jimmy Carter, marvelling at their spectacular uneasiness in the realm of ideas, language and conviction. As front-runners, all they have to do is avoid, or minimise, the horrendous gaffes that seem ever ready to spring from their mouths. It is as if they can only just stop themselves from yelling out — 'I hate blacks!' or 'Who is Anwar Sadat?' Reagan is justly famous for his howlers, blind spots, mangled statistics and wishful inaccuracies. Each time he goes up to speak, you sense that the pollsters are reaching for their telephones, the aides for their aspirins.

Reagan likes to end his sessions with a bit of down-home give-and-take with his audience — 'You, the American people'. He points to each raised hand with a jerk of hip and shoulder, like a man drawing six-guns, and he listens to each question with his head shyly inclined. The more personal the question, the more he enjoys his own reply. 'Of all the people in America, sir, why you for President?' Reagan grins. 'Well, I'm not smart enough to tell a lie.' Laughter, applause. 'But why do you *want* it, sir?' Reagan flexes his worn, snipped, tucked, mottled face. 'This country needs a good Republican and I feel I can do the job. Why? I'm happy. I'm feeling good.' Here he turns. 'And I have Nancy to tuck me up at night.' Laughter, applause, hats in the air. Right on! Hot damn! You got it!

Then you realise: they love this actor. And I don't mean 'ex-actor'. I mean *actor*. He would have been one anyway, with or without Hollywood. He may not be smart, but there is plenty of cunning in him; and his ambitions are as tangled and cumbrous as anyone else's. 'I am one of you' is his boast, and the American people blush at his flattery. Watching him talk, his off-centred smile, his frown of concentration, his chest-swelling affirmations, you feel moved in that reluctant way you feel moved by bad art — like coming out of *Kramer versus Kramer*, denouncing the film with tears drying on your cheeks. Reagan is an affable old ham, no question. He would make a good head waiter, a good Butlins redcoat, a good host for *New Faces*. But would he make a good leader of the free world?

This is serious. How did it happen?

Reagan grew up in respectable poverty in rural Illinois, the second son of stoical Presbyterian parents. His father, Jack, worked in a shoe shop; his mother, Nelle, worked in a dress shop. During the early years of the Depression, the young Ronald attended little-known Eureka College, a Christian Church establishment near Peoria; he moonlighted to supplement his modest scholarship. Reaganites often boast that their man is the only candidate with a degree in economics. Reagan himself sometimes cautiously mentions this fact too. But he was no scholar, to put it mildly (even today his reading consists entirely of the Bible, *Reader's Digest* and assorted press-clippings). When Eureka gave him an honorary degree in 1957, Reagan cracked, 'I always figured the *first* one you gave me was honorary.'

Eureka saw the emergence of the early radical vein in Reagan's political thinking — if that isn't too exalted a phrase for the gruff simplicities he now trades in. When there was talk of a cut-back in the academic courses offered by the college, Reagan organised a student strike. Like his father, Reagan was at this time a faithful devotee of Roosevelt and the New Deal. (He remains an admirer of Roosevelt – and of Ike and Coolidge, partly because they didn't work too hard. 'Show me an executive who works all the time', Reagan is fond of saying, 'and I'll show you a bad executive.') Reagan continued to be a registered Democrat well into his forties. Towards the end of his Hollywood heyday Reagan led another successful strike: as president of the radical Screen Actors Guild. And during the days of the McCarthy witch hunts, he made a tough, shrewd stand against the Committee of Un-American Activities.

Reagan worked his way into films through sportscasting (for the World of Chiropractic station in Des Moines, Iowa) and through his own natural good fortune. He signed for Warner Brothers in 1937, at the age of twenty-six. He made about sixty films. They include *Cowboy from Brooklyn*, *An Angel from Texas*, *Sergeant Murphy*, *Swing Your Lady*, *Brother Rat*, *Brother Rat and a Baby*, *Bedtime for Bonzo* (about a baby chimp: Reagan refused to star in the sequel, *Bonzo Goes To College* – 'Who could believe a chimp could go to college? Lacked credibility,' said Reagan sternly), *Hellcats of the Navy*, *She's Working Her Way Through College*, *The Winning Team*, *Law and Order*, *All American*. Towards the end of his career Reagan's looks cragged up and he started playing villains. It was time to quit.

During the war Reagan served as a captain with the US Air Force, assigned mainly to the production of training films. In 1948 his eight-year marriage to actress Jane Wyman ended. Her career was just taking off at this point, with *The Lost Weekend* (1945); Reagan was her second husband and she went on to have two more. Reagan was luckier. In 1952 he married another of his leading ladies, Nancy Davis. They met through SAG. Nancy was accused of Un-American Activities and turned to her Guild President for help. It looks as though Nancy might have turned Reagan rightwards, perhaps simply by re-sanctifying the domestic verities. She is well known to be the woman behind the man, but her contribution seems to involve nothing more sinister than tireless idolatry. There is no hint, as yet, of the manipulative power that Rosalynn Carter is said to exercise over the wretched Jimmy.

At this point Reagan was freelancing with several studios, playing steadily smaller and less attractive parts. His career was temporarily revived by television. After a three-year stint as host of the 'Death Valley Days' Western anthology series, Reagan worked for eight years as MC and occasional guest-star for 'General Electric's Theatre of the Air'. To earn his annual $125,000 he was also obliged to tour the country giving uplift lectures to GE employees. Reagan's high-point was his televised speech in praise of GE's latest product, the nuclear submarine. A trio of rich businessmen were attracted by the way Ronnie carried himself on screen. With their backing, Reagan threw himself into Goldwater's disastrous presidential bid against Lyndon Johnson in 1964. Showing his usual talent for survival, Reagan came through the débâcle and in 1966 emerged blinking into the light — as Governor of California.

'I'll run on my record,' says Reagan these days, and points with pride to his achievements as two-term Governor of the richest state in the Union. 'In real terms California is the eighth richest nation in the world,' he points out, failing to add that California never had much in the way of foreign policy. 'When I took office in Sacramento, California was like America is now: bankrupt!' He fixed things there, he claims, and 'I believe I can do all that on the national level too.'

How good is Reagan's record? True, Reagan was Governor for eight years, and California was still there when he left. But one thing is clear: Reagan's record is nothing like as good as he keeps saying it is. His chief contentions are that he cut taxes, reined in a profligate government, and reformed welfare. The facts are as follows. Reagan doubled the per capita tax burden — $244 to $488 — and then softened the blow with tax rebates and credits. Similarly, there were 158,404 government employees when he took office and 203,548 when he left. As for the crucial issue of welfare, Reagan says he saved $2 billion with his reforms, turned a 40,000-a-month increase in recipients into an 8,000 decrease, and raised benefits for the 'truly needy'. Several legislators now maintain that the real saving was closer to $40 million. The welfare load was reduced, willy-nilly, by the economic boom, with parallel effects nationwide. And the benefits Reagan claims to have increased had been static since 1958. They rose — after liberal federal pressure — *two years* behind the deadline mandated by Congress. Reagan stonewalled with a series of court actions, and Washington remained conveniently lax. 'I remember it very well,' says Elliot Richardson, who was Nixon's Secretary for Health, Education and Welfare at the time: 'It was made quite clear to me that we should be nice to Reagan. The 1972 election was coming up and Nixon didn't want to upset him.'

Statistics, of course, are malleable — as Reagan himself has frequently demonstrated. But his governmental style is clear enough. Despite liberal aberrations like ecological control bills, conjugal visits for prison inmates, and a wide-open abortion law (which he now thinks of as his worst legacy), Reagan in California showed steady indifference to the poor, the sick, the dissident — and to the tragic mess of the inner cities. The cities are not his base, as he well knows. And while Reagan is no racist (his remark about 'bucks' in welfare queues can be matched by Carter's gaffe about 'ethnic purity'), he has made no progress whatever in winning the confidence of the blacks. As black leader Aaron Henry said recently, 'With him, any black that can *crawl* will be finding a place somewhere to vote against him.' The question of Reagan's age may have disappeared as an issue; but his ideas still look very elderly. He is a throw-back, and an undistinguished one.

Americans are, perforce, getting used to the idea of President Reagan. Wary at first, big business is getting to like him; he is even finding a base in the trade unions. As this piece goes to press, Reagan is ten percentage points ahead in the polls. The force of John Anderson's independent candidacy remains unpredictable: so does John Anderson. As Gore Vidal has pointed out: 'Compared to Carter and Reagan, Anderson looks like Lincoln. Compared to Lincoln, he looks like Anderson.' At this stage of things, ex-President Gerald Ford is being held up as a Bismarck, a Napoleon, an Alexander. The year 1980 has seen the unchallenged ascendancy of the politics of *faute de mieux*. If Reagan wins this autumn, we will all know where to put the blame: on the bumbling, canting presidency of Jimmy Carter. Carter gave us Tehran. He gave us Afghanistan. He may yet give us President Ronald Reagan.

Sunday Telegraph 1979

*   *   *

Postscript Governor Reagan prospered. Indeed, he is now floundering through his second term. And they still love him.

I have nothing new to say about this phenomenon. Two lines in American life, not quite parallel, were moving towards each other: Ronald Reagan and television. And then they met. In retrospect, it is not entirely frivolous to view the 1980 election as a vanished Reagan Western, a lost outline for 'Death Valley Days'. Carter was the prosing weakie who kept the store. Anderson was the gesticulating frontier preacher who just held up the action. But Ronnie was the man who came riding into town, his head held high, not afraid to use his fists – well prepared, if asked, to become the next sheriff of the United States.

What is this televisual mastery of Reagan's? It is a celebration of good intentions and unexceptional abilities. His style is one of hammy self-effacement, a wry dismay at his own limited talents and their drastic elevation. We feel the discrepancy too – over here in this Prime Target. For President Reagan is not just America's keeper: like his opposite number, he is the keeper of the planet, of all life, of the past and of the future. Until 1988, old Ronnie, that actor, is the Lord of Time.

Mr Vidal: Unpatriotic Gore

Novelist, essayist, dramatist, epigrammatist, television polemicist, controversialist, pansexualist, socialist and socialite: if there is a key to Gore Vidal's public character, it has something to do with his towering immodesty, the enjoyable superbity of his self-love. No, this is not infatuation; this is the real thing. 'I can understand companionship. I can understand bought sex in the afternoon, but I cannot understand the love affair,' Vidal has said; perhaps love is blind after all. Indeed, Vidal's paraded auto-crush has a way of summoning the most wistful refrains. It is a love whose month is ever May. Here is a man, you feel, who would walk a thousand miles for one of Gore's smiles.

It could be argued, of course, that Gore Vidal has a lot to be self-loving about. Gore Vidal has certainly argued as much. 'My critics resent everything I represent: sex, wealth and talent' is a remark attributed to him. Vidal is, for a start, preposterously well-preserved for someone who, according to my records, will soon be fifty. Whereas early photographs of the growing Gore are almost embarrassing to behold (who is this strapping exquisite?), he even now resembles a pampered heart-throb cruising easily into mid-career. Unpleasant rumour has it that Vidal's pulchritude owes as much to the cosmetic surgeon as it does to natural health and proportion — one hears talk of face-lifts, lid-tucks, teeth-capping, etc. But those vigilant, ironic brown eyes, together with his melli-fluous, patrician voice, are the energy-centres of Vidal's person, and age will not wither *them*. They strongly contribute to his immediate, knowing, slightly foxy charm.

The gates to Vidal's Ravello villa are released by a hidden electronic device. With a shy smile, Vidal operates the powerful current to allow us entry, and explains: 'Kidnappers . . . I'm not big enough for them really — but someone might be dumb enough to think I'm Jackie Kennedy's brother.' He saunters on down the path, his hysterical terrier, Rat, patrolling the steep terraces.

Approached from the side, the villa seems impossibly narrow, wedged into the Mediterranean cliff-face. But once we were within, the white passages spanned out impressively in unexpected directions. A courteous if uneffusive host, Vidal parked me in his wood-and-leather library, seated himself opposite and began to talk, dividing his lustrous gaze between me and our photographer (who cavorted acrobatically round him throughout the afternoon, to Vidal's occasional unease). 'That's my bad side,' Vidal would say. 'My left side is my good side.'

Vidal's looks, in common with everything else about Vidal, are dear to Vidal's heart. He minds about them: they are a source of both exhilaration and anxiety. The same applies to his varied talents and the extent to which society honours them with gratitude and rewards. This is not a love affair built on complacence: it is one grounded in ceaseless reassessment ('Am I *really* that great? . . . Yes' is how the soliloquy probably goes). Vidal is perhaps one of the best-selling serious writers in the world, and certainly one of the most prolific; in addition, he has shone brightly in several careers (politics, television, theatre, cinema), any of which might have satisfied a less restively arrogant man. And yet success has not brought serenity: although he has little of the paranoia worryingly frequent among well-known writers, he is someone who delightedly cultivates the envies and rivalries of his peers; although he is assured of his eminence, he has no desire whatever to be above it all. Why?

A recent much-publicised punch-up with his rival Norman Mailer is illuminating in this respect — and highly entertaining, let me say. Vidal's eyes flood with dissimulated pleasure as he prepares to tell the oft-told story; he is looking forward to coming well out of it.

The scene was a New York party, thrown by Lally Weymouth for publisher Lord Weidenfeld (freshly arrived Ambassador Peter Jay was among the startled guests). Vidal was talking to a group of people, when he felt an agitated hand on his shoulder. It belonged to Mailer. The two men had been wary friends for years; but their polarities grew intolerable after Mailer's *The Prisoner of Sex*, and they nearly came to blows on a Dick Cavett television show in 1971.

'It was Norman, looking small, fat and out of shape. "Gore," he said, "you look like an old Jew."

'"Well, Norman," I said in my witty way, "*you* look like an old Jew, too."' (Mailer, by the way, is Jewish. Gore is, if anything, oppressively Aryan in appearance and ancestry.)

'Then he threw the contents of his glass in my face, and punched me gently on the side of the mouth. It didn't hurt. Then I pushed him. Norman has always hated the fact that, apart from everything else, I'm much taller and stronger than he is. He went flying backward six or seven feet, landing — to our alarm — on top of the man who invented Xerox.'

Order then laboriously re-established itself. But Mailer is said to have gone round the room attempting to enlist an anti-Gore faction and demanding that the hostess eject him. She refused. Dourly, Mailer reapproached his foe. It is at this point that the tale turns brutal.

'"Come outside," he said to me. His mouth was working and you could smell the fear. "Norman," I said, "you can't go *on* this way. You're too old for all this." At that point, my friend Howard [Howard Austen, Vidal's aide/secretary/companion for the past twenty-eight years] turned on Norman. Howard is Jewish; he grew up on the same streets as Norman; he knew what Norman was doing. Howard advanced on him steadily, saying, "You flea! Get out, you fucking asshole loser, you fucking asshole *loser*." That was it. No more Norman. The next day he was on the phone to the gossip columnists, convincing them that there had been a fight, that he was some sort of — what's his word? — "existential hero".'

According to the press reports, Vidal had the last word: 'Once again, words failed him.' All Mailer could manage was: 'Vidal? He's just a mouth.'

Mailer had had an early word, though, which goes a bit nearer home. It's the sort of he-man dismissal one would expect from an existential hero; but there may be something to it. 'Vidal', said Mailer once, 'lacks the wound.'

Vidal would no doubt be happy to concur. 'My God, what a lucky life,' he confesses. 'I was born into Washington society. Both sides of

my family were political. Money, fame, power — I was never in awe
of any of that. It had no spell over me.'

His family was grand, but it was also scattered. His father, Eugene
Vidal, was on F.D. Roosevelt's cabinet as the first chief aviation
administrator. ('I was the youngest person ever to land a plane,' says
Vidal, nodding proudly at a framed photograph of father and son in
the cockpit. One wonders, confusedly, whether he still is.) He spent
most of his childhood, however, under the tutelage of his grandfather, Senator Gore, Oklahoma's first elected senator. Gore senior
had been blind from the age of ten, and Gore junior often used to
guide the old man to and from the Capitol (one summer Gore junior
wore a swimsuit when he went to collect his grandfather; Gore
senior was none the wiser, until he overheard catty speculations
about the family's red-neck origins).

The Gores were Anglo-Irish, settling in America in the 1690s, the
Vidals Alpine newcomers arriving in 1848: Gore Vidal combined
the family names in a melodious clinch, one that I take to be an
indispensable ingredient of his glamour. At an early age little Gore
acquired a further sprig to the family tree. His mother divorced his
father and became the second wife of Hugh Auchincloss, a
descendant of Aaron Burr, whom Vidal would eventually write a
novel about. Mr Auchincloss was plainly a lucky man: his *third* wife
was the mother of Jackie Bouvier, who later became Jackie Kennedy,
and who is now Jackie Onassis.

Vidal 'quit schooling' at the age of seventeen, and has been a
tireless autodidact ever since. Recent reading includes Balzac and
D.H. Lawrence: 'Balzac is giving me *great* pleasure. Lawrence — my
God — every page I think, "Jesus, what a fag. Jesus, what a *faggot*
this guy sounds."'

As the war was petering out, Vidal saw peripheral service in the
Aleutians. 'For all my generation, the war was just a great interruption.' He was committed to hospital in mid-service with premature
arthritis; the break nevertheless allowed him to complete his first
novel *Williwaw*, a cool look at war from the edges, at the age of
nineteen. The book was a *succès*, but hardly a success. Sales were
indifferent, and Vidal now found that he had to write a novel a year
to stay alive. Contrary to popular belief, Vidal was no princeling: he
got a handsome send-off when he came of age, but nothing since.
Between 1945 and 1949 he wrote six novels, living frugally in cheap
countries like Guatemala. One of these novels was a notorious work

called *The City and the Pillar*. It was enough to evaporate the little repute Vidal had.

'I took on the whole heterosexual dictatorship of America at the age of twenty-three. Enough wounds were given and received in that battle to satisfy even Norman Mailer.' *The City and the Pillar* was about 'the essential naturalness, if not normality, of homosexuality'. It seems mild enough – even evasively cerebral – today; but all the closets were locked in the American 1940s, and the book scuppered Vidal as a serious novelist. A few more fictions trickled out until 1953 (including three detective novels under the quibbling name of Edgar Box – 'they took eight days each to write'), then Vidal put down his quill, opened his eyes and looked round about himself.

There followed a busy, public decade. Spreading his wings, Vidal became one of the last contract writers for MGM. 'It wasn't like working as a writer. It was like working for General Motors,' he admits coolly. One of his (uncredited) screenplays was for *Ben Hur*: 'By the time I arrived on the set, everything had already been built – including Charlton Heston.' He wrote plays for television and Broadway; he wrote essays and political pieces; Vidal embarked on his long career as a television pundit. At one point there was surprising talk of a romance and engagement between Vidal and Joanne Woodward. They ended up living *à trois* for a time in California, the third member of this curious *ménage* being Paul Newman.

In 1960, he submitted to the old tug of politics and ran for Congress: he stood as a Democratic-Liberal candidate for a safe Republican seat in upstate New York. He lost, of course, 78,789 to 103,325, but he trebled the Democratic showing and won 20,000 more votes than John Kennedy – 'as I never ceased to remind him'. Two years later, he was asked to stand for the US Senate. Vidal pondered the offer carefully – then fled the country.

'Why did you give up politics?'

'I would never have gone far enough to be of any use. But I *could* have made it. I am just perfect for television, and that's all a President has to be these days. No – I would have become a drunken Senator who said something interesting once a year.'

'Why did you want to be President?'

'Why not? Admittedly I lack the character and wisdom of Johnson, Nixon, Ford and Carter. But the office itself ennobles. Anyway, I left the country. I wanted to be a writer again.'

'Why couldn't you be that in America?'

'Because I didn't want to become an alcoholic, basically. They all are there, for some reason. Fitzgerald, Hemingway and Faulkner are the classic examples, but it didn't stop with them. Apart from the Jews, all American writers do seem to booze a great deal. After all, there's something to be said for being an alcoholic in America.

'Either that or they barricade themselves away, like Salinger. But I wonder how he passes the time. It is very cold where he lives ... '

Besides, Vidal had a specific novel to research and compose, and it was this that brought him to Italy. The book was called *Julian*: it turned out to be the start of a fresh track in Vidal's career as a writer. A study of the fourth-century apostate Roman Emperor, the new novel combined imaginative passion (Vidal's suspended nostalgia for pre-Christian grandeur and chaos) with intellectual distance (a chance to be rigorous and erudite). *Julian* was his first fiction for ten years: it was a huge success, critically and commercially, and prepared the way for his equally redoubtable trilogy about the American political past, *Washington, DC*, *Burr* and (well-timed for the bicentennial year) *1876*. These novels, together with the problematical *Myra Breckinridge*, have made him world famous – and a millionaire at least a couple of times over.

Although there is almost total unanimity about Vidal's quality as an essayist, assessments of his fiction vary to an unusual degree. To some, Vidal's gifts are primarily analytical and expository. So long as his fiction is tied to argument – as in the historical novels – it has all the wit and conviction of his essays, with an added spaciousness and poise, a sense of intimacy with the way the world works. Once freed from this reality, though – as in the satirical fantasies *Myra Breckinridge* and *Myron* – his imagination founders in a kind of puerile vivacity, mere low-campery. Auberon Waugh remarked of *Myron* that only humourless people seemed to find it funny. And such people would, on Vidal's admission, include a great many Americans.

While he forged ahead with his fiction during the Sixties, Vidal became, if anything, even more trenchant and ubiquitous as a commentator on the American scene. 'Living outside America helps: you see things more sharply and can say what you want.' Undiminished controversy shadowed his exile. In 1961 he launched his famous feud with Bobby Kennedy. 'Jack was tremendous company – really droll. But with Bobby . . . it was chemical. Put us in the same room and I'd want to kick him. He was a McCarthyite tough.'

In 1967, he wrote two remarkably clear-headed attacks on the Kennedy political machine, *The Holy Family* and *The Manchester Book*; he was later to say of Teddy's presidential aspirations, 'Well, he would have made a very good bartender.'

During elections he returned to gallivant round the US television circuit, eliciting on one occasion this lucid retort from William Buckley Junior: 'Listen, you queer. Stop calling me a crypto-Nazi or I'll sock you in your goddamn face.' During the 1970 election Vidal became co-chairman of Dr Spock's New Party, a wet-lib fringe group running on a collection of fashionable issues (a protest-vote, surely?). Two years later his play *An Evening with Richard Nixon* earned him an impressive bundle of death threats. ('Well-written death threats, too. They weren't just lunatics.') Vidal is, and will remain, an energetic, increasingly Parnassian monitor of his homeland – 'a national treasure,' as one critic put it, 'one of the very few sane voices amidst the babble'.

'Oh to be in England, now that England's here,' drawled Gore when, on arrival at my Ravello hotel, I diffidently telephoned his villa. I had reviewed Mr Vidal's work on two occasions, and with sufficient hostility to win his amused disdain, or so a common friend told me. I had met him once, last year, and he was geniality incarnate (later describing me, in a student-magazine interview, as 'a cute little thing'). Now Vidal is well known to harbour grudges, and for a moment I suspected that some small, patrician revenge might await me. A bit of lordly hetero bashing, perhaps, or at least several hours of Vidal's expertly decadent taunts.

Nothing – or very little – of the kind. He is excellent company and a superlative talker, aphoristic, funny, learned, with a delightful line in brutal mimicry (his Tennessee Williams is an unforgettable, croaky mixture of affection and savagery). There *is* that fundamental coldness in him, and occasionally one catches glimpses of it. But it is not something that a day-tripper would be permitted to inspect.

Vidal's life at present seems to be a masterpiece of order and productivity. He does most of his writing in the Ravello villa, an ivory palace slapped on the cliff-face, with occasional diversionary visits to his opulent apartment in Rome (it is there – if the late Tom

Driberg was to be believed — that most of his startling socio-sexual escapades take place. 'So Tom sang, did he?' said Vidal grimly). He has a living-out maid, and there is always the devoted Howard to mastermind the running of villa and estate. Among other things, they make their own wine. On the ground floor, between Vidal's bedroom and Howard's, is a well-equipped bathroom/sauna/ gymnasium, complete with dumb-bells, where 'I work out irreligiously every day'. He looks fit. He is fit, as I discovered during a back-breaking walk down the cliff to Amalfi.

As I wheezed down the endless steps behind him, Vidal chatted melodiously on. The two-year débâcle over his recent screenplay, *Caligula*, continues to vex him. The producer, Bob Guccione of *Penthouse*, intended to call the film *Gore Vidal's Caligula*; having seen some of the revised script, Vidal set a lawsuit in train to have his name removed from the title. One of the stars, Maria Schneider (*Last Tango in Paris*), hardly an actress famed for her fastidiousness, quit the film rather than enact the sex scenes required of her by the Italian director.

'Oh, it's hard-core all right. Nothing wrong with that, in itself. It's just that the director has no talent. As for the producer . . . ' Some exuberantly libellous comments ensued.

'Right, give me some gossip,' Vidal demanded, producing wine as I recuperated after the walk.

Vidal is on record as saying that he always perks up at news of catastrophe among his friends. And, as I did my best with tales of professional failure, neurosis and marital collapse, a new intensity began to invade his features. In a curious way, despite his ameliorist image, you feel that he wishes everything were worse than it is — America, the modern marriage, the trials of his friends. It would be neater that way, and more fun to think about. He has removed pain from his own life, or narrowed it down to manageable areas; and it is one thing he cannot convincingly re-create in his fiction. But his deeply competitive nature is still reassured to know that there is plenty of pain about.

I have never met an American so English in his irony. No issue is serious enough for him to resist its satirical possibilities, a habit that reinforces his stirring pessimism about the way the world is changing. 'As cheerful as a leper-bell,' was how Simon Raven described his prognosis, a verdict which Vidal prizes. But the phrase misses his grisly relish of human folly, the sense you get that his world-view is obedient to a personal rhetoric, a private enjoyment of the badness of things.

* * *

Postscript In agreeing to the interview Mr Vidal had armed himself with the stipulation that he would be able to see and check the piece before it was published. There was nothing sinister in this: naturally he wouldn't attempt to trim my opinions. Nevertheless I had the ticklish task of calling on Vidal at the Connaught in London and sitting there in his room while he inspected the galleys. In the first paragraph he changed 'homosexual' to 'pansexual'. A little later he said, in his grandest voice, 'Now if you print that I shall most certainly sue,' and deleted a chance scurrility with a stroke of his pen. ('As one gets older', Vidal has remarked, 'litigation replaces sex.') Thereafter he merely did a bit of gardening, corrected some misquotations ('No, that's not my style at all'), and inserted a new joke or two ('If you take that out, I'll give you this'). We haggled over a number of points; there were no real cruces. Occasionally, as he read on, he gave a reluctant laugh. 'Mm,' he concluded. 'A bit thin on the *work*.'

This was perfectly true. I had read *Myra* and *Myron* (with difficulty), some of *Williwaw*, half of *The City and the Pillar* and most of *Julian*; I had also spent three weeks reading three chapters of *Burr*. I cannot get through Vidal's fiction. The books are too long. Life is too short. In the interests of balance I append a piece about Vidal's essays, where I am a little older and a little more forthright.

May I also take the opportunity here to pit Vidal's account of his fight with Mailer against Mailer's account of his fight with Vidal? Needless to say, at no point do they tally. When I asked Mailer for his version, he nodded, squared his shoulders, and spoke with solemn deliberation.

'Vidal had written things about me. I had resolved that the next time I saw him, I was going to hit him. You understand? The next time I saw him was at Lally's. I walked up and banged him over the head with a glass — a heavy cocktail glass. He looked very scared. I asked him to come outside. Then his little friend started in on me.

"All right," I said. "Come on. I'll take out the two of yous." They stayed where they were. I walked away.'

Perhaps, towards the end, I am guilty of importing the accents of De Niro's Jake la Motta; but that was it, in substance. One day I must triangulate the story with the version of an impartial onlooker, if any such exist. Whom to believe, though? In my experience of fights and fighting, it is invariably the aggressor who keeps getting everything wrong.

*   *   *

Gore Vidal is probably the cleverest book-reviewer in the world. This needn't sound like faint praise, even to someone as exhaustively lauded as Mr Vidal. He is too clever to write effective Hollywood screenplays, too clever to be an effective politician (he flunked in the senatorial primaries in 1982), too clever, really, to be an effective novelist. Essays are what he is good at: you can't be too clever for them.

Vidal is the unchallengeable master of the droll stroll. Rightly indulged by his editors, who give their star performer all the rope he wants, Vidal saunters at his leisure through the books tendered for review, with many a delightful diversion, racy short-cut, startling turn of speed. He is learned, funny and exceptionally clear-sighted. Even his blindspots are illuminating.

Roughly half the essays in *Pink Triangle and Yellow Star* are literary, half socio-political. When writing about the real world, Vidal sounds like the only grown-up in America — indeed, his tone is that of a superevolved stellar sage gazing down on the globe in pitying hilarity. There are two reasons for this. First, Vidal was born into the governing classes, and has never regarded them with anything but profound suspicion. In 1940, following the death of the virtuous Senator William Borah ('the lion of Idaho'), a large stash was found in his safety deposit box, causing uneasy speculation. Vidal approached his grandfather, Senator Gore, and asked him who had paid Borah off: 'The Nazis,' came the reply. 'To keep us out of the war.' This is traumatic news, even now. Vidal must have been fifteen at the time. It is easy to see how such disclosures would have shaped and hardened his thinking.

The second and closely related reason for Vidal's bracing hauteur is that Vidal is incorrigibly anti-American. My, is Gore unpatriotic!

No pomaded Hanoverian swaggerer could have such natural contempt for that coarse and greedy colony. Writing about the Framing
of the First Constitution, Vidal does not accept 'the view that a
consortium of intellectual giants met in Philadelphia in order to
answer once and for all the vexing questions of how men are to be
governed'. He finds, rather, that their 'general tone is that of a
meeting of the trust department of Sullivan and Cromwell'. In
another essay Vidal resolutely fails to distinguish between American
polity and the workings of the Chase Manhattan Bank: bureaucrats
are 'tellers', voters are 'depositors'; and when Banksman Nixon goes
to Peking or Moscow, he goes 'in search of new accounts'. As for the
judiciary, and the moral code it enforces, Vidal claims that the
prisons throng 'with people who get drunk, take dope, gamble, have
sex in a way that is not approved by the holy book of a Bronze Age
nomad tribe as reinterpreted by a group of world-weary Greeks in
the first centuries of the last millennium' − i.e. the Bible (or 'the
Babble', as many of its adherents seem to call it). How true or
'helpful' all this is remains unclear. But the gleeful iconoclasm has
the conviction of satirical truth.

Vidal's flag-scragging extends from public life through literary
questions to social mores. In 'the land of the tin ear', where
'stupidity . . . is deeply revered', where humourlessness is endemic
('what other culture could have produced Hemingway and *not* seen
the joke?'), cultural conspiracies flourish unchecked. 'Americans will
never accept any literature that does not plainly support . . . a
powerful and bigoted middle class', a state of affairs institutiona-
lised by the universities, which are themselves torpid bureaucracies
of preferment and tenure. Among the bigotries of this powerful
middle class is a deep and mindless 'homophobia', the American
establishment being militantly heterosexual. Vidal has written about
this before, of course, but never quite so virulently. 'In the German
concentration camps, Jews wore yellow stars while homosexualists
wore pink triangles' − hence the book's title. The moral stakes could
hardly be raised any higher; Vidal's *tic nerveux* has developed into
an obsession, a crusade, and the effect on his writing is everywhere
apparent.

In the opening essay, on Scott Fitzgerald's *Notebooks*, we learn
that Fitzgerald makes 'rather too many nervous references to fairies
and pansies'. In the second, on Edmund Wilson, we learn that
Wilson's notebooks, too, 'are filled with innumerable references to

'fairies that range from derisive to nervous'. What does 'nervous' mean here exactly? Does it mean that Fitzgerald and Wilson are 'nervous' about being fairies themselves? Yes, because Vidal has always believed that heterosexuals got that way purely through the conditioning of that powerful middle class. The third essay, on Isherwood's *Christopher and His Kind,* ends with a plangent clarion call: 'one can only hope that thanks to Christopher's life and work, his true kind will increase even as they refuse, so wisely, to multiply'. A few pages earlier Vidal has called Isherwood 'the best prose writer in English'. This is a meaningless tribute anyway, but by now the nervous hets among Vidal's readers will be wondering whether the verdict is really a literary one. It sounds like a manic-depressive overpraising Sylvia Plath, a postmaster general making excessive claims for Trollope, a midget going ape for Pope.

Vidal expands his platform. The ruling classes fear the gays because they aren't as easily dominated by the hen-pecked, ball-broken straights with their nagging wives and grasping children. Everyone – oh, happy day – is potentially bisexual. This is a terrific plus because 'we have more babies than we know what to do with'. Finally, and clinchingly, 'the family is an economic, not a biological, unit'. Actually, of course, the family is both: how could a parent-child relationship *not* be biological? But what the family mainly is is a unit, willy-nilly. To disapprove of this fact is as futile as disapproving of oxygen or bipedalism.

Besides, the whole line sounds rather ... American, does it not, tending to reduce argument to a babble of interested personalities, an exchange of stricture and veto, with money as the bottom line? Well, if Vidal sounds unusually shrill, 'there is a good deal to be shrill about'. He sees his freedoms as being under particular threat, and maybe he is right. More likely, the stand just happens to suit his antic pessimism. 'Real stupidity does excite me,' he once said. America is the perfect rumpus-room for this witty invigilator. Meanwhile it should be stressed that the new book is a peach. It will give everyone many hours of nervous pleasure.

Sunday Telegraph 1977 and *Observer* 1982

Too Much Monkey Business: The New Evangelical Right

'I call it Mickey Mouse mentality,' proclaimed Judge Braswell Deen, referring to the theories of Charles Darwin: 'monkey mythology methodology monopoly, mysterious musings and mundane dreams of all this monkey business!' The audience of 15,000 — most of them Baptists, Methodists, charismatics, fundamentalists, pentecostalists and journalists — applauded and whooped.

Elsewhere in the Reunion Arena, Dallas, Texas, a frowning Ronald Reagan told a press conference that he had 'a great many questions about evolution'. 'I believe schools should be even-handed on the issue,' he added. This was a nervous moment for gaffe-dreading Ronnie, in the week of Taiwan. And, sure enough, here was another howler jumping out of his mouth. But who cared? Perhaps this particular gaffe would win him 50 million votes.

Meanwhile, wearing a press badge that identified me as 'Marty Amis', I strolled the Reunion Arena concourses, sampling the pro-family propaganda on offer there. New in Dallas, I returned to the hotel restaurant and ate The American Way (hamburger and cottage cheese), plus an Elite Pastry. Beside my plate lay a stack of pamphlets. What was going on around here?

Some of the leaflets were simply illiterate hate-sheets; others were glossy and well produced. *Why a Bankrupt America?* explains how the Trilateral Commission is helping 'Russia Enslave the World!' *When You Were Formed in Secret* tells of the miracle of birth and the 'homicide of abortion'. *The Family Issues Voting Index* helps you to sort 'the good guys from the bad guys' ('The bad guys need our prayers. The good guys need our votes'). *Is Humanism Molesting Your Child?* urges you to 'examine your child's library for immoral, anti-family, and anti-American contents'. *Your Five*

Duties as a Christian Citizen are as follows: Pray, Register, Become Informed, Help Elect Godly People, and Vote ... Then I found the pamphlet I was looking for.

'Today the evolution controversy seems as remote as the Homeric era to intellectuals in the East,' wrote the historian Richard Hofstadter in 1962. But elsewhere there are still many Americans who, in the words of William Bryan, prosecutor at the Scopes trial of 1925, are 'more interested in the Rock of Ages than the age of rocks'.

Are Evolutionary Scientists Like Three Blind Mice? is the pamphlet's title. And, yes, apparently they are. Because evolution is 'a vicious lie!' There follows a sarcastic résumé of the atheist argument, with the clincher: 'QUESTION: IF GOD HAD TO DO ALL THE WORK ANYWAY WHY DID HE STRETCH IT OUT OVER MILLIONS OF YEARS? SURELY THEY DON'T THINK GOD WAS TOO WEAK TO CREATE EVERYTHING IN 6 DAYS!' The last page carries special offers of anti-evolution T-shirts ($6.95) and creationist bumper-stickers (40 cents). I finished my meal and returned to the National Affairs Briefing at the Reunion Arena to hear Reagan — Reagan, and his new champions, the electronic ministers of the air.

This is a good deal more serious than it may at first sound. The mobilisation of the Evangelical Right could influence the outcome of the 1980 presidential election and determine that of 1984 — though many of the new evangelists claim that a free 1984 election will not take place unless their man gets in this time. Their man, naturally, is the Republican nominee: the movement claims to be non-partisan, but it is about as neutral as Nancy Reagan. (Ironically, Nancy is the chief Evangelical reservation about Ronnie, who is a divorcee. According to them, the Reagans have been living in adultery for nearly thirty years.) By informing their congregations about the 'pro-family' issues, by setting up vote-registration booths in their aisles, the Evangelicals have already ousted left-wing incumbents in mid-term elections, have thwarted pro-homosexual and women's-rights legislation in key states, and have played a part in the shaping of the Republican platform. And these are early days.

Ronald Reagan, Jimmy Carter and John Anderson are all 'born-again' Christians. They are not alone. One in three Americans takes the lesson of Nicodemus in John 3: 'unless one is born anew, he cannot see the kingdom of God'. Reaching back to the Great

Awakening of the early eighteenth century, the Evangelical faith is the most proletarian and anti-intellectual of the many mansions of American religion. It rests on a personal experience of the Saviour; it is Manichaean and eschatological; for all its hatred and rejection of modernity, it maintains that the Earth is only 6,000 years old.

The latest surge in Evangelical activism is entirely new. Like so much else in America, it has to do with money, power and, above all, television. There are 36 wholly religious TV stations in America (and 1,300 radio stations). Jerry Falwell's *Old-Time Gospel Hour* is seen on 374 stations nationwide, outstripping *Dallas*. Pat Robertson's daily devotional chat show has more viewers than Johnny Carson. The TV preachers turn over billions of tax-free dollars every year (Falwell alone raises more than a million dollars a week, $300,000 of which goes on buying more air-time). Their mailing lists are kept on guarded computer tapes. The electronic ministries have a combined congregation of 115 million people attending every week.

The political wing of the movement has developed only in the last fifteen months. Its names are legion: Moral Majority Inc., Religious Roundtable, Christian Voice, Christian Voters' Victory Fund, Campus Crusade for Christ, Christians for Reagan – all loosely grouped under the pro-family banner. American religion has always been popular rather than hieratic in character, concerned not with theology but morality; and it has always, until now, been politically quietist, with low registration and a tendency to vote for the incumbent. The Evangelical message is plain – 'out of the pews and into the polls'. 'Not voting is a sin,' says Falwell: 'Repent of it.'

'And the Lord turned to him and said, "My precious child, I never left you in your hours of trial. When you look back along the pathway of your life and see only one pair of footprints in the sand – why, that was when I carried you."'

This wasn't the ghost of the Rev. Billy Sunday: it was a close-to-tears Ronald Reagan, winding up his address to the 15,000 Evangelicals (10,000 pastors, 5,000 lay people) at the Reunion Arena in Dallas. Reagan is taking these people seriously all right: he has hired a Moral Majority operative to liaise with the born-again community. 'Religious America is awakening, perhaps just in time,' said

Reagan hopefully. He praised the freedom-fighters of Poland and their leader, the Pope — 'just the son of simple farm folk'. He tied himself up in knots trying to pronounce 'Sollsy Neetsin' and his friend, 'Archie Pelaygo'. He spoke of the dream of all true Americans to attain 'that shining city on the hill'. But this was mild, hammy stuff compared to the kick-'em-down oratory of the electronic preachers.

Reagan was preceded at the podium by Dr James Robison, the good-angel JR of the Dallas–Fort Worth metroplex, whose TV show reaches ten million people (and has twice been taken off the air for its anti-homosexual virulence). Robison is six foot three of US prime, with a sensual, predatory manner and the tumbling unstoppability of the natural demagogue. He strode onstage to a rock star's welcome — a deafening wall of whistles and wolf-howls. A-men! Ooh-hah! Wah-who! Ee-haw!

Robison brandished his Bible a good deal, and often seemed about to wrestle his lectern to the ground. His language was violent, even scabrous. He spoke, or hollered, about 'the cancerous visible sores' afflicting America, sores which Christians were obliged to 'fight'. Jesus was no sissy, no sir. 'You slap my cheek', said Robison, slapping his own cheek resoundingly, 'and I'll turn it. But you slap my wife or my children, boy, and I'll *put you on the floor!*' (Dog-barks, coyote-calls. Why-haw! How-he!) 'Scientists', Robison believes, 'don't know what they're talking about.' The Bible, on the other hand, is 'more relevant than tomorrow's newspaper'. In his wind-up Robison advised 'the perverts to get back in the closet and not parade on Main Street!' Ow-wee! Who-how! Aaa-*mien!* . . . Reagan applauded. Back in Washington, Carter must have been wondering about the size of the pervert vote. Perverts for Carter — that's all he needs.

When Reagan's speech was over (and before anyone could get away) Jerry Falwell eased himself up on to the stage. Jerry's job was to complement Robison's brimstone with the other side of the Evangelical hard-sell: the cajoling demand for money. There wasn't much ooh-hawing now, as grim stewards passed out envelopes and plastic buckets to the multitude, which had already paid $25 apiece to get in. Falwell wanted a thousand people to 'pledge' $100 each, to help tab the Dallas experiment; he then coaxed and nagged some smaller contributions out of the audience for various circulars and devotional knick-knacks. 'One hundred dollars! This is a tax-deductible gift . . . Stand up all those who have pledged one hundred dollars. Or more.'

Money is the two-way traffic of the religious TV industry: money is taken from the viewers in the form of sacramental contributions; money is 'returned' to them in the form of celestial jackpots. The tax-free status of American religions (including the Californian cults) is constantly assailed. But all challenges are repulsed by the First Amendment — and by the age-old analogy between sectarian competition and free enterprise. Furthermore, Americans don't feel the same way about money as we feel about it. They are not embarrassable on the subject. Money is its own vindication; money is its own just cause.

By no means all of the uplift shows are consciously political. Some electronic preachers do nothing more sinister with their millions than aggrandise themselves and their sanctuaries. Oral Roberts (yes, *Oral* Roberts), whose programme is centred on mere semi-hysterical folksiness, is going ahead with a $200-million City of Faith in Tulsa, Oklahoma. Robert Schuller, who has a drive-in ministry one exit past Disneyland in Southern California, is building a twenty-two-acre Shopping Centre for Jesus Christ, featuring an all-glass Crystal Cathedral.

Styles vary. Some preachers tout health instead of money, which in America often means the same thing. Gene Profeta, who looks like Frankie Vaughan at the London Palladium, stands surrounded by the remnants of slum families who have found togetherness again with the Lord. 'Yeah, Gene, since I been praying and everything, I ain't had no seizures.' Gene grabs the mike: 'Oh praise Jesus.' Dr W.V. Grant's televisual pantheon looks like a field hospital at Gettysburg. Grant interrupts a spiritual to solace a crippled negro. 'The name's *Jim*, right?' 'Yeah.' 'You don't know me, do you, Jim?' 'No.' 'Jim, how long you been crippled up like that? Long time?' 'Yeah.' 'Jim, I want you to throw down these crutches and *walk!*' 'Okay.' Jim gets lithely to his feet, without looking pleased or grateful or even mildly surprised, and troops morosely up the aisle. 'Oh, hallelujah, praise that Lord!' sings Brother Grant. 'The Lord has healed him!' At this point, you begin to wonder Who crippled him. But Grant does not tarry with points of theodicy; he has his sales pitch to make.

Pat Robertson, chairman of the Christian Broadcasting Network, the great Sanctimoney genius of Portsmouth, Virginia, goes one further: he heals and rewards his flock over the airwaves. In the miracle-facility section of his show, the kneeling Robertson is granted visions of various recoveries, reunions and windfalls throughout the land. Robertson describes the miracles, and people ring in to claim them. His poorer viewers send him their rent cheques and disability allowances — because the gamble works better 'if you give out of your need'. Like all the TV preachers, Robertson also does big business in what the trade calls 'the pretty-pretties': sacred key-rings, beatified pen-clips and whatnot. CBN takes in over $1 million a week.

Robert Schuller's line typifies the logic of the holy sting, and he articulates it with all the unction of sweet reason. Gently waving his arms about and baring his practised false smile, Schuller explains that 'the major decision' in his life was 'tithing' — 'or the giving of 10 per cent of one's income *back* to the Church'. This of course means the giving of 10 per cent of one's income *back* to Robert Schuller. 'And it turned me into a very *good* business manager,' he adds, without a blush. 'If you can't live on the 90 per cent, you couldn't live on the 100 per cent. No way . . . ' And, in return, 'God will give you management skills.'

Schuller's show is entitled, candidly enough, *Hour of Power*. Of course, there is nothing peculiarly American, or peculiarly Western, about the religious emphasis on material reward. Present-day Hinduism, for example, is very largely structured on the principle of worldly success. However, the Midas tradition in American worship has little to do with modern laxity. It shocked de Tocqueville in 1831. A century later it effloresced in a host of how-to books on harmonial and self-bettering themes, under a thin shine of gnosticism: Dale Carnegie's *How to Win Friends and Influence People*, Norman Vincent Peale's *Power of Positive Thinking*, Billy Graham's *Peace with God*. What could be more American, in its way, than a version of Christ as the eternal miracle-worker and faith-healer — bringer of salubrity and cash, here and now?

The Rev. Jerry Falwell is the most powerful, most convincing, most committed — and the least vulgar — of all the electronic Evangelicals. He is without the messianic stridency of James Robison (with his talk of 'prophets' and 'new Jeremiahs'), and without the frank hucksterism of Pat Robertson. Falwell will last when the others are too bored, frightened or mad to continue usefully on the political wing. And if you ask *him* about his colonial mansion in Lynchburg, Virginia, his private aeroplane and airport, his tax-avoiding loans within his corporation, his bodyguards and gofers, he will tell you that material wealth is 'God's way of blessing people who put Him first'.

'I known Jerry Falwell since he was knee-high to a duck,' said the old Lynchburger in the bar (which took some finding). 'Knew his daddy too, biggest bootlegger ever hit this state. I seen Jerry Falwell so drunk he couldn't stand up – thirty years back, must be. But don't you trash Jerry now, you hear? Bet he earns more money than *you* ever will.'

Most of Lynchburg, Virginia, resembles an outsize drive-in shopping-mall. If you ask, with some desperation, to be taken to the centre of town, you end up in a different shopping-mall called Main Street. Moving around on foot, you feel vulnerable and isolated, like the next-to-go in *The Amityville Horror*. The township was founded by Colonel Charles Lynch – the man who got so memorably carried away when dealing out rough justice to loyalists after the American Revolution. It has a population of sixty-odd thousand, nearly a third of which owes allegiance to the Thomas Road Baptist Church, Jerry Falwell's home ministry.

Lynchburg is Jerryburg now, more or less. Falwell runs his *Old-Time Gospel Hour* from here, and his fund-raising computers glisten in the redbrick buildings behind the strapping new church. He also runs a children's academy, a Bible institute, a correspondence school, a seminary, and Liberty Baptist College itself, where 'leaders are trained for the generation to come, learning good character traits and how to become good moms and pops'.

Accompanied by Perry, a honey-toned young blonde from Falwell's PR department, I went up to Liberty Mountain to inspect the campus. 'Are *you* saved?' Perry asked me early on. I had grown used to fielding this kind of question over the past week. 'Well, not exactly,' I began. Perry was saved all right. 'I felt the Lord coming into my heart with – such love . . . ' Perry had been born again at the age of four, good going even for these parts.

Liberty Baptist College is a Southern-fried crag lined with bungalow-style lecture halls, the students' living-quarters situated further up the hill. No smoking, no drinking, no swearing. The fresh-faced pupils stroll peacefully from class to class, or sit reading their Bibles, or chat by the Coke machines. Not all the courses are theological — though I assumed that a lecture on, say, sociology would consist of an hour-long denunciation of the subject. Perry herself had majored here in psychology. 'How do they teach Freud?' I asked. 'Well, you take Freud, and see where he disagreed with the Bible,' said Perry. 'I mean, sometimes they agree. But we all know the Bible got there first.'

Thomas Road Baptist Church is more like a cinema than a place of worship, with its scalloped stalls sloping downwards to the stage, and the TV cameras wedged into the balcony. I mingled unobtrusively (I hoped) with the 4,000 Lynchburg faithful; I had Perry's say-so on this, but still felt uneasy about the imposture . . . There was a busy, socialising air: clumps of gossiping girls, all with a new dollar-bill on their laps for the collection bowl, and fondly watched by the big-chinned boys further back. Everyone opened their much-thumbed, much-underscored Bibles. It was 7 p.m. The two-hour service began.

This was an untelevised service, and so more down-home and gone-fishing in style than Falwell's standard performance. We memorised a verse from the Book of Psalms, slyly invited by a Falwell sidekick to insert the names of Carter and Reagan wherever we thought it appropriate: 'God *is* the judge: he putteth down one and setteth up the other.' We heard a spiritual from an Isley-Brothers-style trio (among the few dark faces in the house) and a squawky ballad from five local sisters on violin. Falwell preached with avuncular cheer — don't listen to the media, God loves you, my little wife, on Judgment Day we'll all be bigshots, sometimes you're up, sometimes you're down. Doubters filed up and then filed back, all born again again. Then Falwell asked us to join in little groups of two and three, and pray together, out loud.

Until that moment I had been performing a nervous, if quite passive, imitation of a devout Virginian. When people jotted down apophthegms, I took notes; when they sang hymns, I mimed along; when they prayed for salvation, I prayed for a Winston King Size and a large gin and tonic. But suddenly the young man on my left, who had kindly shared his Bible with me during the readings, turned to me and said, 'You wanna pray together?' – and I, for some reason, said, 'Surely'.

We hunkered down, hands on brows. 'You wanna go first?' he asked. 'No. You go first.' And as he stuttered on about the Lord helping America in its hour of etc., etc., I thought of the strapping young champions of Christ all about me, and of my own blasphemous intrusion. In five minutes, I thought, you'll be dangling from the rafters – and quite right too. The voice beside me trailed off with some remarks about Sue-Ann's rheumatism and Joe-Bob's mortgage; I turned to see his bashful, expectant face. In rocky Virginian I babbled out something about our people in Tehran and the torment they must feel in their hour of etc., etc. My prayermate wished he had thought of this too. We squeezed our frowning foreheads and nodded together for a very long time.

Falwell is innocuous in his home pulpit, smiling, sensible, protective: he understands the American spiritual yearning, which is the yearning to belong. But my first reaction when I met and talked to him, back in Dallas, was a momentary squeeze of fear. With his people milling about him in the futuristic foyer of the Hyatt Regency Hotel, he reminded me of the standard villain of recent American fiction and film: the corporation man.

Jerry Falwell (born in 1933; born again in 1956) is six foot and then some, with the squashy-nosed face of the friendly policeman. He wore a suit of some incredibly plush and heavy material (taffeta? theatre curtains? old surplices?), adorned with a small gold brooch in the characters of Jesus Christ, the terminal *t* stretched into a cross. (The same thing happens to the *T* in VOTE on his supporters' banners.) A huge aide brought us coffee. We began.

Doggedly I began to rehearse the obvious liberal objections to his platform, mentioning that he had called the Equal Rights Amendment 'a vicious attack on the monogamous Christian home'. 'That's right,' he said blandly. 'I don't believe in equal rights for women. I believe in superior rights for women.' (This is consistent enough: Falwell has always wanted to kick women upstairs.) 'You know, the Women's Lib movement? Many of them are lesbians, you know. They're failures – probably married a man who didn't treat them like a human being,' he added, completing the machocentric circle.

'If you were President,' I said, eliciting a brief smirk, 'how would you stop people being homosexual?'

'Oh, they've got to live, have jobs, same as anybody else. We don't want any Khomeini thing here. It's the sin not the sinner we revile. It's anti-family. When God created the first family in that Garden, he created Adam and Eve, not Adam and Steve.

'Besides, I want influence, not power. But I want global influence. We can't buy more airtime in America, no way. But we'll start buying it worldwide. South America, Europe, Asia ... '

His aides signalled. I asked my final question.

'Yes, sir, every word, quite literally, from Genesis to Revelations, which says there will soon be nuclear holy war over Jerusalem, after which Russia will be a fourth-rate power and Israel will astonish the world. Nice talking to you. Now if you'll excuse me, I have a radio show to attend.'

Easy prey, perhaps. British liberals enjoy being alarmed by commotion on the American Right; we also tend to indulge our vulgar delight in American vulgarity. I don't think the Evangelicals will soon be running the country. Although they have made an appeal to something old and fierce in the native character, it will take years to develop this into any kind of consensus. The movement constitutes a genuine revolution from below, however, and will have to be heeded. To dismiss the beliefs of the Evangelicals is to disdain the intimate thoughts of ordinary people.

Nor is their critique of American society contemptible in itself. One of Falwell's TV specials is called *America, You're Too Young To Die*. It shows leathery gays necking in Times Square, sex-aid emporia, child pornography, aborted foetuses in soiled hospital trays. A predictably alarmist collage, certainly. But some of us who have been born only once find plenty that is cheerless here, and fail to buy the 'humanist package' entire.

'All the ills from which America suffers can be traced back to the teaching of evolution,' wrote William Bryan in 1924. 'It would be better to destroy every other book ever written, and save just the first three verses of Genesis.' The anti-intellectual content in Evangelical feeling is, by definition, a source of pride to its leaders. But it will either ruin or deform the movement eventually. No book but the Bible; Genesis or Darwin, one or the other. This is why the movement will have to be contested. This is why the movement is so wide-open, so abjectly vulnerable, to authoritarian thought.

Observer 1980

Vidal v. Falwell

'I usually start with a prayer. But instead I'll start with the latest Nancy Reagan joke.' The perpetrator of this careful irreverence was Mr Gore Vidal; its setting — Lynchburg, Virginia, the Rev. Jerry Falwell's home town and HQ, the capital of the New Right. 'Actually,' drawled Vidal, an old-Virginian aristo himself, 'it's the capital of the Old Right. If there's anything a Virginian hates to be called, it's *new*.'

It was one of those curious, fixing moments in the swirling American scene. Gore Vidal, lifelong excoriator of the political circus, is once again donning his tutu for the high trapeze: later this year, he hopes to replace California's S.I. Hayakawa in the US Senate. Vidal has often said that any American who is prepared to run for President should automatically, by definition, be disqualified from ever doing so. Yet he confessed over dinner (or, rather, over a Virginian meat tea, before his speech) that he is intending to go the whole way. And so, last Monday night, Vidal strolled sturdily up to the lectern at Lynchburg College and gave his annual State of the Union address, his mocking echo of the Presidential bulletin of the previous week. But this is no longer Vidal's lecture-circuit, after-dinner oration: it is his stump speech, and it is sweepingly, piercingly radical.

Meanwhile, across town, Jerry Falwell lurked brooding behind the walls of his $300,000 house. Jerry's house is a Doric mansion, but it lies in the wrong end of town: 'among the cracker boxes', in the local parlance. For all his Hugh-Hefner trappings, Jerry remains a rockbottom grass-roots figure, regarded as riff-raff even by petit-bourgeois Lynchburgers. (Jerry minds about this; Vidal's new-Virginian remark was meant to sting.) Asked along that night by the local anti-Falwell group, which arranged Vidal's talk, Jerry had silently declined. Perhaps he was watching the first episode in a new soap-opera about a video evangelist, called – with an appropriate glance at Pay TV – *Pray TV*. Or perhaps, like everyone else in America, he was monitoring the depravities of Charles and Sebastian, in *Brideshead Revisited*.

Against this varied opposition, Vidal still attracted a full house. After a few preliminary jokes and jabs (enough to make a few heavy citizens walk from the hall shaking their heads), he kicked off with the proposition that America was run by a single-party system. The party happened to have two factions – Democrats and Republicans. 'It's supposed to give you the feeling of choice, like Painkiller X versus Painkiller Y. But they're both just aspirin.'

Ever since the Bust of 1929, Vidal pursued, the US had been in thrall to the notion that 'war is good for business'. Open or covert, hot or cold, war had been waged for the past fifty years; and now Reagan, 'in the bright springtime of his senility', was busy arranging the next war with Nicaragua, say, or El Salvador ('I lie awake at night worrying about the hordes of El Salvadorans pouring across our border in Greyhound buses'). Reagan's $1½ trillion five-year defence budget could result only 'in nuclear war or bankruptcy – one or the other'. The CIA, he claimed, was now as active and ubiquitous as the KGB.

Without too much chapter and verse, Vidal switched from the question of global policing to that of domestic enforcement. He estimated that 50 per cent of all police work was taken up with 'victimless crime'. Why do we meekly accept that our private lives should be run by Washington? If people want to kill themselves with drink, drugs, or indeed bullets, then that is their business; ditto with restraints on sexual morality. Released from their patrols of parlour and bedroom, the police would be free to combat the crimes that really etc., etc.

All this may have surprised – and delighted and scandalised – the gathered Lynchburgers; but it was hardly news to anyone who had read Vidal in the *New York Review* or *Esquire* over the years. Indeed, there is practically nothing in his stump speech that isn't to be found in his *Collected Essays, 1952–1972*. But now Vidal moved on to tax reform, acknowledging the help of certain 'advisers', and we began to get a glimpse of a possible platform.

'To govern', Vidal had written ten years ago in *Homage to Daniel*

Shays, 'is to choose how the revenue from taxes is to be spent.' Nowadays, though, the question is not how to cut the cake but how to bake it. Vidal's new recipe is simple and direct: lay off the poor, and squeeze the corporations. He further suggested that the corporations would include the electronic ministries of the airwaves, and their tax-exempt revenues. By this means alone, $100 billion would be raised, 'enough to service the national debt'.

That was as near as Vidal came to a direct attack on Falwell, and it was taken up again in the question-and-answer period after the talk. Goaded by a journalist in the front row, Vidal confessed that he had always thought of Falwell as 'the banker for the Lord'. Was there *anything* to be said for Falwell? 'Well,' said Vidal weightily, and paused. 'I like his choir. I like his fat little smile . . . '

Poor Jerry. Everyone seems to be getting at him recently, even on his home turf. Eighteen months ago, when I saw Falwell in Dallas, the video pastor had given off a steady glow of beatific anticipation. His awakening of the born-again community, through TV and computer mailing, would surely swing the election for Reagan's 'dream platform'. The silent majority had solidified into the Moral Majority: 'family issues' would soon be catapulted into the forefront of political life.

It came to pass. But then what happened? Within weeks of his victory, Reagan stopped returning Jerry's calls. The President, it seemed, had gone cool on the treasured issues of abortion, homosexuality, welfare cutbacks and the teachings of Genesis. Recently Jerry was obliged to join in the orchestrated howls of betrayal and neglect at a New Right rally in Washington. Reagan, said the Conservative bigwigs (Howard Phillips, Paul Weyrich, Richard Viguerie), had 'the right gut-instincts, the right rhetoric', but had sold out to pragmatism by opting for 'experience' in his advisers (instead of the inexperience of Falwell, Weyrich *et al.*). Some people, you may think, are never satisfied. The New Right had hoped to celebrate Roosevelt's centenary with the dismantling of the New Deal. Such a position, as Reagan knew, has no support whatever among the American people. In fifty years the only proponent of the Old Deal has been Barry Goldwater, who carried half-a-dozen states in 1964.

In Dallas, Falwell confessed to expectations not only of national power but of global influence. The dream had looked so bright, so fresh. A year later he was back in Lynchburg, cranking out *The Old-Time Gospel Hour*. And now here was Gore Vidal — an atheist, a Darwinian, an intellectual, and a faggot — goosing Jerry in his own front yard.

Vidal's address, or history lesson, was given at Lynchburg College, one of the few local establishments of secular education. Falwell himself shepherds a whole string of fundamentalist institutions, from kindergarten schools to postgraduate colleges. His pride is Liberty Baptist College, perched on a dusty tor called Liberty Mountain, just across town.

Up on Liberty Mountain, you get education Falwell's way. The brochure for LBC is a document of some interest. Its photograph of the school's business department, for instance, is in fact a cropped snap of a downtown bank; the chapel featured in the brochure also happens to belong to a school several miles away. LBC rules forbid 'hip-hugging pants-suits', 'personal displays of affection', and sideburns that extend lower than 'the bottom of the earlobe'. The history and biology teachers are under the impression that the Earth is less than 10,000 years old. There have been Falwell-related book-burnings, as chapters of Moral Majority lead search-and-destroy missions into local libraries: *Daffy Duck*, *Slaughterhouse-Five* and *Fifty True Tales of Terror* have all been scorched at Fahrenheit 451. The LBC motto is Knowledge Aflame.

Falwell does not rest from his holy mission, which is to raise lots of money. Jerry's sanctuary is the Thomas Road Baptist Church, known locally as 'Jerry Co.'; in its forum, which resembles that of the Empire, Leicester Square, parishioners can help themselves to prayer letters on the open racks. These letters are part of the Faith Partner kit which Jerry will sell you if you pay — or 'pledge' — $20 a month. The kit includes a Bible, a concordance, and a badge of a baby's foot, tastefully scaled to viable-foetus size. You send in your Faith Partner Prayer Request, and fellow parishioners take them home to pray over.

A glance through the requests is as good a way as any of getting the flavour of Falwell's pitch. 'This is a lonely time for me, Jerry . . . wife scheduled for surgery . . . husband an alcoholic . . . business reverses . . . I also need a car . . . no savings — zero . . . please accept $5 a widow's mite . . . ' Jerry will accept the $5 by the way, but the widow will be demoted on the prayer roster. Mere poverty is no excuse: pay-prayers are supposed to work better if you can't afford them. Pledge now, live later.

Falwell regularly claims that he swung the 1980 election for

Ronald Reagan. No one disputes that the 5 to 7 per cent push provided by the mobilisation of the quietist proletariat had a lot to do with the Republican landslide. It is also axiomatic that Falwell's influence (and his multi-million-dollar business) comes down to one thing: the influence of television.

'As the age of television progresses, the Reagans will be the rule, not the exception.' This prescient remark was made by Gore Vidal, covering the Republican Convention of 1968. Actually, nowadays the Reagans are not just the rule: they are the President. Ten years later, Vidal said in an interview: 'I am perfect for television. And that's all a President has to be these days.' Vidal is a more solid and dependable figure now than he was five years ago (greyer in the temples, heavier in the back); but whether his telly-flair will take him far is open to question. He will need to get his smile fixed, for one thing: it is twitchy, furtive, full of childish malevolence. 'Above all, a politician must not sound clever or wise or proud,' he has said. But that is exactly how Vidal sounds. Unpatriotic Gore: this has always been the key to his invigorating contempt.

What can Vidal achieve in the new babel of the airwaves, while staying recognisably himself? It has never been clearer that the trend of American politics is one of attrition, trimming and compromise. In times of recession, everyone huddles towards the neutral warmth of the centre. Reagan is learning this — if 'learning' is quite the word we want. Falwell and the New Right are learning it too. Gore Vidal, more than anyone, surely, has known it all along.

Observer 1982

Joseph Heller, Giantslayer

A good title isn't exactly a seal of approval, but a bad one will seriously detract from a novel's aura. Interestingly a 'brilliant' title, like *Hangover Square* or *Ballad of the Sad Café*, is almost a guarantor of very minor work. It appears that the classic titles give substance to an idea that, when it comes, seems to have been there all along: *Pride and Prejudice, Hard Times, A Portrait of the Artist As a Young Man, Lolita*. To risk a Hollywood intonation, Joseph Heller's titles vary in quality, and in some sense gauge the quality of the books they give a name to.

The catchy and catching *Catch-22* put its finger on a central modern absurdity, and the catchphrase passed straight into the language. Even more weighty and haunting, in my view, is *Something Happened*, a novel whose refrain is one of unlocatable loss ('something did happen to me somewhere that robbed me of confidence and courage'), a novel where nothing happens until the end, the fateful accident presaged by a random cry in the street: 'Something happened!' With *Good as Gold* the Heller stamp starts to smudge: Bruce Gold is the cheerfully venal hero, and all novels that pun on a character's name tend to seem, well, a bit Sharpe-ish, like *Blott on the Landscape*. It has to be said, too, that *God Knows* sounds particularly flat and perfunctory; it sounds like a God-awful movie starring some grinning octogenarian. Perhaps 'God's Wounds' might have been better (for the novel is dark); and no doubt the obvious contender, 'The Book of David', was disqualified by E.L. Doctorow's *The Book of Daniel*.

At first, *God Knows* reads like God's gift to readers. All novelists in every book are looking for a voice — the right voice in the right place at the right time — and Heller, at first, seems to have found the perfect, the consummate medium. Here he gives us the deathbed memoir of King David ('I've got the best story in the Bible. Where's the competition?'), filtered without apology or embarrassment through the modern, urban, decadent and paranoid consciousness of Joseph Heller. While the comic possibilities are infinite, they are not the only possibilities on view, Heller being a comic writer whose chief interest is pain. David, at seventy, fading, receding, seems the true instrument for Heller's brand of envenomed elegy. 'The older I get, the less interest I take in my children and, for that matter, in everyone and everything else.' Or, in a more familiar cadence: 'I get up with the fucking cricket.'

With a justified smirk Heller furtively maps out his fictional island. And what riches are there, what streams and melons and ores. David agrees that it was odd of God to choose the Jews — but why didn't He *give* them anything? He gave them bread without scarcity

> and that's all that He gave us, along with a complicated set of restrictive dietary laws that have not made life easier. To the *goyim* He gives bacon, sweet pork, juicy sirloin, and rare prime ribs of beef. To us He gives a pastrami . . . Some Promised Land. The honey was there, but the milk we brought in with our goats. To people in California, God gives a magnificent coastline, a movie industry, and Beverly Hills. To us He gives sand. To Cannes He gives a plush film festival. We get the PLO.

Each joke is earned, prepared for and exquisitely timed. When the prose rolls along in its high old style, we brace ourselves for the deflation. Here is the effect, in miniature: 'And the anger of Moses was kindled and he demanded of the Lord: "God damn it, where am I supposed to get the flesh to feed them?"' The interfolding of the ancestral voice with the voice of blasphemous modernity provides the main technical business of the novel. And, for a while, Heller has it pat.

The favourite targets are lined up against the wall: sex, cruelty, Jewishness and universal injustice (for which God is a handy embodiment). 'Like cunnilingus, tending sheep is dark and lonely work; but someone has to do it' — where the first two elements are ordinary enough, and the third is pure genius. 'Are you crazy?' David asks his new mistress Abishag. 'I'm a married man! I don't want Michal, Abigail, Ahinoam, Maccah, Haggith, Abital, or Eglah to find out about us.' David's trials are universal: 'Evil would rise up against me in my own house. So what? This was an eventuality taken for granted by every Jewish parent.' But he is also a man of his times: 'When my lovely daughter Tamar was raped by her half-brother Annon, I was upset, naturally. Mainly, though, I was annoyed.' After all, as he points out later, 'She's only a girl'.

'Girl-crazy Samson was a natural pushover for Philistine twat', but David deplores intermarriage; his first wife is, of course, a Jewish Princess, and she talks like one too. To win Michal's hand, he must pay her father, Saul, the bride-price of 100 Philistine foreskins. 'It takes six strong Israelites, we figured, to circumcise one live Philistine. The job turned easier after I finally got used to the idea of killing the Philistines first.' He tells his men 'to bring back the whole prick' and, sure enough, *bring back the whole prick* becomes the battle-cry of the campaign ... Not to everybody's taste, one has to admit; but I was one happy reviewer until page seventy or so (a fifth of the way through), at which point the novel curls up and dies.

Something happened. God knows what. Initially one assumes that the joke has simply run its course, and that the novel is maintained only by the inertia of its ambition. But in fact the joke, the promise, is boundlessly strong: it is the ambition that fails and retracts. Significantly, the two thematic counterweights to the main action – God and the present day – fade without trace into the vast and sandy background. 'God and I had a pretty good relationship', muses David, 'until he killed the kid.' And indeed God was a lively presence, a nasty piece of work ('the Lord, of course, is not a shepherd, not mine or anyone else's'), a divine underwriter of the nihilism we first glimpsed in *Catch-22*. To the question 'Why me?' He jovially answers, 'Why not?' As David says, 'Go figure Him out'. David never does. Between him and his maker there is only silence, which is poignant, and biblical; but it doesn't fill the pages.

What does fill the pages? Writing that transcends mere repetition and aspires to outright tautology. Here's an accelerated foretaste: 'lugubrious dirge', 'pensive reverie', 'vacillating perplexity', 'seditious uprising', 'domineering viragos', 'henpecking shrews', 'sullen grievance and simmering fury', 'gloating taunts and malignant insults', 'loathed me incessantly with an animosity that was unappeasable', 'tantrums of petulance and tempestuous discharges of irrational antipathies'. The units of spluttering cliché sometimes achieve paragraph-status. They get bigger and bigger — and say less and less.

No reader should be asked to witness an author's private grapplings with his thesaurus. Comic effervescence having been stilled, Heller is left alone with his material — i.e., oft-told yarns from the Holy Book. He churns on through the chaff long after the inspiration has been ground to dust. The *donnée* of *God Knows* must have seemed as lithe and deft as the young David with his sling; the finished book looks more like 'the big bastard' Goliath, brawny, apoplectic, and easily toppled.

The unedifying truth is that Joseph Heller, like all the best athletes, needs a manager, a coach. It is common knowledge that he had one (his editor at Knopf) until part-way through *Good as Gold*, when Heller switched houses. Several New York publishers are owned by hamburger chains; so far as this writer is concerned, Simon and Schuster is simply the House of the Whopper. Is *God Knows* without jewels? Does a bull have tits? Of course not: the unforgiving genius still flares, and the book is worth the price of admission for the first few pages alone. In at least two senses, though, Heller's novels simply refuse to get better.

Observer 1984

Newspeak at Vanity Fair

In these days of cultural Balkanisation, one would expect a new American magazine to have a pretty firm fix on its potential market. A journal targeted at the gourmet jogger, say, or a forum for Buddhist computer experts, or simply a David Soul or John Travolta monthly. Encouraged by its recent successes with *Gentlemen's Quarterly* (aimed at the foppish young male) and *Self* (aimed at the careerist young female), Condé Nast is now launching a general-interest magazine aimed — at whom? According to the handouts and brochures, the new magazine is aimed at fickle readers of *The New Yorker, Atlantic, Rolling Stone* and the *New York Review of Books*. *Architectural Digest, Smithsonian* and *Town and Country* are also cited as possible competitors; so are *Vogue, GEO* and *Sports Illustrated*. Trying to capitalise on their obvious confusion, the promoters are calling it 'a "fun" magazine for the very, very highbrow'.

Its name is *Vanity Fair* and, yes, it is a resuscitaton of the spangled original, the ur-glossy that served café society from 1914 to 1936. *Vanity Fair* in its prequel form is now being cried up as a Parnassus of glamour and distinction. But then all long-lived magazines sound glamorous in précis. Edmund Wilson, Dorothy Parker, D.H. Lawrence, T.S. Eliot, Colette, Cocteau and Houdini contributed to *Vanity Fair*. Yet *Cosmopolitan* and *Penthouse* will eventually be able to produce an equally impressive backlist. Famous people do tend to work for magazines. We forget that there must have been many issues of *Vanity Fair* in which the star writer was Philboyd Studge.

Still, the old *VF* was strong on the visual side too, with its popularisation of European painters and graphic artists, and its photographic features by Edward Steichen and Man Ray. It served a self-conscious élite, and with such glittering insensitivity that the death of the magazine now looks very like a suicide. After the Crash of '29, and well into the Thirties, *VF* was all parties and peppermint creams, even as its readership was turning into a pauperised diaspora. It seems only appropriate that in a 1932 photo feature 'handsome Mr Hitler' was presented as the personification of 'Hope'.

The brains, money and expertise behind the new *VF* are intensely aware of the reasons for the death of its predecessor. In fact, they are intensely aware of everything. The minutes of the *VF* 'Sales Call' — or marketing think-in — are full of beguiling bizspeak. The media-planning director is Doyle Dane Bernbach. Noreen Palardy, associate media director of Kenyon and Eckhardt, Inc., is also at the table. 'Let's take a peek. I've taken stats of selected pieces . . . Right now I'd like to turn this over to Joe . . . Thank you, John . . . A good question, Jay . . . ' They are rightly convinced that a jitter-bugging superclass no longer exists; but they firmly believe in the existence of a new élite out there somewhere, and longing to be tapped. These are the 'meritocrats', the 'integrateds'. 'We're not aiming for a demographic; we're aiming for a *psychographic*,' stresses *VF* publisher Joseph E. Corr.

Here is Corr's vision of the dream couple — from the *VF* targeting point of view, of course. *He* is a 'group product director', an outdoorsman, a hunter, a pianist with musical tastes ranging 'from Bach to the B-52s'. *She* is a market-research director (but who isn't?), a marathon runner, 'an accomplished photographer who's had some things printed'. He and She are, alike, 'achievers, thinkers'. If such terrifying people exist — and if they have any spare time to read it, or even buy it — then *VF* is the magazine for them.

One wonders, though, whether the marketing bigwigs are waffling about *VF* or simply waffling about marketing. The editor of the magazine is an encouragingly unlikely figure whom the media are already fingering as a frontman booked for early departure. He is Richard Locke, trim, fortyish, an ex-deputy editor of *The New York Times Book Review*. He is not a sculptor, hang-glider and corporate lawyer. He is merely a solidly literary personage, as are many of his senior staff.

The *VF* PR-men don't really know what to say about Mr Locke. But they say it anyway. 'In his 12 years [at *NYTBR*] he contributed better than 60 literary essays and reviews ... Richard is president of the National Book Critics Circle ... To say that there's excitement going on at 350 Madison Avenue is an understatement.' A rough equivalent of the Locke appointment would be the elevation of, say, Hermione Lee to the editorship of the *Sunday Times*. It *would* be interesting — but why should it set the pulses racing in the managerial offices of New Printing House Square?

In America, magazines have taken the place of national newspapers; they have also established themselves (by virtue, perhaps, of the country's relative classlessness) as arbiters of cultural etiquette. The success of any general-interest magazine depends on an accidental nimbus of authority, a lucky aura. It is, in every sense, the business of the targeting gurus and marketing mentors to deny or pooh-pooh this fact. The first issue of *Vanity Fair* will contain the Gabriel Garcia Marquez novella *Chronicle of a Death Foretold* in its entirety. Richard Locke wants the magazine to be 'a playground for writers' — literary, critical, political, satirical. He wants it to be full of good things; he hopes it acquires that lucky aura. Enmeshed in their spools, charts, print-outs and psychographics, the media-men are hoping this too. In other words, they are simply waiting and seeing, just like the rest of us.

Observer 1983

Kurt Vonnegut: After the Slaughterhouse

Inveterately regressive, ever the playful infantilist, Kurt Vonnegut recently shuffled his career into a report card, signed it, and tacked it to his study wall. The report was chronological, grading his work from A to D. This is what it looked like:

Player Piano	A
The Sirens of Titan	A
Mother Night	A
Cat's Cradle	A+
God Bless You, Mr Rosewater	A
Slaughterhouse-Five	A+
Breakfast of Champions	C
Slapstick	D
Jailbird	A

The burden of the report seems clear enough: Kurt started confidently, went from strength to strength for a good long spell, then passed into a trough of lassitude and uncertainty, but now shows signs of rallying.

The graph charted by the American literary establishment — viewed by Vonnegut as, at best, a flock of cuecard-readers, at worst a squad of jailers, torturers and funeral directors — would be even starker, and much less auspicious. *Their* report would probably go something like this: B−, B, B−, A, A−, B−, B, D, C.

'Anyway, the card isn't quite up to date,' I said, half-way through lunch in a teeming trattoria on Second Avenue. Vonnegut is a mildly lionised regular here, but it was mid-December, and we took our chances among the parched and panting Christmas shoppers of New York. Our table seemed to be half-way between the lobby and the toilet. I wondered, protectively, whether we'd have done any better during Vonnegut's heyday; perhaps the head waiter hadn't liked *Slapstick* either. 'What about your new novel?' I asked. 'How would you grade *Deadeye Dick*?'

Vonnegut looked doubtful. 'I guess it's sort of a B-minus,' he said.

Even by American standards, Vonnegut's career represents an extreme case of critical revisionism and double-think. He is immensely popular, an unbudgeable bestseller, a cult hero and campus guru; all his books are in print; he is the most widely taught of contemporary American authors. On the other hand, his work has remarkably little currency among the card-carrying literati; his pacifistic, *faux-naïf* 'philosophy' is regarded as hippyish and nugatory; he is the sort of writer, nowadays, whom Serious People are ashamed of ever having liked. Cute, coy, tricksy, mawkish — gee-whiz writing, comic-book stuff.

'It has been my experience with literary critics and academics in this country', he has written, 'that clarity looks a lot like laziness and ignorance and childishness and cheapness to them. Any idea which can be grasped immediately is for them, by definition, something they knew all the time.'

'I have to keep reminding myself', he told me, 'that *I* wrote those early books. *I* wrote that. *I* wrote that. The only way I can regain credit for my early work is — to die.'

The shaping experience of Vonnegut's life and art is easy to pinpoint. It occurred on February 13, 1945. On this night, Vonnegut survived the greatest single massacre in the history of warfare, the Allied fire-bombing of Dresden. Over 135,000 people lost their lives (twice the toll of Hiroshima); and Dresden, the Florence of the Elbe, a city as beautiful, ornate — and militarily negligible — as the city of Oz, was obliterated. Vonnegut, a prisoner of war, a gangly private, was billeted in the basement of a slaughterhouse — *Schlachthof-fünf*. *Slaughterhouse-Five* is the title of his most celebrated novel, the book that in turn reshaped his career and his life. Everything that he wrote before 1969 leads up to *Slaughterhouse-Five*; everything he has written since leads away from it.

In another sense Vonnegut was uniquely well placed to write about Dresden, about war, violence and waste, with maximum irony. He is a German-American. His parents were German-speakers; all eight of his great-grandparents were part of the Teutonic migration to the Midwest between 1820 and 1870, as he reveals in an unreadably ample genealogy in *Palm Sunday* (one of his two volumes of autobiographical meanderings). In the superb early novel *Mother Night*, this genetico-political accident – together with his peculiar charm and moral subtlety as a writer – empowered him to attempt the impossible: to write a funny book about Nazism. He succeeded. Hitler is a longstanding obsession, and duly plays his part in the new novel *Deadeye Dick*.

Vonnegut grew up in Indianapolis, Indiana – a cultural Nothingville, like Swindon or Stoke. The characters in his books come from nowhere: Ilium, Midtown, Midland City. Indianapolis, Vonnegut insists, remains the centre of his cultural universe: 'Not Rome, not Paris – Indianapolis.' In his fiction Vonnegut's most crucial imaginative habit is to gaze down at humanity as if from another world, fascinated by Earthling mores yet baffled by our convulsive quests for order, certainty and justice. 'This attitude was a result of my studies in biochemistry [at Cornell], before the war and anthropology after the war [at Chicago]. I learned to see human culture as an artefact, which it is – vulnerable, precarious and probably futile.' His latest novel, *Galapagos*, concerns itself with Darwinism – 'our only alternative to conventional religion. It's all modern man has.'

Pre-*Slaughterhouse*, Vonnegut was loosely regarded as a science-fiction writer, a genre man. In fact only his first novel, *Player Piano* (1952), and a few short stories can be classified as hard SF. His real mode has always been something dreamier, crazier, more didactic, nearer to Mark Twain than to Fred Pohl. The standard Vonnegut novel works as follows: a semi-fantastical plot (with outrageous vicissitudes and reversals), an attack on some barndoor-sized moral target (atomic warfare, economic inequities, loneliness) and, in between, round the edges, a delightfully weighted satire of ordinary, unreflecting, innocent America.

The early novels were taut, concise and sharply constructed. 'My first trade was newspapering,' said Vonnegut, typically down-home. 'You said as much as you could, as soon as you could, and then shut up.' The later novels, on the other hand ... Well, I was enjoying our lunch, and decided to postpone discussion of the later novels. 'My public stance is not to take myself seriously,' he had remarked. 'I do that in order to be likeable.' Vonnegut is likeable all right. But he takes himself seriously too. Of course he does.

During the Sixties Vonnegut was making 'a good middle-class income' from journalism and from writing short stories 'for the slicks'; yet his responsibilities were considerable. Through a gruesome coincidence, which would sound implausible even in a Vonnegut plot outline, his sister and brother-in-law died within twenty-four hours of each other. He died in a New Jersey rail disaster; she died in hospital the following day, of cancer. Vonnegut and his first wife adopted the three orphaned children. They already had three of their own. Alice was Vonnegut's only sister. He still writes with her in mind. '"Alice would like this," I say to myself. "This would amuse Alice."'

Alice, one gathers, was a little crazy. So was Vonnegut's mother, who eventually killed herself when the family was degentrified by the Crash of 1929. Like craziness, 'suicide is a legacy', says Vonnegut. 'As a problem-solving device, it's in the forefront of my mind all the time. It's like walking along the edge of a cliff. I'm in the country and the pump stops. What'll I do? I know: I'll kill myself. The roof is leaking. What'll I do? I know: I'll blow my brains out.'

Finally, along came *Slaughterhouse-Five*, and everything changed. Vonnegut had been trying to write about Dresden ever since his return from the war. He had filled 5,000 pages and thrown them away. But the book, when it came, was a cunning novella, synthesising all the elements of Vonnegut's earlier work: fact, fantasy, ironic realism and comic SF. In my view, *Slaughterhouse-Five* will retain its status as a dazzling minor classic, as will two or three of its predecessors. But quality alone can hardly explain its spectacular popularity.

Perhaps the answer is, in some sense, demographic. Although the Vietnam war changed the mood of America, it produced no fiction to articulate that change. As a result the protest movements seized on and adopted two Second World War novels as their own, novels that expressed the absurdist tenor of the modern revulsion. Those novels were *Catch 22* and *Slaughterhouse-Five*: they became articles of faith as well as milestones of fiction. *Slaughterhouse*-converts looked back into the early work and found that the same chord was struck again and again. Vonnegut had secured his following.

He had also lost his first wife, Jane: 'It was a good marriage for a long time — and then it wasn't.' Jane Vonnegut 'got' religion; Kurt

Vonnegut still had scepticism – as well as the strange new freedom of hemispheric adulation. He left Cape Cod and came to New York, setting up house with the well-known photographer Jill Krementz. By all accounts – and my own brief impressions tend to bear this out – Jill is the opposite of Jane, and the opposite of Kurt too. She is glamorous, voluble and abrupt; and the Vonneguts are now talked of as a celebrity couple fairly active in society and fringe politics. When success happens to an English writer, he acquires a new typewriter. When success happens to an American writer, he acquires a new life. The transformation is more or less inexorable.

After lunch we walked back to the Vonneguts' house on the East Side of mid-town. We passed the mailbox where, on three separate occasions, Vonnegut had palely loitered in the early morning to retrieve letters written the night before – letters of denunciation, sent to hostile reviewers. 'I don't know what the law is in England,' he said, 'but over here the letters are still your property, and the mailman has to give them back.'

He laughed his wheezy, spluttering laugh. Vonnegut has chain-smoked powerful Pall Malls for forty-five years. He has given up twice. The first time, he blew up to eighteen stone. His second attempt, though, worked like a charm. He felt fine; he was 'enormously happy and proud'. The only trouble was that no one could bear being near him. 'I had stopped writing. I had also gone insane. So I started smoking again.' He is shaggy, candid, reassuring. The big suede shoes on his big American feet are ponderous and pigeon-toed. His blazer is epically stained.

Like its proprietor, the Vonnegut town house stands tall and thin. The furnishings are anonymously handsome. In the basement, Jill runs her business; on the top floor, Kurt runs his. Up there he proceeds with his post-*Slaughterhouse* fiction – vague, wandering parables of American futility, full of nursery games (*Breakfast of Champions* contained dozens of childish drawings; *Deadeye Dick* is dotted with cookbook recipes), full of shrugs, twitches and repetitions, full of catchphrases, adages, baby-talk. So it goes. Poo-tee-weet? Peace. Skeedee wah. Bodey oh doh. And so on. And on and on ...

Until 1969, Vonnegut was in his own words 'a trafficker in climaxes and thrills and characterisation and wonderful dialogue and suspense and confrontations'. Now he is — what, exactly? The later Vonnegut novels are deserts, punctuated by the odd paradisal oasis. These good moments are, simply, reversions to his earlier manner, which is why it is more fun to re-read an old Vonnegut novel than it is to tackle a new one. I switched on the tape-recorder and backed myself into the Big Question. Of all the writers I have met, Vonnegut gives off the mildest prickle of *amour propre*. But no writer likes to be asked if he has lost his way.

He heard me out with a few 'Mm-hms' and said: 'American literary careers are very short. I had very low expectations. I always thought, if I could ever get something down about Dresden, that would be *it*. After *Slaughterhouse-Five* I'd already done much more than I ever expected to do with my life. Now, since I don't have to do anything any more, I've gotten more personal, freer to be idiosyncratic. It's like the history of jazz: musicians reach the point where they play the goddamn things with the mouthpiece upside down and stuff the tube with toilet paper and fuck around and make all the crazy sounds they can.'

An honest and accurate answer. I wondered out loud whether a sense of futility had anything to do with it, with the rejection of melody, phrasing, structure, control, with the rejection of art.

'There was Dresden,' said Vonnegut, 'a beautiful city full of museums and zoos — man at his greatest. And when we came up, the city was gone . . . The raid didn't shorten the war by half a second, didn't weaken a German defence or attack anywhere, didn't free a single person from a death camp. Only one person benefitted.'

'And who was that?'

'Me. I got several dollars for each person killed. Imagine.'

Observer 1983

Gloria Steinem and the Feminist Utopia

Gloria Steinem is the most eloquent and persuasive feminist in America. She is also the most reassuring — i.e. the least frightening, from a male point of view. There are two clear reasons for this. Here is one reason:

> So what would happen if suddenly, magically, men could menstruate and women could not? ... Men would brag about how long and how much ... Street guys would invent slang ('He's a three-pad man') and 'give fives' on the corner with some exchange like, 'Man, you lookin' *good*!'
> 'Yeah, man, I'm on the rag!'

The humour is not only humour (rare enough in these parts): its satirical accuracy is enlivened by affection. The second reason for her wide appeal can be glimpsed in the photograph on the back cover. (She looks nice, and friendly, and feminine.) In the sort of utopia which Gloria Steinem seriously envisages, neither of these considerations would carry much weight. But we aren't there yet.

I sat waiting for Ms Steinem in the midtown offices of *Ms.*, the magazine that she co-founded in 1972. Launched on a shoestring and a wave of female dedication, *Ms.* now has a circulation of 450,000, financing the Ms. Foundation which, in turn, acts as a clearing-house for feminist issues (not rape hotlines and conflict–resolution meetings so much as monetary aid for various programmes and projects). The magazine hires about fifty people, three of whom are men. Ms Steinem's assistant, Ms Hornaday, brought me some coffee, and we chatted away. The atmosphere is purposeful, high-morale, sisterly. Pleasant though I found it, I was also aware of my otherness, my testosterone, among all this female calm.

Two blocks north, Forty-Second Street was crackling through its daily grind of sin and stupor, of go-go, triple-X and hard core. Forty-Second Street wouldn't last forty seconds in Ms Steinem's utopia. Pornography is the pressing feminist topic of 1984 and I had been reading up on the protest literature, finding much good sense and justified outrage — also the faint glare of paranoia. 'Men love death . . . In male culture, slow murder is the heart of Eros' — Andrea Dworkin, and her murderous high-style. Even the commonsensical Ms Steinem believes that pornography is the 'propaganda' of 'anti-woman warfare', sensing conspiracy rather than mere weakness and chaotic venality. In the hot-and-cold hostilities between the sexes, there is still plenty of paranoia on either side.

Ms Steinem emerged from her conference, and we all got ready to leave. Our destination was Suffolk County Community College in Long Island, where Gloria would address the students — the kind of trip she makes once or twice a week. Photographs had not prepared me for Ms Steinem's height and slenderness; her face, too, seemed unexpectedly shrewd and angular beneath the broad, rimless glasses (which she seldom removes). The long hair is expertly layered, the long fingers expertly manicured. Fifty this year, Ms Steinem is unashamedly glamorous: it is a pampered look, a Park Avenue look. Out on the street, a chauffeur-driven limousine mysteriously appeared, and in we climbed.

Now I knew from a half-digested reading of her collected journalism that Ms Steinem was a crystallised and not an accidental feminist. One of the book's many successes is the way it documents the slow politicisation of a contented and prospering individual. After a hard, poor and painful childhood in Toledo (much of it spent caring single-handedly for a crushed, confused mother), and after a spell in show business as a dancer, Gloria pursued a thriving career as a New York journalist. It was the usual freelancing pot-pourri; pieces on stockings, fashion, Truman Capote, John Lennon, Vidal Sassoon. As early as 1963 she wrote the classic exposé, 'I was a Playboy Bunny'. Despite various 'no broads' ground rules, Ms Steinem started working on the campaign trail, both as a journalist and an aide — to George McGovern. This soon led her into the civil rights movement; she found herself writing about migrant workers, Puerto Rican radicals, Martin Luther King. Then, in 1969, it happened: Ms Steinem 'got' feminism — and realised she had had it all along. The experience 'changed my life', she writes. 'It will never be the same.'

Encased by the limousine, and also by a sense of comfortable male irony, I kicked off by asking Ms Steinem whether the movement was now undergoing a phase of retraction or redefinition. Hadn't Nora Ephron recently joked that the only thing feminism had given women was the privilege of going dutch? Hadn't Susan Brownmiller confessed that while she would never remove the hair on her legs, she had started dyeing it (this being the centrist or SDP stance on the leg-hair issue)? Weren't women finding that going out to work and joining the 'pink-collar ghetto' only doubled their hardships, since they were obliged to moonlight with the Hoover? What about Germaine Greer's sudden championship of motherhood, chastity and coitus interruptus?

'Well, I don't know anyone who's into coitus interruptus,' said Ms Steinem, and gave her musical laugh. She then proceeded (pretty gently, it now seems) to put my argument in its place. This was the first lesson of the day: to challenge feminism, in America, in 1984, is to disqualify yourself as a moral contender. It is the equivalent of espousing a return to slavery. One of Ms Steinem's dialectical techniques is that of role-reversal; she puts the (white male) reader in a different racial or sexual circumstance – then asks how *he* likes it. And this is more than a trick of argument. It speaks for a passionate identification with the fate of the American black. Feminism in England lacks that dimension, just as England lacks a history of racial guilt. The second lesson of the day took a little longer to learn. Reasonable and unmenacing though Ms Steinem's logic sounds, it contains the core of something quite revolutionary, indeed millennial.

The previous or 'reformist' school of feminists, she explained, 'wanted a piece of the existing pie. We want to bake a new one.' The more radical view centres on the home – 'on *families*, not *the* "family", which has become a codeword for reactionary power-groups'. When Ms Steinem talks of 'democratic parenthood' she has more in mind than a bit of male nappy-changing. If the rearing of children were undertaken equally then the intractable stereotypes of Male and Female would finally begin to fade. No longer would a child perceive femininity in terms of warmth, care, devotion, and masculinity in terms of energy, action and business elsewhere. 'We grow up dividing our natures because of the way we're raised.' And this is her Children's Crusade in another sense, because 'sex roles', she believes, 'are in the anthropological, long-term view a primary cause of violence. Any peace movement without that kind of challenge to violence — well, it's like putting a Band-Aid on a cancer.'

Then what? If, as she says, 'the sex or race of an individual is one of 20,000 elements that go into making up an individual person', the proliferation of human types would be ceaseless. Sexually 'there would be thousands of ways to be', rather than the existing three or four. 'There would be no average. Sameness would be done away with.'

'And so,' I said, with my last ironic breath, 'there might be an enclave in your utopia where the Victorian marriage still thrived.'

'It's possible,' said Ms Steinem doubtfully. 'But they'd be living that way through *choice*.'

Up on stage in the Arts Theatre at the Community College, Ms Steinem suavely delivered her stump speech, 'Equality: The Future of Humankind'. The audience, like the institution, was modest enough — a mere five or six hundred people, compared to the rock-concert-sized crowds she has attracted elsewhere. Once a painfully nervous speaker, she now performs with brisk panache. She marches up to the mike, returning the applause of the audience. 'Friends,' she begins. There are laughs ('We now have words like *sexual harassment* and *battered women*. A few years ago they were just called *life*'), but no cheap jokes. Maximum clarity and suasion are what she is after. 'Yes,' you keep thinking, 'that's true. That's right.'

After the speech, the applause, the questions ('I'm a homemaker, or a uh "domestic engineer" ... '), I drank a lot of coffee and smoked a lot of cigarettes with Eddie, our young, black chauffeur. I asked him if he worked for the Ms. Foundation, and he revealed, hesitantly (though it's no great secret), that he worked for Ms Steinem's 'friend', a high-level but low-profile company lawyer. Ms Steinem, like most eminent feminists, is unmarried and childless. The nature–nurture axis, one gathers, takes quite a wobble when you have kids of your own — but then Steinem's utopia is many generations away. 'I've driven Gloria out to speak at places three or four times now,' said Eddie. 'It's going to happen a lot more times, I can tell. I'm looking forward to it. I like to hear her speak.'

Eddie went on to say that it had taken only three months of

Gloria's example to 'convert' him to the cause. 'Me and my wife, we had a talk. Now I do my bit in the home. When she goes out — I used to make her take the kids with her. Now she can leave them with me. She can do what she likes. It's better, for her, for me. I never knew my father, and it's too late now. I don't want to make the same mistake. I like to be with my children. Watching them grow.'

Well, by this stage I was on the verge of calling *my* friend in London — to tell her that it would all be different from now on. While Ms Steinem held court in the corner, I strolled round the common room among the dissolving crowd. A noticeboard advertised some forthcoming attractions: Frisbee Tournament, Human Potential Fra-Sority. The average age of the American college student is now twenty-seven, and I marvelled at their variety — not least the variety of the student *body*: some as thin and tightly-cocked as whippets, some like walking haystacks, with all the intervening shapes and sizes fully represented. As soon as you leave New York you see how monstrously various, how humanly balkanised, America really is. And yet in Steinemland — home of the Polymorphous Perverse — such diversity would not be remarkable, and would certainly not be amusing. A sense of humour is a risky thing to have out here, in the big mix, where mere oddity is no cause for laughter. Do all these people actually *have* a human potential? Don't we need the norms? How much variety can a society contain? How much can it stand?

Feminism is a salutary challenge to one's assumptions — including your assumptions about feminism. I wonder, though, how much it has to offer as an all-informing idea. And is the racial analogy, so often claimed, really fully earned? Busy systematisers, with a thing called 'Women's Studies' to erect, the feminists have systematised an ideology, a history, an enemy. Yet surely there has been a good deal of collusion, and dumb human accident, on both sides. Adjustments in thought are necessary, but some of the reparations look alarmingly steep.

Ms Steinem has a literary gift — her prose is swift and sure — yet this is not quite the same thing as a gift for literature. Inevitably her artistic values are now ideologically determined, for the greater good, as is her view of language itself. She is against all idioms that are 'divisive' or 'judgmental', so it's *birth names* for 'maiden names', *back salary* for 'alimony', *preorgasmic* for 'frigid'. 'Peace on Earth, Good Will to People' is the sort of 'rewrite' she recommends. And at this point I have to ask myself: would I want to be a writer in the feminist utopia? Would anybody? People might be happier or less anxious under such a tactful populism, but one wonders about the kinds of personality they would knock up for themselves. The result might simply strengthen the American how-to culture, the general thirst for ready-made or second-hand lives.

We returned to the limousine and headed back for Manhattan. Gloria talked of her forthcoming visit to England, her intention to visit the Greenham Women and 'to seek political asylum' here if Ronald Reagan, 'a smiling fascist', won a second term. The frequency of her smile at first suggests, not falsity, but settled habit; after a time, though, it suggests a real superabundance of warmth — also energy and self-belief. Here is a woman riding the crest of conviction, of achievement. 'Look!' she said with a triumphant laugh (this was one of her daily rewards). 'There are PEOPLE WORKING signs on the road ahead.'

Observer 1984

William Burroughs:
The Bad Bits

Like many novelists whose modernity we indulge, William Burroughs is essentially a writer of 'good bits'. These good bits don't work out or add up to anything; they have nothing to do with the no-good bits: and they needn't be in the particular books they happen to be in. Most of Burroughs is trash, and lazily obsessive trash too – you could chuck it all out and not diminish what status he has as a writer. But the good bits are good. Reading him is like staring for a week at a featureless sky; every few hours a bird will come into view or, if you're lucky, an aeroplane might climb past, but things remain meaningless and monotone. Then, without warning (and not for long, and for no coherent reason, and almost always in *The Naked Lunch*), something happens: abruptly the clouds grow warlike, and the air is full of portents.

The good bits are so fortuitous, indeed (mere reflexes of a large and callous talent), and the no-good bits so monolithic, that the critic's role is properly reduced to one of helpless quotation. Here is a good bit; this is another good bit; take, for example, this good bit. Eric Mottram, however, in his adoring and humourless new study, *William Burroughs: The Algebra of Need*, swallows Burroughs whole: every section of jaded agitprop, every page of trite assertion and denatured rhetoric, every abstract noun finds an honoured place in the inter-disciplinarian's filing-system. John Fletcher, general editor of this Critical Appraisals series, says that to qualify for inclusion writers need to be 'demonstrably "masterly" in the sense of having made a real impact on the contemporary arts' (I think he must mean 'modern-masterly'). Mr Mottram, anyway, has unsmilingly accepted the brief. His book is, in effect, about the bad bits.

Here are two of the funnier insensitivities ensured by this

approach. There is, by common consent, a great deal about drugs in Burroughs's four main novels (or 'tetralogy', as they are here typically dignified). Many of his characters are junkies, they talk about junk a lot, their senses — in common with Burroughs's prose — are peeled by junk: on junk, says Burroughs, 'familiar objects seem to stir with a writhing furtive life'. From Mr Mottram's Delphic lectern, though, 'the junk world is the image of the whole world as a structure of addiction and controls'. Well, this is the radical falsification line of the Beat school, and fair enough in its way. But evaluative criticism of Burroughs (and all criticism of living authors should be evaluative) would be far better off with the unglamorous premise that Burroughs was just a junkie himself, that he got lost for a long time in the junk world, and that it is in this reality that his imagination — and his style — has been conclusively formed. An index of Mr Mottram's futile reverence is that he seldom refers to Burroughs as 'being dependent on' drugs, or 'taking' drugs, or even 'using' drugs. What Burroughs does is 'experiment' with them. (At one point Mr Mottram pictures Burroughs 'experimenting' with *alcohol*. I hereby confess that, during his longer chapters, I conducted a few experiments with the stuff myself.)

Burroughs's militant homosexuality, also, is seen as yet another suave literary device. Mr Burroughs doesn't really like women: one feels safe in this observation, since he has gone on record with the vow that he would kill every woman alive if he could. Although this is not in itself a criticism of his *writing*, it is certainly a clue to it. But here is Mottram, in a biographical stroll-in:

> Burroughs returned to the academy to study psychology . . . Then he went to Mexico (where he accidentally killed his wife with a revolver), and on a GI grant, studied native dialects and was able to obtain drugs with comparative absence of legal restriction.

That parenthesis is all she rates. Similarly — and to take only the most spectacular example — Burroughs's obtrusive interest in the sexual hanging of young boys (orgasm to be synchronised with the pathetic voiding at the moment of death) is duly accorded the status of a 'symbol', a symbol, in this case, of 'critical anarchism'. So it is, though not in the sense intended. At no point will Mr Mottram admit a human value. He does not answer to any of the gods we answer to: he sits up late at night, listening for the knock of The Semiologic Police.

Burroughs's principal 'theme' — in that he goes on about it more than he goes on about anything else — is 'control', social, sexual and political. Mr Mottram annotates this theme with some rigour (his book has good bits too), and he does draw haphazard attention to the things that make Burroughs worth looking at: his great scenes of interrogation and manipulation, the desolate evil of his wound-down cities and inert, vicious bureaucracies, that sense of wasted and pre-doomed humanity which animates his best writing. What Mr Mottram never addresses himself to, however, is the question of artistic control, of the artist's control of his material and his talent. Control is not something one grafts on to natural ability: it is part of that ability. Burroughs has vacated the control tower, if indeed he ever went up there. No living writer has so perfidiously denied his own gifts — most of which are, incidentally, comic and exuberant rather than admonitory and bleak. It may be his just reward, then, to be studied by people who don't find him funny.

New Statesman 1977

Steven Spielberg: Boyish Wonder

Steven Spielberg's films have grossed approximately $1,500 million. He is thirty-four, and well on his way to becoming the most effective popular artist of all time ... What's he got? How do you do it? Can *I* have some?

'Super-intensity' is Spielberg's word for what he comes up with on the screen. His films beam down on an emotion and then subject it to two hours of muscular titillation. In *Jaws* ($410 million) the emotion was terror; in *Close Encounters* ($250 million) it was wonder; in *Raiders of the Lost Ark* ($310 million) it was exhilaration; in *Poltergeist* ($480 million and climbing) it was anxiety; and now in *E.T.* — which looks set to outdo them all — it is love.

Towards the end of *E.T.*, barely able to support my own grief and bewilderment, I turned and looked down the aisle at my fellow sufferers: executive, black dude, Japanese businessman, punk, hippie, mother, teenager, child. Each face was a mask of tears. Staggering out, through a tundra of sodden hankies, I felt drained, pooped, squeezed dry; I felt as though I had lived out a year-long love affair — complete with desire and despair, passion and prostration — in the space of 120 minutes. And we weren't crying for the little extra-terrestrial, nor for little Elliott, nor for little Gertie. We were crying for our lost selves. This is the primal genius of Spielberg, and *E.T.* is the clearest demonstration of his universality. By now a billion Earthlings have seen his films. They have only one thing in common. They have all, at some stage, been children.

It is pretty irresistible to look for Spielberg's 'secret' in the very blandness of his suburban origins — a peripatetic but untroubled childhood spent mostly in the south-west. As I entered his offices in Warner Boulevard, Burbank Studios, I wondered if he had ever really left the chain-line, ranch-style embryos of his youth. The Spielberg bungalow resembles a dormitory cottage or beach-house – sliding windows, palm-strewn backyard. The only *outré* touch is an adjacent office door marked TWILIGHT ZONE ACCOUNTING: perhaps it is into this fiscal warp that the millions are eventually fed, passing on to a plane beyond time and substance . . .

Within, all is feminine good humour. Spielberg has always surrounded himself with women – surrogate aunts, mothers, kid sisters. These gently wise-cracking ladies give you coffee and idly shoot the breeze as you wait to see the great man. That girl might be a secretary; this girl might be an executive producer, sitting on a few million of her own. Suddenly a tousled, shrugging figure lopes into the ante-room. You assume he has come to fix the Coke-dispenser. But no. It is Mr Spielberg.

His demeanour is uncoordinated, itchy, boyish: five foot nine or so, 150 pounds, baggy T-shirt, jeans, running-shoes. The beard, in particular, looks like a stick-on afterthought, a bid for adulthood and anonymity. Early photographs show the shaven Spielberg as craggy and distinctive; with the beard, he could be anyone. 'Some people look at the ground when they walk,' he said later. 'Others look straight ahead. I always look upward, at the sky. This means that when you walk into things, you don't cut your forehead, you cut your chin. I've had plenty of cuts on my chin.' Perhaps this explains the beard. Perhaps this explains the whole phenomenon.

Spielberg sank on to a sofa in his gadget-crammed den, a wide, low room whose walls bear the usual mementoes of movie artwork and framed magazine covers. 'I had three younger sisters,' he began. 'I was isolated, left alone with my thoughts. I imagined the very best things that could happen and the very worst, simply to relieve the tedium. The most frightening thing, the most uplifting thing.' He stared round the room, seemingly flustered by the obligation to explain himself for the thousandth time – weighed down, indeed, by the burden of all these mega-hits, these blockbusters and smasher-oos. 'I was the weird, skinny kid with the acne. I was a wimp.'

His mother, Leah, has confirmed that Steven 'was not a cuddly child'. Evidently he kept a flock of parakeets flapping around wild in his room. Leah never liked birds, and only reached a hand through the door once a week to grope for the laundry bag. She didn't go in there for years. Steven also kept an 8mm camera. According to his sister Anne, big brother would systematically 'dole out punishment' while forcing the three girls to participate in his home movies. This technique is well-tried in Hollywood: it is known as *directing*.

Spielberg's films deal in hells and heavens. Against the bullying and bedevilled tike, we can set the adolescent dreamer, the boy who tenderly nursed his apocalyptic hopes. One night, when he was six, Steven was woken by his father and bundled into the car. He was driven to a nearby field, where hundreds of suburbanites stood staring in wonder (this is probably the most dominant image in his films). The night sky was full of portents. 'My father was a computer scientist,' said Spielberg. 'He gave me a technical explanation of what was happening. "These meteors are space debris attracted by the gravitational . . . " But I didn't want to hear that. I wanted to think of them as falling stars.'

All his life Spielberg has believed in things: vengeful ten-yard sharks, whooping ghosts, beautiful beings from other worlds. 'Comics and TV always portrayed aliens as malevolent. I *never* believed that. If they had the technology to get here, they could only be benign . . . I know they're out there.' The conviction, and desire, lead in a straight line from *Firelight* (one of his SF home movies) to the consummation of *E.T.* 'Just before I made *Close Encounters* I went outside one night, looked up at the sky and started crying. I thought I was falling apart.'

In *Poltergeist*, a suburban family is terrorised by demons that emerge from the household television set. When Spielberg describes the film as 'my revenge on TV', he isn't referring to his own apprenticeship on the small-screen networks. 'TV was my third parent.' His father used to barricade and boobytrap the set, leaving a strand of hair on the aperture, to keep tabs on Steven's illegal viewing. 'I always found the hair, memorised its position, and replaced it when I was through.'

Rather to the alarm of his girlfriend, Kathleen Carey, Spielberg still soaks up a great deal of nightly trivia. 'All I see is junk,' she says, 'but he looks for ideas.' It is clear from the annuals and pot-boilers on his office shelves that Spielberg is no bookworm (this is Hollywood after all, where high culture means an after-dinner game of Botticelli). TV is popular art: Spielberg is a popular artist who has outstripped but not outgrown the medium that shaped him. Like Disney – and, more remotely, like Dickens – his approach is entirely non-intellectual, heading straight for the heart, the spine, the guts.

'All right,' conceded Spielberg, shifting up a gear in his own defence. 'I do not paint in the strong browns and greens of Francis [Coppola], or in Marty's [Martin Scorsese's] sombre greys and whites. Francis makes films about power and loyalty; Marty makes films about paranoia and rage. I use primary colours, pastel colours. But these colours make strange squiggles when they run together on the palette ... I'm coming out of my pyrotechnic stage now. I'm going in for close-ups. Maybe I will move on to explore the darker side of my make-up.'

The line of thought is interrupted, as telephones ring and doors swing open. During the interview Spielberg has been attentive enough in his restless way, but some sort of minor crisis is rumbling through the office. His youthful co-producer, Kathleen Kennedy, peers into the room. 'What's happening?' Spielberg asks. 'No, Steven, you don't even want to hear about this.' But Steven does. The row has something to do with a music-publishing spin-off. Later, as I prepared to leave, I could hear Spielberg coping with his stacked calls. 'I'd rather dump the song than get involved in a political war ... We think it'll go to number one, which is good ... This has to be solved, and not tomorrow. Two hours.' He doesn't sound like a dreamy kid any more. He sounds like Daryl Zanuck with a bit of a hangover.

Spielberg's career has on occasion resembled that of the old-time Hollywood moguls – and it will do so again, perhaps much more closely. His induction into the studios wasn't quite a case of 'Kid, I'm going to give you a break', but it had its classic aspects. At eighteen, the weird, skinny kid more or less abandoned his studies at California State College and started hanging round the Universal lot. He was thrown off a Hitchcock set; John Cassavetes gave him some unofficial tuition. He raised $10,000 and made a twenty-minute film called *Amblin'*. (His office now bears the nostalgic logo, Amblin' Productions – though these days Sprintin' would be nearer the mark.) On the basis of this modest short, which was designed to show that he could do the simple things, Spielberg became the youngest director to be signed up by a major studio, and was set to work in television.

The full apprenticeship was never served out. Spielberg made episodes of *Columbo*, *The Name of the Game* and *The Psychiatrist*. He made TV specials. One of these was called *Duel*. It was pure Spielberg, and showed just how quickly the tiro found his line. A faceless suburbanite makes a business trip by car; he is inexplicably menaced by a steam truck whose driver is never seen. By the end of the seventy-five-minute film, the truck is as monstrous, blind and elemental as anything out of *Poltergeist* or *Jaws*. Released in Europe as a feature, *Duel* made its money back thirty times over. Spielberg was shifted up into the real league. After an inconclusive sortie on *The Sugarland Express* (a chase movie whose only Spielbergian ingredient was its concern with a mother's forcible separation from her child — a recurring crux), the twenty-five-year-old went on to make *Jaws*. The rest is history: box-office history.

After *Close Encounters*, however, Spielberg's career did take a salutary wobble with the chaotic Second World War satire, *1941*. Characteristically in a way, the movie was a megaflop — a snowballing fiasco. By now it has laboriously recouped its $30 million budget, yet Spielberg still shows a surprising touchiness about his only brush with failure: 'I haven't read a review of that movie to this day . . . I just flew into it and forgot to read the script. It taught me that creative compromise is more challenging than the blank cheque-book. And it taught me that I'm not funny when I'm just being funny. There *has* to be a dramatic context.'

In all his major films, that context has not varied. It places ordinary people, of average resources, in situations of extraordinary crisis. How would *you* shape up to a shark? Would *you* enter that cathedral-organ of a mothership and journey to the heavens, never to return? Accordingly, as the strength of his bargaining position has increased, Spielberg has been less and less inclined to use star actors in his films. One scans the cast-lists of *Poltergeist* and *E.T.* in search of a vaguely familiar name. Craig T. Nelson? Dee Williams? Peter Coyote? These are useful performers, but they are not headliners, and never will be.

Coppola, for instance, has another way of ducking the star system. Look at the constellation that was formed by *Godfather I* alone: Robert Duvall, Diane Keaton, James Caan, Al Pacino. Spielberg uses a more radical technique for avoiding the big salaries and big egos that always accompany the big names. He casts his actors for their *anti*-charismatic qualities. 'The play's the thing,' says Spielberg. 'In every movie I have made, the movie is the star.' He is the first director with the nerve to capitalise on something very obvious: audiences are composed of ordinary people.

After his *1941* débâcle, Spielberg brought himself violently to heel with *Raiders of the Lost Ark*, and this perhaps explains why it is the most anonymous of his major films. (It was the most personally profitable too, before *E.T.*: Spielberg and producer George Lucas simply offered the studios distribution rights – in other words, they kept it *all*.) With *Raiders*, Spielberg completed a movie under budget and within schedule for the first time, and has not erred since. A perfectionist and non-delegator, a galvanised handyman on the set, he worked 100-hour weeks to keep the production under tight control. '*Raiders* was popcorn,' he admits, 'but great popcorn.' It also brought him to the end of something. It marked the apotheosis of Spielberg the pyrotechnician.

Up until this point in his career it was just about possible to regard Spielberg as merely a brilliant hack. Flitting from studio to studio, he was the lucky mercenary, the big-budget boy with a flair for astronomical profits. *Poltergeist* and, far more centrally, *E.T.* put such dismissals quietly out of their misery. The time had come to acknowledge that Spielberg was unique.

Spielberg produced and co-wrote *Poltergeist* but leased the direction out to Tobe Hooper, the horror-buff and gore-bandit who gave us *The Texas Chainsaw Massacre*. Like the bygone nabobs of the Forties and Fifties Spielberg had hired his director and yet was unwilling to relinquish his original conception. Later, he ran apologetic ads in the trade-papers, saluting Hooper's contribution. As it turned out, Hooper's contribution was all too palpable. The film's ambitions were in any case pretty limited. 'I started out', says Spielberg, 'just to scare the be-Jesus out of anybody who dared to walk into the theatre.' The film is more than that – and exploits the mother-and-lost-child theme with harrowing relish. But Spielberg's humour and clarity are in the end barely visible through the miasma of Hooper's Gothic-graphic mediocrity.

E.T. is something else again. It is all Spielberg, essential Spielberg, and far and away his most personal film. 'Throughout, *E.T.* was conceived by me as a love story – the love between a ten-year-old boy and a nine-hundred-year-old alien. In a way I was terrified. I didn't think I was ready to make this movie – I had never taken my shirt off in public before. But I think the result is a very intimate, seductive meeting of minds.'

Intimacy is certainly the keynote of *E.T.* Using a predominantly female production team, Spielberg effectively re-created the tremulous warmth of his own childhood: a ranch-style suburban home, full of women and kids, with Spielberg the dreaming nucleus of the action. His well-attested empathy with children is tied to a precise understanding of how they have changed since he was a boy. 'The years of childhood have been subject to a kind of inflation. At sixteen, I was the equivalent of a ten-year-old today.' In the movie, the kids have a wised-up naïveté, a callow, TV-fed sophistication. Reared on video games and Spielberg movies, with their Space-Invader T-shirts, robot toys and electronic gizmos, they are in a way exhaustively well-prepared for the intrusion of the supernatural, the superevolved.

Despite his new-deal self-discipline, Spielberg decided to 'wing' *E.T.*, to play it by ear and instinct. (He brought the movie in on the nail anyway, at $10 million.) 'If you over-rehearse kids, you risk a bad case of the cutes. We shot *E.T.* chronologically, with plenty of improvisation. I let the kids feel their way into the scenes. An extraordinary atmosphere developed on the set.' E.T. is, after all, only an elaborate special effect (costing $1.5 million − 'Brando would cost three times that,' as Spielberg points out); but 'a very intense relationship' developed between E.T. and his young co-star, Henry Thomas. 'The emotion of the last scene was genuine. The final days of shooting were the saddest I've ever experienced on a film set.' Little Henry agrees, and still pines for his vanished friend. 'E.T. was a person,' he insists.

Later, while scoring the film, Spielberg's regular composer John Williams shied away from what he considered to be an over-ripe modulation on the sound-track. 'It's shameless,' said Williams: 'will we get away with it?' '*Movies* are shameless,' was Spielberg's reply. *E.T.* is shameless all right, but there is nothing meretricious about it. Its purity is utopian, and quite unfakeable.

You can ask around Los Angeles − around the smoggy pool-sides, the oak and formica rumpus-rooms, the squeaky-clean bars and restaurants − in search of damaging gossip about Steven Spielberg, and come away sorely disappointed. There isn't any. No, he does not 'do' ten grand's worth of cocaine a day. No, he does not consort with heavily-set young men. In this capital of ambition, trivia and perversity, you hear only mild or neutral things about Spielberg, spiced with many examples of his generosity and diffidence.

He has walked out with starlets, notably Amy Irving. He blows a lot of money on gadgets, computers, video games. He owns a mansion, a beach-house; he has just spent $4 million on a four-acre hillock in Bel Air. He seldom goes to parties: 'When I do go, I'm the guy in the corner eating all the dip.' Spielberg, it appears, is a pretty regular guy. Apart from his genius, his technique, his energy, his millions, his burgeoning empire (rivalling Coppola's Zoetrope and Lucas's Marin County co-operative), he sometimes seems almost ordinary.

Towards the end of the interview, I asked him why he had never dealt with 'adult relationships', with sex, in his movies. After all, he de-eroticised Indiana Jones in *Raiders*, who was originally conceived as a playboy, and he excised the adultery from *Jaws* (the sex-interest in the novel Spielberg attributes to 'bad editorial advice'; actually the culprit was bad writing – but this is California). For the first time Spielberg grew indignant. 'I think I have an *incredibly* erotic imagination. It's one of my ambitions to make everyone in an 800-seat theatre come at the same time.' Well, we'll have to wait until he has completed *Raiders II, E.T. II*, and, possibly, *Star Wars IV*, as well as the host of minor projects he is currently supervising. But if Spielberg does for sex what he has done for dread and yearning, then he can expect a prompt visit from the Vice Squad.

'I just make the kind of films that I would like to see.' This flat remark explains a great deal. Film-makers today – with their target boys and marketing men – tie themselves up in knots trying to divine the LCD among the American public. The rule is: no one ever lost money underestimating the intelligence of the audience. Spielberg doesn't need to do this because in a sense he is there already, uncynically. As an artist, Spielberg is a mirror, not a lamp. His line to the common heart is so direct that he unmans you with the frailty of your own defences, and the transparency of your most intimate fears and hopes.

Observer 1982

John Updike: Rabbitland and Bechville

John Updike's 'Rabbit' novels are fattening into a sequence — a wahooing, down-home barn dance to the music of time. *Rabbit, Run* (1960) gave us Harry 'Rabbit' Angstrom's disastrous early marriage, *Rabbit Redux* (1971) his chaotic experiments with adulthood. *Rabbit Is Rich,* the latest but not the last in the line, traces with appalled affection the contours of Rabbit's maturity: it is about middle-aged spread, physical, mental and (above all) material.

Rabbit has never looked a less likely hero for an American epic. Equipped with a troublesome family and a prosperous car show-room, Rabbit is meant to seem provincial and vulgar even by the unexacting standards of suburban Pennsylvania. His reading consists of *Consumer Reports* and the odd newspaper — 'mostly human-interest stories, like where the Shah is heading next and how sick he really is'. His mind is a jabbering mess of possessions, prejudice and pornography. But then Rabbit is an extreme middle-American, a voluble and foul-mouthed representative of the silent majority.

The time is 1979 — the time of petrol shortages, the Three Mile Island radiation leak, the hostage crisis, the invasion of Afghanistan. Like its predecessors, the novel is crammed with allusive topicalities; in a few years' time it will probably read like a Ben Jonson comedy. Rabbit, however, is quick to reinterpret global events in the light of furtive self-interest. Will the Iranian revolution give a boost to his precious-metal investments? Is OPEC going to louse up his car-dealership?

The previous Rabbit books had their share of incident — deaths, desertions — but Rabbit is rich now, and largely protected from contingencies. His life, he feels, has devolved to an 'inner dwindling'. The reader is bound to feel a bit like this too, since the novel's structure is not linear so much as quotidian or seasonal. Updike toys with plot and incident, then flirtatiously retreats. Rabbit's son pushes his pregnant wife down the stairs! But she is fine, and so is baby. The leggy blonde at the showroom might be Rabbit's long-lost daughter! But she isn't, and that's that. In the end, the most dramatic events in the book centre on things like car dents, mortgage rates and gold futures.

If *Rabbit Is Rich* has a central theme – and it is by no means clear that it wants or needs one – it has to do with the one-directional nature of life: life, always heading towards death. Not surprisingly, Updike injects a little low-church churchiness here. 'I always felt I was very innocent, actually,' says Rabbit's fat, busted ex-mistress. 'We all are, Ruth,' consoles Rabbit. A few pages later we read: 'Like what souls must feel when they awaken in a baby's body so far from Heaven: not only scared so they cry but guilty, guilty.' It is a fruitful confusion: We Are All Not Guilty, though we keep on thinking we must be. Rabbit, of course, is only lightly touched by this knowledge. He swans on down the long slide, clumsy, lax and brutish, but vaguely trying.

The technical difficulty posed by Rabbit is a familiar and fascinating one. How to see the world through the eyes of the occluded, the myopic, the wilfully blind? At its best the narrative is a rollicking comedy of ironic omission, as author and reader collude in their enjoyment of Rabbit's pitiable constriction. Conversely – and this is the difficult part – the empty corners and hollow spaces of the story fill with pathos, the more poignant for being unremarked.

Not remarking on things, however, isn't one of Updike's strengths. There is just no stopping him remarking on things. The Rabbit books are not first-person but localised third-person: Updike's voice can therefore flit freely in and out of Rabbit's hick musings. A certain nervousness about this device perhaps explains the two derisory sorties into the consciousness of Rabbit Jr. More seriously, in his desire to keep the emotional content topped up, Updike repeatedly lapses into winsome editorials, as if to fill the spiritual gaps. 'Her blurred dark eyes gaze beyond him into time . . . love floods clumsily the hesitant space . . . saying, in a voice tears have stained . . . '

Being a boor and a goon, Rabbit is on the whole a healthy

influence on Updike's style; but Updike's style remains a difficulty. In every sense it constitutes an embarrassment of riches — alert, funny and sensuous, yet also garrulous, mawkish and cranky. Updike often seems wantonly, uncontrollably fertile, like a polygamous Mormon. His recent novel about Africa, *The Coup*, was praised as an astounding 'departure' from his usual beat; in fact, though, the very facility of the experiment gave grounds for alarm. Plainly, here is a writer who can do more or less as he likes. But what ought he to like?

Furnished with such gifts, a novelist's main challenge is one of self-contraception. A talent like Updike's will always tend towards the encyclopaedic. *Rabbit Is Rich* is a big novel, and in some ways it would be churlish to wish it any thinner. It is never boring but it is frequently frustrating. You feel that a better-proportioned book is basking and snoozing deep beneath its covers, and that Updike never really tried to coax it out.

*   *   *

After *Rabbit, Run* came *Rabbit Redux*. After *Rabbit Redux*, *Rabbit Is Rich*. Now after *Bech: A Book*, we are offered *Bech Is Back*. What next? *Bech Is Broke?*

Actually Bech is in pretty good shape by the end of *Back Is Back*, financially at least. In the Rabbit books John Updike delivers a commentary on the unreflecting side of human nature (at a certain, unspecifiable distance from his own): this is what the unexamined life would be like: venality, fear, and the innocence born of knowing no better. Rabbits are the victims of whatever set of values gets to them first. They are the people whom you see every day and dismiss as junior aspirants, junior sufferers, unvexed by soul. But the Rabbit, like the Babbit, does have his inner life, his private culture, and Updike dissects it with tingling fascination.

Bech is the opposite, though equally remote from the real Updike: he is smart, learned, artistic, cosmopolitan, alienated, Jewish, single and promiscuous. Bech is a blocked writer, and this calls for a spectacular feat of authorial empathy, since Updike himself can hardly let a month go by without blurting out a new novel, short-story collection, book of poems, essay hold-all. If Rabbit is an alter ego, then Bech is a super ego. Or maybe he is just an alter id.

Like *Bech: A Book*, *Bech Is Back* concerns itself with the subsidiaries of authorship: it is about what writers get up to when they aren't writing. In Bech's case, not writing consumes his every waking hour, and yet his reputation grows as his powers decline. The Superoil Corporation sends him to the Caribbean to sign 28,500 copies of his elderly second novel at $1.50 a pop. Here, Bech's block reaches its cramped epiphany. 'He gazed deep into the negative perfection to which his career had been brought. He could not even write his own name.'

Bech is pestered by autograph hounds, Ph.D. students, women's institutes. He is swept off on cultural exchanges (chapter title: 'Bech Third-Worlds It'), during which he is lionised, bored, traduced and menaced (chapter coda: 'He vowed never to Third-World it again, unless someone asked him to'). Showing that mixture of awe, terror and gratitude characteristic of famous, middle-aged American novelists, he is regularly seduced by briskly adoring co-eds, models and cultural stewardesses. But Bech's unfinished novel, *Think Big*, remains unfinished, even as his privileged gloom nears burnished completion.

At this point (half-way through the novel), Bech decides to marry his patient mistress, Bea, who has been hanging around ever since *Bech: A Book* (1970). Bea of course longs to be Bea Bech. An improbably bland divorcée with three kids, Bea wants to translate Bech to the Waspy suburbs of Westchester, to install him in a little hardwood study, and have him finish *Think Big*. Manhattan-based Bech has always refused to become a 'one-man ghetto' in yet another thriving outpost of bohunk America, but he submits to 'his plump suburban softy . . . and vowed to marry her, to be safe'.

The prospect, for the reader, is enthralling. Bech, long mangled by citified cynicism, will now enter Rabbitland, with its safety, its squabbling, its marathon acquisitiveness. But the confrontation, when it happens, is a quiet one, and the book stays muted until Bech completes *Think Big*, escapes the idyll, and returns to Manhattan and his old ways. Rabbitland, quite rightly, is left to the Rabbits. It seems that the literary dystopia − even the gentle, suburban dystopia − is best evoked by the satisfied citizen, not by the brooding insurrectionary.

One's disappointment, however, inevitably seeps through into the rest of the novel. The book feels patched together, invisibly mended, as if travel notes and a shelved novella have been busily revamped. (In particular, the harassments of *Think Big* have only a lackadaisical bearing on those of *Bech Is Back.*) The new novel is inferior to its predecessor and both Bechs bear the signs of authorial thrift.

Something needs to be added, in a tone of baffled admiration, about Mr Updike's prose. In common with all his post-*Couples* fiction, the new novel is 'beautifully written'. That phrase has of course been devalued − it now means little more than freedom from gross infelicity; but Updike's style is melodious, risky, detailed, funny and fresh. (An example, more or less at random: 'He flopped into a canvas chair and kept crossing and recrossing his legs, which were so short he seemed to Bech to be twiddling his thumbs.') This is so *good*, you keep thinking; why isn't it the best? Such prose is never easily achieved, and yet Updike produces an awful lot of the stuff ... In the end, it reminds you of the best cinematography. Using talent and technique, lens and filter, the artist enjoys a weird infallibility, producing effects that are always rich, ravishing and suspiciously frictionless.

Observer 1982 and 1983

Joan Didion's Style

Joan Didion is the poet of the Great Californian Emptiness. She sings of a land where it is easier to Dial-A-Devotion than to buy a book, where the freeway sniper feels 'real bad' about picking off a family of five, where kids in High Kindergarten are given LSD and peyote by their parents, where young hustlers get lethally carried away while rolling elderly filmstars, where six-foot-two drag queens shop for fishnet bikinis, where a twenty-six-year-old woman can consign her five-year-old daughter to the centre divider of Interstate 5 (when her fingers were prised loose from the fence twelve hours later, the child pointed out that she had run after the car containing her family for 'a long time').

All of us are excited by what we most deplore – 'especially,' as Miss Didion says in another context, 'if we are writers'. Miss Didion used to be excited by human stupidity and viciousness. *Slouching towards Bethlehem* (1968), her previous collection of journalism and essays, begins with a piece about a murder in the San Bernadino Valley – Mormon country. On October 7, 1964, Lucille Miller took her depressive and generally below-par husband, Cork, out for a moonlight drive in their Volkswagen. After a visit to a nearby supermarket, Mrs Miller stopped the car in the middle of the road, poured a can of petrol over her husband, set fire to him, and then attempted to propel the VW over a four-foot drop. As it happened, the car got stuck on the ledge; Mrs Miller seemed to have a change of heart at this point, and spent the next seventy-five minutes trying to save her husband by poking at him with a stick ('I just thought if I had a stick, I'd push him out'); but by now, anyway, Cork was 'just black'. The trial was surprisingly protracted, considering that the tirelessly hysterical Mrs Miller had a boyfriend and $120,000 coming to her in the event of Cork's accidental death. 'It wasn't a very interesting murder as murders go,' Miss Didion quotes the DA as saying 'laconically', intending a gentle laugh on him. Actually the DA was right. It wasn't a very interesting murder. But it was certainly very stupid and vicious, and Miss Didion used to be excited by that kind of thing.

She isn't any more. No longer can Miss Didion regard the neurotic waywardness and vulgar infamies of California as simply 'good material'. *The White Album* deals with the late Sixties and early Seventies. During these menacing years Miss Didion lived with her husband and daughter in a large house in Hollywood, at the heart of what a friend described as a 'senseless-killing neighborhood'. Across the street, the one-time Japanese Consulate had become a group-therapy squat for unrelated adults. Scientologists used to pop by and explain to Miss Didion about E-meters and how to become a Clear. High-minded narcotics dealers would call her on the telephone ('what we're talking about, basically, is applying the Zen philosophy to money and business, dig?'). Pentecostalist Brother Theobald informed her that there were bound to be more earthquakes these days, what with the end of time being just round the corner. One night a baby-sitter remarked that she saw death in Miss Didion's aura; in response, Miss Didion slept downstairs on the sofa, with the windows open. Then it happened – not to Joan Didion, but to Jay Sebring, Abigail Folger, Voytek Frykowski, Steven Parent, Rosemary and Leno LaBianca, and Sharon Tate:

> On August 9, 1969, I was sitting in the shallow end of my sister-in-law's swimming pool in Beverly Hills when she received a telephone call from a friend who had just heard about the murders at Sharon Tate Polanski's house on Cielo Drive. The phone rang many times during the next hour. These early reports were garbled and contradictory. One caller would say hoods, the next would say chains. There were twenty dead, no, twelve, ten, eighteen. Black masses were imagined, and bad trips blamed. I remember all of the day's misinformation very clearly, and I also remember this, and wish I did not: *I remember that no one was surprised.*

And, at a stroke, the Sixties ended – 'the paranoia was fulfilled'.

Miss Didion reached her own breaking-point almost exactly a year before Charles Manson reached his. Alerted by an attack of nausea and vertigo (and such an attack 'does not now seem to [her] an inappropriate response to the summer of 1968'), Miss Didion enrolled as a private outpatient of the psychiatric clinic at St John's Hospital in Santa Monica, where she underwent the Rorschach Test, the Thematic Apperception Test, the Sentence Completion Test and the Minnesota Multiphasic Personality Index. Miss Didion quotes at italicised length from the ensuing psychiatric report: *'a personality in process of deterioration ... regressive, libidinal preoccupations ... fundamentally pessimistic, fatalistic ... feels deeply that all human effort is foredoomed to failure ... '*. Following a series of periodic visual disturbances, she then submits to three electroencephalograms, two sets of skull and neck X-rays, one five-hour glucose-tolerance test, two electromyelograms, a variety of chemical tests and consultations with two ophthalmologists, one internist and three neurologists. Damage to the central nervous system is diagnosed and given a nasty name by the sinister doctors. 'The startling fact was this,' writes Miss Didion: 'my body was offering a precise physiological equivalent to what had been going on in my mind.' At that moment she had a sharp apprehension 'of what it was like to open the door to a stranger and find that the stranger did indeed have the knife.' Charles Manson had come calling, but under the name of Multiple Sclerosis. 'Lead a simple life,' the neurologist concluded: 'Not that it makes any difference we know about.'

In her relatively self-effacing preface to *Slouching towards Bethlehem* Miss Didion admitted: 'whatever I write reflects, sometimes gratuitously, how I feel.' Ten years on, the emphasis has changed; you might even say, after 200 pages of these high-profile musings, that whatever Miss Didion feels reflects how she writes. 'Gratuitous' hardly comes into it any more – and this doesn't apply only to the essays specifically addressed to her migraines, marital problems, book-promotion activities, and so on. 'I am talking here about being a child of my time,' begins one essay. 'I had better tell you where I am, and why,' begins another. Having told us where she is and why (Honolulu, to save her marriage), Miss Didion proceeds: 'I tell you this not as aimless revelation but because I want you to know, as you read me, precisely who I am and where I am and what is on my mind. I want you to understand exactly what you are getting: you are getting a woman who for some time now has felt radically separated from most of the ideas that seem to interest other people. You are getting a woman who . . . ' And so on. You learn a good deal more about what you are getting.

Only someone fairly assured about certain of her bearings would presume to address her readers in this (in fact) markedly high-handed style. The style bespeaks celebrity, a concerned and captive following; it is inconceivable, for instance, that any beginner would risk such a take-me-or-leave-me tone. It occurs to you that Miss Didion's reasons for disliking Woody Allen's *Manhattan*, and for attacking it at length in the *New York Review*, are perhaps largely defensive in origin. What is objectionable about *Manhattan* is not that it is knowing, cute, 'in', as Miss Didion claimed. What is objectionable about *Manhattan*, and *Annie Hall*, is that Woody Allen is publicly analysing a past love affair, *with* his past lover, *on screen* (Woody used to be with Diane, as is well known; as is also well known, Diane is now with Warren, or was at the time of writing). Such self-advertisement feels cheap and, for all its coy alienations, looks thick-skinned. Miss Didion would dismiss the comparison as footling when compared to the inescapability of her new-found emotional rawness. She feels that she is responding accurately to some extremity in the observed life – in the great and desperate human action she reads about in the newspapers, listens to on the radio, and fragmentarily witnesses. Yet it remains true that writing, unlike living, is artificial, disinterested: it is not just another facet of reality, however clamorous and incorrigible that reality may sometimes feel.

Miss Didion, though, has come out. She stands revealed, in *The White Album*, as a human being who has managed to gouge another book out of herself, rather than as a writer who gets her living done on the side, or between the lines. The result is a volatile, occasionally brilliant, distinctly female contribution to the new New Journalism, diffident and imperious by turns, intimate yet categorical, self-effacingly listless and at the same time often subtly self-serving. She can still find her own perfect pitch for long stretches, and she has an almost embarrassingly sharp ear and unblinking eye for the Californian inanity. Seemingly obedient, though, to the verdicts of her psychiatric report, Miss Didion writes about everything with the same doom-conscious yet faintly abstract intensity of interest, whether remarking on the dress sense of one of Manson's hench-

women, or indulging her curious obsession with Californian water-
works. In these pieces, Miss Didion's writing does not 'reflect' her
moods so much as dramatise them. 'How she feels' has become, for
the time being, how it is.

The effect on her style is everywhere apparent. In the middle of a
piece about the design of shopping-centres, Miss Didion abruptly
announces: 'If I had a center I would have monkeys, and Chinese
restaurants, and Mylar kites and bands of small girls playing
tambourine.' That sentence could have been written by Richard
Brautigan; it is peculiarly Californian style, a schlepping style. Bouts
of wooziness affect the judgment too. After a wearily lucid analysis
of the Women's Movement and a precise appraisal of Doris Lessing,
Miss Didion moves on to a bizarre hymn to Georgia O'Keeffe, the
veteran American painter. Miss Didion makes the mistake, at the
outset, of taking along her seven-year-old daughter to see a Chicago
retrospective of the painter's work:

> One of the vast O'Keeffe *Sky Above Clouds* canvasses floated over
> the back stairs in the Chicago Art Institute that day, dominating
> what seemed to be several stories of empty light, and my daughter
> looked at it once, ran to the landing, and kept on looking. 'Who
> drew it,' she whispered after a while. I told her. 'I need to talk to
> her,' she said finally.
>
> My daughter was making, that day in Chicago, an entirely
> unconscious but quite basic assumption about people and the
> work they do. She was assuming that the glory she saw in the
> work reflected a glory in its maker . . . that every choice one made
> alone . . . betrayed one's character. *Style is character.*

It is easy to see here how quickly sentimentality proceeds to
nonsense. The extent to which style isn't character can be gauged by
(for example) reading a literary biography, or by trying to imagine a
genuinely fruitful discussion between Georgia O'Keeffe and Miss
Didion's seven-year-old daughter: a scene of painful mawkishness
springs unavoidably to mind. When the child whispered, 'I need to
talk to her,' Miss Didion should have whispered back, 'Quiet, I'm
working,' and got on with her job. As it is, Miss Didion gives us a
tremulous pep-talk on O'Keeffe's career, fondly stressing the 'crusti-
ness' and 'pepperiness' of 'this hard woman', 'this angelic rattle-
snake'. She sums up:

In Texas there was only the horizon she craved. In Texas she had her sister Claudia with her for a while, and in the late afternoons they would walk away from town and toward the horizon and watch the evening star come out. 'That evening star fascinated me,' she wrote ' . . . My sister had a gun, and as we walked she would throw bottles into the air and shoot them. I had nothing but to walk into nowhere and the wide sunset space with the star. Ten watercolors were made from that star.' In a way one's interest is compelled as much by the sister Claudia with the gun as by the painter Georgia with the star, but only the painter left us this shining record. Ten watercolors were made from that star.

A tribute to 'hardness', from one tough performer to another, becomes a husky gasp of shared prostration.

'Style is character.' Or, as Miss Didion puts it: *Style is character*. If style were character, everyone would write as self-revealingly as Miss Didion. Not everyone does. Miss Didion's style relishes emphasis, repetition, re-emphasis. Her style likes looking at the same things from different angles. Her style likes starting and finishing successive sentences with identical phrases. Take these two little strophes, separated by a hundred-odd pages in the present book:

In the years after World War I my mother had put pennies for Grace [Episcopal Cathedral] in her mite box but Grace would never be finished. In the years after World War II I would put pennies for Grace in my mite box but Grace would never be finished.

And:

In 1973 the five pillboxes on Makapuu Head had seemed to James Jones exactly as he had left them in 1942. In 1973 the Royal Hawaiian Hotel had seemed to James Jones less formidably rich than he had left it in 1942 . . .

Both passages evoke the passing of time with the same reflexive cross-hatching. Equally, you know when to ready yourself for some uplift, because each sentence – like the one about Miss Didion's shopping-centre – contains more 'and's than a song by Leonard Cohen: 'I thought about barrack rats and I thought about Prewitt and Maggio and I thought about Army hatred and it seemed to me that night in Honolulu ... ' That night in Honolulu, that day in Chicago. It is a style that has become set in its own modulations, proclaiming its individuality by means of a few recurrent quirks and lilts. In other words, it has become mannered.

It could be argued that the same thing happened to Miss Didion's fiction. *Run, River* (1963) is an exemplarily solid first novel, mildly ambitious in construction and restrained in delivery and scope — contentedly minor, above all. It is set in rural California during and after the Second World War, and examines familial and community power-balances in relaxed, elegant, clichéless prose. Miss Didion's somewhat top-heavy interest in madness and stupefaction — the vanished knack of 'making things matter' — puts in an early appearance here, but it is at least placed against a background where not everything is mad and stupefied. The trouble starts with *Play It As It Lays* (1970). This is when the Californian emptiness arrives and Miss Didion attempts to evolve a style, or a manner, to answer to it. Here come divorces, breakdowns, suicide bids, spiced-up paragraphs, forty-word chapters, and the sort of italicised wedges of prose that used to be called 'fractured'. The 'bad' characters are movie people who drink and take drugs to excess, sleep with one another a lot, and don't go crazy. The 'good' characters are movie people who drink and take drugs to excess, sleep with one another a lot, and do go crazy. The bad characters are shallow pragmatists. The good characters are (between ourselves) shallow nihilists. We are meant to think that BZ, the ruefully degenerate producer, is acting with perversely heroic decorum when he kills himself with vodka and Seconal at the end of the book ('Don't start faking me now ... Take my hand'). And we are meant to think that Marie, the ruefully degenerate actress, is actually trumping BZ in the nihilism stakes by the shrewd expedient of *not* killing herself. The book closes:

> *I know what 'nothing' means, and keep on playing.*
> *Why, BZ would say.*
> *Why not, I say.*

Her italics.

The area occupied by *A Book of Common Prayer* (1977) might be called the aftermath of breakdown. Told by one woman about another, the novel's catalogue of lost husbands, lost children and lost lucidity – its endless 'revisions and erasures' (*erasures*: a very Didionian word) – is glimpsed through a mesh of distortion and dislocation. From the outset, the prose tangles with a good deal of counterpoint, elision and italicisation, and gets more hectic as the novel proceeds. Towards the end, such is the indirection on display, Miss Didion seems incapable of starting a new subordinate clause without splintering off into a new paragraph.

> In fact she had.
> Told Leonard what she was going to do.
> She was going to stay.
> Not 'stay' precisely.
> 'Not leave' is more like it.

and

> I am told, and so she said.
> I heard later.
> According to her passport. It was reported.
> Apparently.

are examples. I find this kind of writing as resonant as a pop-gun. The most poetic thing about Miss Didion's prose in this novel is that it doesn't go all the way across the page.

However much she would resist the idea, Miss Didion's talent is primarily discursive in tendency. As is the case with Gore Vidal, the essays are far more interesting than the fiction. The novels get taken up, with the enthusiasm, the unanimity, the relief which American critics and readers often show when they discover a new and distinctly OK writer. Miss Didion is already being called 'major', a judgment that some might think premature, to say the least: but she is far more rewarding than many writers similarly saluted. In particular, the candour of her femaleness is highly arresting and original. She doesn't try for the virile virtues of robustness and infallibility; she tries to find a female way of being serious. Nevertheless, there are hollow places in even her best writing, a thinness, a sense of things missing.

There are two main things that aren't there. The first is a social dimension. At no point in *The White Album* does Miss Didion think about the sort of people she would never normally have cause to come across: the 'cunning Okie' who doesn't actually commit the crime and hit the headlines, the quietly crazy mother who never gets round to leaving her daughter on the centre divider of Interstate 5, the male-prostitute flop who will never have the chance to roll and murder a Ramon Novarro and win a place in Miss Didion's clippings file. Lucille Miller was alive and ill and living in San Bernadino Valley long before she tried to burn her husband to death. Miss Didion sensed this, in *Slouching towards Bethlehem*, and had the energy to follow it up: but in *The White Album* her imaginative withdrawal seems pretty well complete. It must be easier to get like this in California than anywhere else on earth. Even the black revolutionaries Miss Didion goes to see chat about their Medicare schemes and the royalties on their memoirs. It is interesting, though, that Miss Didion fails to identify a strong element in the 'motives' behind the Manson killings: the revenge of the insignificant on the affluent. What frightened Miss Didion's friends was the idea that wealth and celebrity might be considered sufficient provocation to murder. But Miss Didion never looks at things from this point of view. It is a pity. If you are rich and neurotic it is salutary in all kinds of ways to think hard about people who are poor and neurotic: i.e. people who have more to be neurotic about. If you don't, and especially if you are a writer, then it is not merely therapy you miss out on.

The other main thing that isn't there is any kind of literary spaciousness or solidity. Miss Didion has excellent sport with the culturelessness of her fellow Californians. 'As a matter of fact I hear that no man is an island once or twice a week, quite often from people who think they are quoting Ernest Hemingway.' Or again, writing about Hollywood: 'A book or a story is a "property" only until the deal; after that it is "the basic material", as in "I haven't read the basic material on *Gatsby*."' Miss Didion has read the basic material on *Gatsby*; she has even read *The Last Tycoon*. But what else has she read, and how recently? A few texts from her Berkeley days like *Madame Bovary* and *Heart of Darkness* get a mention. Lionel Trilling gets two. And while holidaying in Colombia she takes the opportunity to quote from *One Hundred Years of Solitude* ('by the Colombian novelist Gabriel García Márquez') and Robert Lowell's 'Caracas'. Yet at no point does Miss Didion give a sense of being someone who uses literature as a constant model or ideal, something shored up against the randomness and babble that is fundamental to her distress. When Miss Didion herself attempts an erudite modulation we tend to get phrases like 'there would ever be world enough and time' or 'the improvement of marriages would not a revolution make' or 'all the ignorant armies jostling in the night' – which might be gems from a creative-writing correspondence course.

'Slouching towards Bethlehem' is, of course, a literary reference itself. As Miss Didion dramatically points out in her preface: 'This book is called *Slouching towards Bethlehem* because for several years now certain lines from the Yeats poem which appears two pages back have reverberated in my inner ear as if they were surgically implanted there.' The whole of 'The Second Coming' is indeed printed a few pages back, along with a deflationary extract from the sayings of Miss Peggy Lee ('I learned courage from Buddha, Jesus, Lincoln, Einstein, and Cary Grant'). The title essay duly begins: 'The centre wasn't holding'. It doesn't seem to have occurred to her with the necessary force that 'The Second Coming' was written half a century ago. The centre hasn't been holding for some time now; actually the centre was never holding, and never will hold. Probably all writers are at some point briefly under the impression that they are in the forefront of disintegration and chaos, that they are among the first to live and work after things fell apart. The continuity such an impression ignores is a literary continuity. It routinely assimilates and domesticates more pressing burdens than Miss Didion's particular share of vivid, ephemeral terrors.

London Review of Books 1980

In Hefnerland

1. The Playboy Party

At last, that very special moment. Playmate of the Year Barbara Edwards composed herself at the far end of the astroturfed marquee. The stage she stood on recalled the train motif of her 'pictorial' in the current magazine; the blancmange-coloured dress she wore matched the press-kits that lay on every table. With her make-up scored by tears of pride, Barbara thanked the assembly for sharing this very special day. 'And now, the man who makes the dreams come true, ladies and gentlemen, Mr Hugh M. Hefner!' Barbara faltered, then added, on the brink of crack-up: 'I love him *so much*.'

Hef took the stage. For a man who never goes out, who rises at mid-afternoon, who wanders his draped mansion in slippers and robe (whose lifestyle, on paper, resembles nothing so much as a study in terminal depression), Hef looks good — surprisingly, even scandalously so. A little haggard, maybe, a little etiolated, but trim and ferret-fit in blazer and slacks. It was 4.30, so Hef had presumably just rubbed the sleepy dust from his eyes and climbed from the trembling, twirling bed which he so seldom leaves. 'I work in it, play in it, eat and sleep in it,' he has said. What *doesn't* he do in it? Well, perhaps this is the look you get, when the day's most onerous chore is your twilight visit to the men's room.

'It's a very special day for us,' Hef confirmed — and Barbara was a very special lady. She was also an exception to the recent 'run of blondes': why, the last brunette he'd crowned was Patti McGuire, 'who went on to marry Jimmy Connors'. At this point Barbara seemed suddenly subdued, no doubt by the prospect of going on to marry John McEnroe. 'Without further ado', however, Hef gave

Barbara her special gifts, all of them taxable: $100,000, a new car (not a pink Porsche or a crimson Cadillac but a dinky black Jaguar), and the title itself: Playboy Playmate of the Year.

The assembled shower of pressmen, PR operatives, hangers-on and sub-celebrities – Robert Culp and Vince Van Patten were perhaps the most dazzling stars in this pastel galaxy – listened to the speeches, applauded zestlessly, and returned to their lite beers and tea-time vodka-tonics. More animated, in every sense, was the tableful of centrefold also-rans to the left of the podium, who greeted each remark with approving yelps of 'Yeah!' and 'Wha-hoo!' and 'Owl-*right*'. These are the special girls who languish in semi-residence at Playboy Mansion West, sunbathers, jacuzzi-fillers, party-prettifiers. Now what is it with these girls? The look aspired to is one of the expensive innocence of pampered maiden-hood, frill and tracery in pink and white, flounced frocks for summer lawns. They also have a racehorse quality, cantilevered, genetically tuned or souped-up, the skin monotonously perfect, the hair sculpted and plumed; the body-tone at its brief optimum. Compared to these girls, the ordinary woman (the wife, the secre-tary, the non-goddess) looks lived-in or only half-completed, eccen-trically and interestingly human.

Now Hef partied – Hef made the scene. Behind him at all times stood his bodyguard, a representative of the balding, gum-chewing, bodyguarding caste. Don't be a bodyguard, if you can possibly help it. You have to stand there all day with your arms folded, frowning watchfully. If you don't look grim and serious, you aren't doing your job. Diversified only by a bit of Pepsi-ferrying to the boss, that's what Hef's bodyguard does all day: look serious, while Hef horses around. A teenage playmate nuzzled Hef's chest and giggled. The bodyguard watched her watchfully.

As the thrash thrashed on, I slipped out of the tent and strolled the grounds. The man-made, bloodheat rockpool, the jacuzzi-infested grotto, the mini-zoos with their hunched, peanut-addict monkeys, smiling parrots, demonic macaws, the tennis court, the vast satellite receiver, curved like a giantess's brassière, which enables Hef to watch even more TV than he does already ... Hef would later describe an average day in his life. 'Get up in the early afternoon, have a meeting, there's a regular buffet, a couple of movies, go upstairs around 1 a.m. with a girlfriend or whoever, make love then, have a meal, watch a movie or two.' Now that's four movies a day we're looking at. In the early Seventies Hef left the 'controlled environment' of his sealed and gardenless mansion in Chicago and moved out to California — itself a kind of controlled environment. Here the sun's controls are turned up all year long, and the girls are bigger, better, blonder, browner. But Hef isn't much of a fresh-air buff, even now ... On the edge of the tropical fishpond stands an ornamental barrel, full of feed. Scatter a handful of the smelly pellets, and the fish — gorgeously shell-coloured — will rush to the bank, scores of them, mouths open, like benign but very greedy piranha. 'God, that's so gross,' said a passing partygoer. It is, too. The fish mass so tightly that for a moment, a special moment, there is no water beneath you — only squirming suicide. They look netted, beached, like a fisherman's haul.

2. The Playboy Salad

Keyholder turns Bunny Back cards into Bunny for issuance of desired Certificate. (This offer is not valid in conjunction with any other special promotional offer.) — Playboy Club Leaflet

To the Playboy Club in Century City, just off the Avenue of the Stars. In the foyer of this desperate establishment you will find a squad of strict-faced, corseted Bunnies, a gift shop featuring various 'celebrity purchases', and a big TV screen showing a big Playmate as she soaps herself in the tub ... This is hot footage from the Playboy Channel — yes, a whole channel of the stuff, nine or ten hours a day. Playboy Inc. is changing its act: once a paunchy conglomerate kept afloat by gambling profits, it is now a solid publishing company nursing high hopes for cable TV. Hef believes that this is the way forward as the trend of American leisure increasingly shuns the street and huddles up in the home. Hef ought to know. He *is* home-smart, having put in thirty years' experience of never going out. In the submarine sanctum of the club itself you will find a Playboy pinball machine (the artwork depicts Hef flanked by two playmates in their nighties), a video game with a handwritten Out of Order notice taped to its screen, some backgammon tables, a wall of framed centrefolds, and an oval bar where two or three swarthy loners sit slumped over their drinks, staring at the waitresses with an air of parched and scornful gloom. The wine glasses bear the Playboy logo: the little black rabbit-head does such a good imitation of a drowned insect that the young woman in our party shrieked out loud as she raised the glass to her lips. A 747-load of Japanese tourists in modified beachwear filed cautiously past. The manager or greeter, who looked like the rumba-instructor or tango-tutor of a Miami hotel, showed us to our table with a flourish. The Playboy Club, we knew, was LA's premier talent showcase, and tonight's act, we learned, was straight in from Las Vegas. When questioned, the manager proudly agreed that the club did a lot of package-tour business, as well as 'Greyline Tour bus groups. But the bus groups are very minimal tonight.' We gazed over the shining mops of the Japanese, and over the coiff, frizz, rug and bald-patch of the bus groups, as tonight's act did its thing: three girls in tutus, singing popular hits. At the incitement of the lead singer, the audience clapped its hands to the beat. The sound they made was as random as weak applause.

Over a Playboy Salad (remarkably similar to a non-Playboy salad, though rather heavy on the Thousand Island), I unwrapped my Playboy gift-pack. A dime-store garter belt for the special person in my life, two Playboy bookmatches, a blizzard of promotional offers, and a scrap of paper bearing the tremulous signature of Hugh M. Hefner. According to the new Bunny Pack bonus program, all I had to do was 'enjoy dinner Playboy style' 2,531 times, and I'd win a new VCR. There were other offers: 'Easy-to-take drink prices and complimentary chili every Monday through Friday from four to seven.' Even as I finished my steak, the $1.50 all-you-can-eat brunch was being assembled on the sideboards.

'Playboy Style ... live it!' say the ads for the club in the parent magazine. But Playboy Style, nowadays, is something you'd have to ask your father about. In this den of innocuousness, you see that the Playboy dream has submitted to the heroic consumerism of everyday America: it has been proletarianised, kitsched, disappearing in the direction it came from, back to Chicago, the Fifties, Korea, the furtive world of *Dude, Gent, Rogue, Flirt, Sir, Male, Cutie, Eyeful, Giggles, Titter, Modern Sunbathing and Hygiene*. Then, suddenly, there was Kinsey, the bikini, talk of the Pill, penicillin and *Playboy*. In the proud dawn of the Playboy dream, Hef hung out with Ella Fitzgerald, Dizzy Gillespie, Lenny Bruce and Jack Kerouac. Now it's Sammy Davis Jr, Jimmy Caan, John and Bo Derek, and Tom Jones. As it fades, the dream must reach down deeper into lumpen America, searching for the bedroom fevers of someone very like Hef in 1953: the son of stalwart Methodist parents, a fried-chicken and pork-chop kind of guy, miserably married, naïve, ambitious and repressed, someone who connected sex with upward mobility, someone who knew just how expensive the best things in life could be.

3. The Playboy Playmate

My friends all asked me why I wanted to become a Playmate, and I told them I thought the women of Playboy *were the epitome of beauty, class, taste and femininity.* – Shannon Tweed, ex-Playmate

Overworked, it seemed, to the point of inanition or actual brain death, Hef's PR man Don was having problems firming up the Hefner interview and Mansion tour. Where, I wondered, was Hef's famous in-depth back-up? But then I remembered what had happened when *Playboy* wanted to interview its own Editor-Publisher, six years ago: 'Hef says call back in a year' was the message from the Mansion. 'We have a problem,' droned Don. And yet problem-solving is his business, as it is with all the corporation Roys and Rays and Phils and Bills. Equally ponderous and evasive, Don is one of the many middlemen hired to interpose between Hef and the outside world. Nearly everybody in LA retains one or two of these reality-softeners. What do you get at the end of every line? The smooth interceptions of answering services; the forensic clearances of security people; Hispanic incomprehension.

I drove to Don's office in the Playboy building, up on Sunset, to meet and chat with a 'representative Playmate'. In the sunny, genial, nude-decked PR department I was introduced to Penny Baker and provided with the relevant issue of *Playboy*. Miss Baker was the beneficiary of The Great Thirtieth Anniversary Playmate Search: 250,000 polaroids later, they settled on Penny: 'And now that we've found her, our greatest reward is in sharing her beauty with you.' What do they look for, exactly? 'Great nipples', 'sincere bush', 'Is there a problem with the breasts?' – these are the sort of concepts (I had read) that are tossed back and forth by Hef's creative consultants. For eight pages plus centrefold, at any rate, Penny's beauty, her charms, were glisteningly revealed. Her turn-ons were 'Mountains and music'. Among her turn-offs were 'big talkers and humidity'. Her ideal man? 'Someone who knows what he wants.' Penny is eighteen.

Monitored by Don's ponderous presence (he lurked there with his little tape recorder – company policy, no doubt), the interview began. Within a minute, I had run out of questions. I would get nothing but company policy from Penny, and we both knew it. Yes, she now worked on the Playboy promo circuit. No, her parents didn't object to the spread: they both thought it was neat. Yes, she belonged to the Shannon Tweed school of Playmate philosophy. 'I have a beautiful baddy,' explained Penny – and why should she be ashamed to share it with *Playboy* subscribers? 'How do you feel about Hugh Hefner?' I asked, and felt Don give a sluggish twitch. Penny's young face went misty. Sweetness, sincerity, sensitivity: like a big family. 'I saw him cry one time,' she confessed. 'It was his birthday. I went up and said Happy Birthday. And he, and he – well . . .' A very special moment, this one, a very special memory, not to be shared.

4. The Playboy Interview

With another side of the same story comes iconoclast Buck Henry who reveals . . . that those really close to Hef always refer to him as Ner. – 'Playbill', *Playboy*

What a scoop. I arrived at the Playboy Mansion for my interview to find that a quite extraordinary thing had happened: Ner had gone out! Now as we all know this is something that Ner hardly ever does. He hasn't been in a cab or a shop for twenty years. Only once in that period has he walked a street – back in 1967. At that time Ner still nestled in the sealed and soundproofed Chicago Mansion: he never knew the time of day, or even the season. Playboy Inc. had purchased a new property. Struck by the desire to see the place, Ner decided on a rare sortie: he would walk the eight blocks to North Michigan Avenue. Venturing out of his controlled environment, he found that it was raining. It was also the middle of the night. Legend does not record whether he was still in his pyjamas at the time . . . Today, Ner had *gone out* to the doctor's. But he would shortly return.

You pull up at the gates – Charing Cross Road, Holmby Hills. On my previous visit I'd been unsmilingly cleared by a young man with tweed jacket, guest-list clipboard and turbulent complexion (peanut-butter plus pimple problem). Today the closed gates were unattended. My cab idled. Suddenly a mounted camera jerked its head in my direction – surprised, affronted. 'Let me have your name, sir,' I was asked by an ornamental boulder on my left. After several unfriendly questions and delays, the gates grudgingly parted. WARNING, says a sign on the curved drive: YOUR VISIT MAY BE RECORDED OR TELEVISED.

'An elegant English Tudor home, L-shaped, with slate roof and leaded windows', Playboy Mansion West teems with car-boys, handimen, minders, butlers, bunnies. Everyone is brisk with corporation *esprit*, with problem-solving know-how. They bear themselves strictly, in accordance with some vague but exacting model of efficiency and calm. Their life's work, you feel, is to ensure that nothing ever gets on Ner's nerves.

The library sports a double backgammon table, a panelled, Pepsi-crammed icebox, various framed mag-covers featuring Ner, and a wall of books: bound editions of *Playboy* and the *Encyclopaedia Britannica*, a modest collection of hardbacks – *The Supercrooks, Sex Forever, Luck be a Lady, Winning at the Track with Money Management*. Over the fireplace hangs a jokey, Renaissance-style portrait of Ner, emphasising his close resemblance to Olivier's Richard III. (I later telephoned Don and asked him if this visual reference was an intentional one. Bemused, Don trudged off to check, and returned with an indignant denial.) As I walked to the window two limousines pulled up self-importantly in the forecourt. Slamming doors, busy car-boys, watchfully craning bodyguards. Having *gone out*, Ner had now *come back*. The interview would soon begin. Normally, I had read, recording equipment is set up to monitor a Hefner interview; also, the drapes are carefully drawn. 'Security request we close the drapes whenever Mr Hefner is in a room.' But things are laxer now. The sun can shine, and it's still OK if Ner is in a room.

And in he came, wearing scarlet silk pyjamas, with pipe and Pepsi – all as advertised. He apologised for being late and, in answer to my query, gave assurances that all had gone well at the doctor's. We settled down. The interview went through two phases, quite distinct in timbre. For the first hour or so, Ner talked like a politician: he has a hundred well-thumbed paragraphs in his head, each of them swiftly triggered by the normal run of questions. He is comfortable with criticism from the Right (abortion, censorship), rather less so with criticism from the Left (misogyny, philistinism). Actually Ner believes that these orthodoxies go in cycles: now that pornography has become – ironically – a civil-rights issue, he can imagine himself 'returning to the sexual avant garde' and reliving his old crusade. If such a challenge were to arise, the father of sexual liberation won't duck it. Nor shall Ner's sword sleep in his hand – no sir.

During the second part of the interview Ner relaxed: that is to say, he became highly agitated, showing the wounded restlessness of a man who thinks himself persistently misunderstood. His eyes, previously as opaque as limo-glass, now glittered and fizzed. So did his Pepsi: he took such violent swigs that the bottle kept foaming to the brim. His language grew saltier. 'That's all *bullshit*,' he said repeatedly, swiping a finger through the air. You saw the Chicagoan in him then – the tight-jawed, almost ventriloquial delivery, the hard vowels, the human hardness of the windy city, the city that works.

What changed Ner's mood? First, a discussion of Bobbie Arnstein, the private secretary who committed suicide after involving Playboy in a drugs scandal during the mid-Seventies. Ner was able to give himself a quickfire exoneration on this 'very scummy case'. He was far less convincing, though, when talk turned to the case of Dorothy Stratten. There is clearly something central and unshirkable about the Stratten story; it is the other side of the Playboy dream: it is the Playboy nightmare. All set for stardom, likely to become the first Playboy-endorsed Hollywood success, Stratten was murdered by her rejected husband in circumstances of hideous squalor. The controversy has been ceaseless (and deeply unwelcome to the corporation), with the TV film *Death of a Centrefold*, Bob Fosse's *Star 80* and now Peter Bogdanovich's memoir *The Killing of the Unicorn*. Dorothy Stratten was Playmate of the Year for 1980, but she never saw 1981.

'Dorothy', he said, his face briefly wistful, 'was a very special person, very trusting, a very special . . . human being.' People talked about the connections between Dorothy's death and the mores of the Playboy world – 'But that's all bullshit. There is not and never has been a casting-couch thing here.' He then went on to slander Bob Fosse (off the record: a private thing between Ner and me). 'Recreational sex can still be moral – and that's what I'm all about. You have responsibilities as a bachelor. Nobody has ever had an abortion because of me. Nobody. It's like a family here. People stay with us for a very long time: my night-time secretary was a Playmate in 1960! I am a warm and caring person and so is the company. That's the kind of guy I am.'

The interview ended with some deliberation about the photographs that would illustrate this article. A recent and idealised portrait of Ner was produced in its frame – the sort of thing a sports or nightclub personality might hang over his bed. Wouldn't this do? 'It's never been used before,' droned Don (who had, of course, been ponderously present throughout). I hesitated. Did they seriously think that any magazine other than *People* – or *Playboy* – would publish such an 'official' study? Was the Editor-Publisher of genius losing his grip? Should I be frank? Was now the time to start calling Hef Ner? I said nothing. We sat there admiring the photograph, all agreeing how very special it looked.

The girls are always saying they feel 'safe' in the Mansion, and yet the Easterner is pretty happy to take his leave – to leave the atmosphere of surveillance, corporation propaganda and PR p's and q's. Ner cruised out of the library and into the hall. An average evening was beginning. In the dining-room two elderly celebrities (Max Lerner and Richard Brook) were ordering complicated meals, with many doctorial vetos and provisos, while in the adjacent room the little squad of playmates and playthings, of honeys and bunnies, sat quietly around a table with their glasses (soft drinks only: Ner doesn't want them sloppy). Momentarily hushed and alert, the girls seemed ornamental and yet not quite passive, on call, expected to disport themselves in a certain way, expected to do whatever is expected.

5. The Playboy Philosophy

Publishing a sophisticated men's magazine seemed to me the best possible way of fulfilling a dream I'd been nurturing ever since I was a teenager: to get laid a lot – Hugh M. Hefner

Hefner has been inviting moral judgments for over thirty years. It shows. It takes it out of a guy. Never altogether cynical, not yet entirely deluded, he is nonetheless committed to a sanitised, an authorised version of his life. The tendency is common enough, especially out here in the land of the innumerate billionaire, where a game of Scrabble is a literary event, where the prevailing values are those of the pocket calculator. 'There are times', Gloria Steinem has said, 'when a woman reading *Playboy* feels like a Jew reading a Nazi manual.' This is a frivolous remark, and blasphemous, too. Say that about *Playboy*, and what's left for *Der Sturmer*? If commercial pornography is imagined as a flophouse, with bestiality in the basement, then *Playboy* is a relatively clean and tidy attic. It is hardly pornography at all, more a kind of mawkish iconography for eternal adolescents. *Playboy* 'objectifies women' all right, in Joyce Wolfe's quaint phrase — but let's be objective here. According to the old Chicago axiom, there are two areas of wrongdoing: ethics and morals. Ethics is money and morals is sex. With Hefner, the line between the two is blurred or wobbly. It is a very American mix.

Three points need to be made about Hefner's oft-repeated contention that Playboy is like a family. First, it is a family in which Poppa Bear gets to go to bed with his daughters. Secondly, it is a family in which the turnover in daughters is high. Thirdly, it is a family in which no tensions, resentments or power-struggles are admitted to or tolerated: at Playboy, everyone is happy all the time. Of every conceivable human institution, a family is what Playboy least resembles. True, Hefner's daughter Christie is now the figurehead of the company; true also that he has recently opened his arms, *Dynasty*-style, to a second, putative son (though he admitted to me that there was, of all things, 'a problem' with young Mark). But they're grown up now: they're on the payroll, under the wing, like everybody else. Hefner isn't paternal — he is exclusively paternalistic, wedded only to the daily exercise of power.

At the time of the interview I had not read Bogdanovich's *The Killing of the Unicorn*. More to the point, neither had Hefner. I assume that his tone would have been very different — less spirited and aggrieved, more furtive and beleaguered. The Bogdanovich memoir is a labour of love, verging on a kind of sentimental mysticism, and its central accusation (that Hefner bears a measure of responsibility for Stratten's death, not only metaphorically but directly too) carries more emotion than weight. Some unpleasant facts, however, are now on record; and one is less disturbed by the sexual delinquencies than by the corporation automatism, the commercialised unreality with which Playboy glosses everything it does. Expediency, double-think, self-interest posing as philanthropy —

179

this is the Playboy philosophy, powder-puffed and airbrushed by all the doltish euphemism of conglomerate America.

You are an eighteen-year-old from some dismal ex-prairie state, a receptionist from Wyoming, or a local beauty queen – Miss Nowhere, Nebraska, perhaps. Your boyfriend's salacious Polaroid suddenly transforms itself into a first-class air ticket to Los Angeles. Limoed to the Mansion guest-house, you are schooled by smiling PR girls, aides, secretaries. No outside boyfriends are allowed into the Mansion – and these are, indisputably, 'healthy young girls'. Natural selection will decide whether you will be orgy-fodder, good for one of the gang, or whether you have what it takes to join the élite of Hefner's 'special ladies'. Signed up, set to work in the Playboy Club or on the promo or modelling circuits, you will find the divisions between public and private obligations hard to determine. You will also experience a wildly selective generosity, the also-rans routinely overworked and underpaid, the front-runners smothered in celebrity purchases – jewels, furs, paintings, cars and what Californians call a 'home'. If Hefner wants you to be a special lady then so does everyone else at the ranch. And when the call comes for you to join the boss in the inexorable jacuzzi, it isn't Hef on the line: it's his night-time secretary . . . This process used to be called seigneurism. 'Warm and caring'? Nowadays every business in America says how warm it is and how much it cares – loan companies, supermarkets, hamburger chains.

'Without you', Hefner once joked to a gaggle of Playmates, 'I'd have a literary magazine.' Yes, but what would he have without the literature? He'd have the Playboy Channel for one thing, and all the footling vapidity of unrelieved soft core. Sexcetera, Melody in Love, Pillow Previews, Alternative Lifestyle Features, 'nudity', 'strong language' and what are laughingly known as 'mature situations'. Christ, a week of this and you'd be like Don the PR man . . . And so we leave him, strolling his games parlour (there are bedrooms in back), his paradise of pinball, Pepsi and pyjama-parties – the remorselessly, the indefinitely gratified self. It is in the very nature of such appetites that they will deride him in time. One wonders what will happen to the girls when they grow up. One wonders what will happen to Hefner, if he ever gives it a try.

Hef at seventy. Ner at ninety. Now wouldn't that be something special?

Observer 1985

Paul Theroux's Enthusiasms

'I have always disliked being a man,' writes Paul Theroux, in a brief essay called 'Being a Man'. 'The whole idea of manhood in America is pitiful, in my opinion.' Not only pitiful: also 'stupid', 'unfeeling', 'right-wing', 'puritanical', 'cowardly', 'grotesque', 'primitive', 'hideous', 'crippling' − and 'a bore', too, what's more. Although there is some truth in these iterations, the adult male has no practicable alternative to being a man − certainly no cheap or painless one. But maybe Mr Theroux *has* found a way round being a man (I concluded, towards the end of this hefty selection of occasional pieces, *Sunrise with Seamonsters*). Being a boy!

As a novelist, Theroux is attracted to the dark, the haunted, the hidden; he is also attracted to the theme of childhood, though more for its terrors than its exhilarations. As a literary odd-jobber, however, as a left-handed gun, he is breezy, temperate and mild − often downright sunny. Nothing makes him blue. A tour of a crammed and rotting madhouse in Afghanistan can't spoil his spirits. He contrives to have a fun-filled week on the New York subway, strolling among the mangled Morlocks with the transit police. He even hits it off with John McEnroe.

Sunrise with Seamonsters is full of jaunts and larks and treats and sprees, obsessions, hobbies, self-indulgences. First, there are the trains. Theroux has already written two whole books about trains, but the choo-choos and chuff-chuffs feature prominently in this one too. The Aztec Eagle, The Lake Shore Limited, The London Ferry, The Frontier Mail, The Izmir Express − The Nine Forty-Five! The whistles, the manifests, the long waits and chance buttonholings still provide endless fascination for this dark-spectacled Bradshaw, train-spotting from the wrong side of the glass. Perhaps the most reckless piece in the book is a seduction fantasy (young man, mature woman — 'her sobs of pleasure', etc.), followed by an essay in praise of the older ladies. 'At her age she could know every trick in the book and, if it weren't for her pride . . . she could probably make a fortune as a hooker.' *Cor.* The seduction takes place in the South of France. On a train.

The book bristles with other enthusiasms. Theroux dabbles in photography; he is crazy about maps; he writes and then personally publishes a special Christmas story for his kids; he goes 'harbour-hopping' round the Cape in his boat, *Goldeneye*. Mr Thoreau (I mean Mr Theroux, but is there any relation?) is a Cape Cod buff, a true-blue Cape Codder, romping and gambolling there annually with his extended family. 'I get sad', moons Theroux, 'thinking that the summer is about to end.' After dinner there are parlour games: Kemps, Up Jenkins, The Parson's Cat, and Murder. Or else he rows along the coast to his folks' house, and horses around with his middle-aged brothers. 'We were not writers, husbands, or fathers. We were three big boys fooling in front of their parents.'

About a dozen of the pieces collected here are about writers; but the approach remains personal rather than literary. A couple (on S.J. Perelman and V.S. Naipaul) are warm pen-portraits inspired by friendship. Others get in as one-time idols (Henry Miller, Kipling, James) who have influenced or liberated Mr Theroux. And occasionally his pen will flash from its scabbard to defend undervalued heroes and neglected favourites (Joyce Cary, John Collier, V.S. Pritchett's *Dead Man Leading*). Theroux praises Pritchett's criticism for its non-academic slant, and obviously sees himself as following in this line himself. But I don't think Pritchett is ever quite as non-academic as his young admirer. A naturally alert and energetic reader, Theroux is nevertheless much happier with the particular rather than the general. When he does venture into theory ('from the Jacobeans onward [there are] villains who are truer and vastly more enjoyable than saintly heroes who never put a foot wrong'), you get a sense of something callow and furtive, as if Mr Theroux still does his reading in the small hours — under the blankets with a flashlight.

In his travels, both mental and actual, Theroux does of course address himself to harsh truths and ugly realities. He could hardly avoid them, having spent his twenties in the equatorial Third World, with the Peace Corps: 'it was a way of virtuously dropping out and delicately circumventing Vietnam'. In a brave piece called 'Cowardice' Theroux makes an amusing boast of his own gutlessness. But all travel is brave, in a sense. To some writers, leaving the house can seem quite an exploit. And, boy, Mr Theroux certainly gets around.

Uganda, Mozambique, Malawi, Tanzania, Burma, India, Malaysia: these are among the poorest and most chaotic countries on earth, and Theroux confronts them with what strikes me as an entirely boyish intrepidity. Beady-eyed, sensual and unflinching, he writes with concern, with feeling, with pity — but with no obvious distress. It is possible that his early experiences in Africa inured him to such spectacles. Certainly his one attempt at a compassionate High Style, 'Leper Colony' (1966) — 'limbs are clubs to thump dirt pits for trash, to wish for knives' — is the only example of literary posing, and the only profound embarrassment, in this engaging and endearing book.

Again, it is curious how neatly Theroux sheds his complexities when he writes left-handed. *Sunrise with Seamonsters* is more a holiday from authorship than an extension of it. (The writing is much looser than the fictional prose, with many a ready-made formulation: 'howling snobs', 'stifling heat', 'whiff of romance', 'hive of activity'.) Why *do* writers travel and then tell their tales? Graham Greene, whom Theroux much admires, travels to escape spleen and to embrace *nostalgie*. V.S. Naipaul, another mentor, attempts to take psychological readings of foreign cultures by way of a risky self-exposure. With both Greene and Naipaul, the traveller and the writer are the same man. Paul Theroux, who has more readers per book than either, tells traveller's tales mostly for the hell of it: long letters home. His mature responses to the things he sees are to be found elsewhere — in *Jungle Lovers, Saint Jack, The Mosquito Coast*.

Observer 1985

Gay Talese: Sex-Affirmative

Just over half-way through this interminable book (*Thy Neighbour's Wife*), we are given a welcome pen-portrait of Dr Alex Comfort, the aged author of *Joy of Sex* and its sequel, *More Joy of Sex*. Comfort is glimpsed in one of the rumpus-rooms of Sandstone Retreat, a Californian holiday camp dedicated to the proposition that everyone should go to bed with everyone else. Strolling naked through the clumps of threesomes and foursomes, the pot-bellies and appendix scars, suntans and tattoos, Dr Comfort regularly megs his cigar to 'join a friendly clutch of bodies and contribute to the merriment.'

But what is 'the nude biologist' up to here? You or I might think that the old goat was simply having a good time at the expense of equally deluded, undignified – but much younger – married couples. Actually, though, the Doc is hard at work. In the argot of Gay Talese (similarly engrossed in another part of the room), Comfort is a 'participating sex researcher' working in a 'non-laboratory situation': i.e. getting laid. Well, it's a living.

This is sexual quango-land. Mr Talese took a very long time to write and 'research' *Thy Neighbour's Wife*. His nine-year mission: to explore 'the social and sexual trends of the entire nation'. The research might have been fun, but the writing was a waste of time. As Mr Talese naïvely snoops from porno film-set to massage parlour, from obscenity trial to the offices of *Screw* magazine, as he talks to 'ordinary' troilists, wife-swappers and haggard masturbators, it slowly becomes clear that he has nothing of any interest to say on his chosen subject. Mr Talese calls this clueless style 'non-judgmental' – and he isn't kidding. Out goes judgment, and in comes jargon, stock-response and humourlessness through the same door. The book is a rag-bag of clichés, most of them about twenty years out of date.

Language is the key to the imposture. Although Mr Talese thinks that, for instance, a 'voluptuary' is a woman with big breasts, his book is not particularly ill-written. It is conscientious, even earnest. The trouble is that almost anyone could have written it. Mr Talese's prose has the stilted, rolling, lip-smacking nullity that has been satirised by Kurt Vonnegut and, more subtly, by J.G. Ballard. The style may be parodied at random: 'Each evening that summer, Keith Krankwinkel would motor out in his cream convertible to the Santa Monica duplex of Doris Dorkburger. As Doris prepared their first evening drinks, Keith would admire the graceful contours of her . . . ' Ballard, most notably in *Vermilion Sands*, uses this style to suggest a kind of existence that is at once affluent and denatured, an existence free of volition or irony. Non-judgmental Talese, however, doesn't 'use' this style: it uses him.

In one of his many chapters on wife-swapping, Mr Talese explains that 'body pleasure' is 'wholesome' and 'therapeutic', it contributes to everyone's 'welfare and personal growth', leading to 'a healthier, more sex-affirmative and open society'. As Barbara Williamson sleeps with David in one chalet bedroom, and John Williamson sleeps with Carol next door, Barbara feels that she and her husband are sharing 'a gift of loving trust', in Mr Talese's ghastly phrase. Having slept with David again at dawn, Barbara makes breakfast, and is 'greeted in the living room by her husband's approving smile and kiss'.

Pleasure is good, Mr Talese believes, and guilt is bad; the idea is to have a lot of pleasure without feeling any guilt. It is indeed a noble dream. Mr Talese's hero in this department is Hugh Hefner, who claims a sizeable chunk of his book. Talese really has to hand it to Hef, and writes of him throughout with envious admiration. Here, after all, is a man who spends the leisure of his mature years being massaged by 'four or five' robotic Playmates of the Month on his circular $15,000 bed, constantly monitored by an Ampex television camera designed to produce 'instantaneous and delayed trans-missions' on the wall screen above. Meanwhile, outside the jacuzzi-infested mansion the 'sprawling green lawns' recede over 'gently rolling hills'.

Mr Talese raptly follows Hefner's seduction of a Texan beauty called Karen Christy, who was lured up to Chicago by one of

Playboy's roving talent scouts. Hef, with his 'infectious enthusiasm' and love of 'variety and spice', successfully chats Karen up on their first night and installs her as court favourite. Hefner goes on to give Karen a diamond watch, a white mink coat, a silver fox jacket, a diamond cocktail ring, a Matisse painting, a Persian cat, a white Mark IV Lincoln, 'a beautiful metallic reproduction of the *Playboy* cover on which she was featured', and a nightly Mazola party on his circular bed. Mr Talese has this to say about the effect on Karen's personality: 'she remained essentially the same country girl she had been on the day of her arrival from Texas.' How extraordinary, if true. But the thought leads nowhere. Karen is a cliché, after all, for Hefner and for Talese.

In his final chapters Mr Talese records that at one point during his decade of energetic fieldwork, his wife suffered a 'negative reaction' to all the publicity he was getting: she left him. At this juncture (page 543), you might expect a suspicion of doubt, or of judgment, to intrude. Perhaps 'body pleasure' can't be sanitised; perhaps sex is as contingent as most aspects of life are. But Mr Talese went out to dinner and an interview with *New York* magazine. Two days later Mrs Talese came home. Lucky man. *Thy Neighbour's Wife* might have had some edge to it if she had stayed away.

Observer 1980

Double Jeopardy: Making Sense of AIDS

Witness this banal and quotidian incident. And then consider the ways in which it might affect all our lives.

A young man is walking home to his flat in Camden Town. In appearance he is, as they say, a 'Castro clone', modelled on the all-gay Castro Street area of San Francisco (where they have gay groceries, gay policemen, gay banks): short hair, regulation moustache, denim shirt and jeans, running shoes. In his path are two young women. They have their standard equipment too: lit cigarettes, tabloids under the arm, a push-chair apiece. As the young man passes the girls (and these are tough girls), they decide to say something. A year ago they might have contented themselves with 'Fucking queen!' or 'Fucking queer!' or 'Fucking poof!' But this year they have something new to say (remember those tabloids). It is: 'Fucking AIDS-carrier!' The young man walks on. End of incident.

Now, let us imagine that the accusation is unfounded. The young man gets back to his flat. He feels shaken-up, he feels *hurt*, in every sense. He wonders if he *is* an AIDS-carrier: conceivably (and he has done his reading too), he might be asymptomatic HTLV3-infected! He is At Risk, after all, and the symptoms are so damnably vague: fevers, chills, swollen glands, diarrhoea, dry cough, breathlessness. That bad night last week – was it a tummy upset, or was it Death? The young man has been considering whether to go down to Hammersmith and take the antibody test. He now decides against it. How can he safeguard his job, his flat? He feels no consensus of decency out there. Meanwhile the stress of the incident and the anxieties it has awakened are, infinitesimally, running him down, making inroads on his defences, weakening him for another kind of attack.

The two young mothers have also done themselves a bit of no good. By the time those babies are as old as their parents, AIDS will probably have shrugged off its homosexual associations (its origins may well be heterosexual anyway, but let that pass for now) and will be established in all areas of society. By then, AIDS could be the most common cause of disease-related death in young people, not just in young men − a status it already enjoys in New York and San Francisco. The young mothers have also done their bit to impede any early control of the epidemic, because such an effort will depend on an atmosphere of unwonted candour and trust. Incidentally, since the cost of caring for AIDS patients may reach £200 million annually by 1989, they have also helped deplete the health services on which their children will rely.

Finally let us re-run the incident and imagine that the accusation − the taunt − is true. The young man returns to his flat − and doesn't leave it for several days. As one of the large pool of 'AIDS-Related Complex' and 'Lesser AIDS' sufferers, his illnesses come and go in cycles, depending on natural resilience and general morale. Now they all begin again: the miseries of recurrence. This is the unique double bind of AIDS. The virus attacks the immune system, which (it appears) must be weakened enough to receive it; symptoms and prognosis invisibly interact; the sicker you are the sicker you get ... Those words on the street. Sticks and stones, perhaps. But, with AIDS, words too can break your bones.

Everywhere you look you see the double bind, the double jeopardy. In America − land of the profit-making casualty ward, home of the taxi-metered ambulance − the bipartite attack assumes its most heartless form. Growing ever weaker, the sick man faces medical bills that average $75,000 and have been known to reach half a million. The medical-insurance system is a shambles of pedantry and expedience. Some policies are soon exhausted; insurance companies often renege, claiming 'prior conditions'; if you lose your job you might lose your cover; and with the two-year waiting period to establish eligibility, 80 per cent of AIDS patients do not survive to draw their first cheque.

'What happens, usually, is a process of *spend-down*,' said Mark Senak of the AIDS Resource Centre.

'Spend-down?' I asked. I sat in Senak's chambers in downtown

Manhattan. He is one of many young lawyers active on the
AIDS-relief front. AIDS-sufferers need lawyers: to defend themselves
against employers and landlords (in America, as in England, you can
legally discriminate against homosexuals but not against the dis-
abled); to transfer assets, to wrangle with insurance companies, to
formulate declarations of bankruptcy. Lawyers like Senak have
drafted wills for young men barely out of college. Wills, bills, audits,
lawsuits − all that extra worry, boredom and threat.

Spend-down turns out to be one of those cutely hyphenated
nightmares of American life. Briefly, it means that you spend
everything you have before qualifying for Medicaid. Until recently
there were further complications. One AIDS patient was suffering
from a rare opportunistic disease called cryptosporidiosis, normally
found only in calves. He applied for social security, and was told
that he couldn't have the money. Why? Because he couldn't have the
disease.

Duly pauperised by *spend-down*, all spent out, the patient
becomes eligible for a bed in one of the city hospitals. Here he will
encounter the suspicion and contempt that America traditionally
accords to its poor. There is no out-patient care, no intermediate
care. He is not legally dischargeable unless he has a home to go to.
And AIDS sufferers often do not know if they have a home to go to.
You might return to find your remaining possessions stacked outside
the door of your apartment. The locks might have been changed −
by your landlord, or by your lover.

'What we have', said Senak, 'are diseased bag-persons living on
the street. No one will house them. No one will *feed* them.' Senak's
personal project is an accommodation centre for sufferers, on the
San Francisco model. But the ruinous cost of real estate is only one
of the difficulties. The risk categories for AIDS form a hetero-
geneous group, colloquially known as 'the 5-H club': haemophiliacs,
Haitians, homosexuals, hookers and heroin-addicts (these last two
frequently overlapping). How do you house a haemophiliac stock-
broker with a Puerto Rican junkie? One of the reasons why AIDS is
seen as a scourge of the homosexual community is that there *is* a
homosexual community, however divided.

'I think we've made progress, in changing general attitudes, since
the panic began in 1983. Tonight I'm going to see someone in
hospital. A year ago I would have had to stop off and buy him some
food. The hospital staff wouldn't take in his tray. But they do now.'

That same week in New York a TV crew — battle-scarred *conquistadores*, veterans of wars, revolutions, terrorist sieges — walked off a set rather than affix a microphone to an AIDS-sufferer's clothing. *No one has ever caught AIDS through casual contact.* After four years of handling patients' food, laundry, bed-pans, drips and bandages, no health worker has yet succumbed. You cannot say this often enough. But how often will you have to say it? In the end one cannot avoid the conclusion that AIDS unites certain human themes — homosexuality, sexual disease, and death — about which society actively resists enlightenment. These are things that we are unwilling to address or think about. We don't *want* to understand them. We would rather fear them.

In New York, everyone on the public wing refers to AIDS patients as PWAs: persons with AIDS. 'Why?' I asked a young administrator at the AIDS Medical Foundation. 'It's to avoid any suggestion of victim, sufferer and so on.' 'Why?' I asked again. They are victims; they are sufferers. But the answer is of course 'political', New York being the most politicised city on earth. New York, where even supermarkets and greasy-spoons have their 'policies'; where all action seems to result from pressure, and never from a sane initiative.

Other euphemisms in this sphere include 'sexual preference' ('orientation' being considered 'judgmental'), 'sexually active' (some go further and talk of 'distributive' as opposed to 'focal' sex) and 'intravenous substance-abuser' (as if a junkie is going to feel much cheered or ennobled by this description). Over here, handicapped people are merely 'challenged', and the 'exceptional' child is the child with brain damage. It is a very American dishonesty — antiseptic spray from the verbal-sanitation department. Having named a painful reality (the belief seems to be), you also dispatch it; you get it off your desk.

In 1983 the total federal budget for the AIDS crisis was $28 million; in 1984 it was $61 million. But this was all grant-hound money, Nobel-race money: not a cent had been allocated to the treatment of patients. During the time of my stay in New York (this was late March 1985), the old tightrope-artist Mayor Koch came across with a $6.5 million package. He was responding to countless protests and petitions; more important (according to many observers), he was responding to the fact that 1985 is election year. The truth is that the New York record on AIDS compares woefully with that of San Francisco, which has long been a coordinated network of treatment and educational services, everything from bereavement-counselling to meals-on-wheels. San Francisco has also taken the controversial step of closing the gay bathhouses, by order of the health authorities. The *Village Voice* claimed that Koch has always been terrified of any association, pro or anti, with the gay cause. Remember the slogan: 'Vote for Cuomo, Not the Homo'? Koch quickly denounced this 'slander' as 'vile' and 'outrageous' – also 'irrelevant'. His confusions are plain enough; but so are those of the gay population, which remains as brittle and fragmented as any other stratum in this volatile city, the city of the omni-partisan.

In New York you will find every permutation of human response to the AIDS crisis. The bathhouses are still open here, and commercialised gay sex is still big business. Many gays see any move to limit their activity as an attack on the civil-rights front, an attempt to isolate, to 'pathologise'. More extreme are the 'disco dummies' who, even after contracting AIDS themselves, maintain or actually increase their sexual output. You hear talk of 'medical scenarios' in the bathhouses; you hear talk of sado-masochistic routines featuring AIDS as the ultimate 'sex death'; you hear talk of just about everything. The heterosexual community has reacted more predictably: the National Gay Task Force estimates incidents of violent harassment at about a thousand a month.

Throughout the history of sexual disease, injunctions to enforce celibacy or monogamy have never had the slightest effect. Then again, the stakes have never been so high. It is quite clear from statistics on routine complaints like gonorrhoea (down 50 per cent in some studies) that sexual activity has drastically decreased. Plainly a lot of thought, and lively improvisation, has already gone into this matter. Strategies include libido-suppressors and vitamin combinations, stress-reduction seminars, 'jerk-off' circles and closed groups of 'clear' gays. There are even Orgiasts Anonymous services, where a sponsor 'talks you down' from an urge to visit the bathhouse. Such expedients may seem bizarre to the straight world. But that is because the straight world expects the gay man to follow its own sexual master-mould. And he doesn't. Homosexuality isn't a *version* of heterosexuality. It is something else again.

*

The consoling idea of the quietly monogamous gay couple is an indolent and sentimental myth. With a large number of exceptions, and all sorts of varieties of degree, it just isn't like that. Friendship, companionship, fellowship — these are paramount; but pairing-and-bonding on the wedlock model is our own dated fiction. Gay lovers seldom maintain any sexual interest in each other for more than a year or two. The relationship may remain 'focal', may well be lifelong, yet the sex soon reverts to the 'distributive'.

Gay men routinely achieve feats of promiscuity that the most fanatical womaniser could only whistle at. In the heterosexual world you might encounter the odd champion satyromaniac who — doing nothing else, all his life — accumulates perhaps a thousand conquests. On some fringes of the gay world (where a man might average ninety 'contacts' a month) you could reach this total in less than a year. In the right club or bathhouse, you could have sex with half a dozen different men without once exchanging a word.

However this may be, the median number of sexual partners for gay American AIDS patients is over eleven hundred. The exponential leap is easily explained. Most obviously, both actors in the sexual drama have the same role; they are both hunters, and can dispense with the usual preliminaries and reassurances (try taking someone to the opera ninety times a week). Also the gay man, more often than not, is making up for lost time. Throughout his youth he has felt excluded, unstable — illegal; even as an adult much of his daily life is spent incognito, in imitation of a mainstream citizen; but at night he joins an extraverted and hedonistic brotherhood. You could cite genetic factors too. Just as the gay woman seems to exemplify the usual feminine imperatives (monogamy, inconspi-cuousness, site-tenacity), so the gay man, in equally intense, redou-bled form, does as his DNA tells him: he is mobile, aggressive and disseminatory.

There is certainly a political dimension also, as many gay leaders claim. In America, homosexuality is illegal in twenty-three states plus the District of Columbia. In England we have the consenting-adults package: no sex until you are twenty-one, no 'public' sex in clubs and bars, and no group-sex whatever (even troilism is indict-able). Despite much harassment and entrapment, these provisos are quite clearly unenforceable. Naturally, then, there is defiance involved, and celebration of the gains already made. Some gay activists even argue that the sexual liberation has worked as an opiate, deflecting the movement from progress of a more tangible kind.

'For fifteen years, we all had a party.' It was a time of dazzling freedoms and self-discoveries. In their new world, the distinctions of class, race, money and privilege were all triumphantly erased. Of course there were the expected perils and boredoms of any long party — the occupational hazard known as feeling 'gayed out'. How many more times (the gay man would wonder) will I wake up to hear myself saying, 'Well, Clint/Skip/Didier/Luigi/Piotr/Basim, what brings you to our fair land?' But the great mix was, on the whole, a vivid and innocuous adventure, one that seemed to redress many past confusions. 'It was so good', as I was told many times, 'that you couldn't help thinking how it was going to end.'

There has been understandable resistance to the idea that AIDS is 'caused' by promiscuity. 'Life-styles don't kill people — germs do', says the New York pamphlet (perhaps a conscious echo of the National Rifle Association's maxim, 'Guns don't kill people — people do'). One vein of paranoia extends to the view that the epidemic was initiated by the CIA as a form of biological warfare. Certainly the profile of the high-risk groups — the 5-H club — is politically effaced. As Larry Kramer, the author of one of five plays about AIDS recently staged in Manhattan, has pointed out: 'The lowliest of streetsweeper associations has twenty-five lobbyists in Washington, and we [24 million Americans] have one part-timer.' If the AIDS virus had chosen, say, real-estate agents or young mothers for attack, then the medical and social context would now look very different. Yet AIDS has chosen homosexual men. The proportion will certainly decrease (and the African epidemic has shown no sexual preference at all), but so far it has remained fairly steady at around 70 per cent.

Throughout the past decade, in New York, gay men were oppressed by an escalating series of health hazards. To begin with, crabs, gonorrhoea and syphilis, the ancient enemies. Then herpes, then cytomegalovirus, then gay-bowel syndrome, then hepatitis B. All venereal diseases compromise the immune system. And so, crucially, does semen. The vagina is evolutionarily designed to deactivate the antigens in semen, the foreign elements which stimulate the production of antibodies. The rectum does the opposite: it is designed to withdraw water from faeces, and so efficiently absorbs antigenic matter through the rectal walls. At each reception the immune system goes on red alert. Ironically, it too becomes paranoid. Repeated reception, repeated infection and repeated trauma prolong the crisis until the cells lose the capacity to correct their own over-corrections. The analogy is as much with cervical cancer as with standard sexual disease. Again, the double bind. It seems that there is a 'natural' – i.e. viciously arbitrary – limit to trauma, to bodily invasion.

There are two lines of thought. One is the single-factor or new-virus theory. This has always been more acceptable to the gay population because it passes no verdict and necessitates no change. The second theory is multi-factorial, the theory of immune-overload, which was immediately perceived in America as 'judgmental', suggesting also that the visitation of AIDS was not a bolt from the blue but a process or a journey. The virus – a retrovirus of a type found only in animals – has been cautiously identified. Yet it seems clear that the two theories are not mutually exclusive; indeed, they go hand in hand.

The secret may lie in an uncertainty principle, in the balance or *potentia* between two factors: the strength of the virus and the weakness of the host. A damaged immune system is susceptible to the AIDS virus, which then destroys that system, so inviting opportunistic infection. Some epidemiologists believe that AIDS is an ancient and world-wide disease of poverty (ineradicable by medicine alone), given passage into society at large through the incubation chambers of the bathhouses. In a sense, perhaps AIDS itself is opportunistic. This is the double jeopardy.

The Gay Men's Health Crisis Centre is just off rugged Eighth Avenue; but the offices are neat, modern, positively *bijou*. Up on the bulletin board is a list of the day's meetings: Volunteer Moral Committee, Care Partner Group One. There are bottle-glass partitions, basketed plants. I asked for the AIDS-information kit and was given a hefty dossier of facts and figures, dos and don'ts, posters and leaflets. The soft-voiced, tiptoeing advisers talk to the worried supplicants, like waiters in a gentle gay restaurant. 'Win With Us', says the slogan on the donation tin. 'We're Winning', says a pamphlet, ' ... Together. We're winning ... Through Respect'.

There are buddy programs, therapy groups, crisis counsellors, PR men. 'Our community keeps on fighting. Keeps on caring. Keeps on loving.' Here they are coping in the American way.

The British equivalent of GMHC, the Terence Higgins Trust, is at first as unwelcoming as its address: Block E, Room 10, number 38, on a street inaccurately called Mount Pleasant, near the Gray's Inn Road. Once you have blundered about a bit in this old warehouse, you enter the tiny, bumf-crammed office of THT. As the outpost in a revolution of consciousness and the epicentre in the fight against a latent epidemic, the premises are not immediately reassuring. But funds, private and public, are gathering, and Tony Whitehead, Chair of the Trust, is clearly exceptionally able and sympathetic. Until a year ago he was running the entire operation from his own flat. This is the English way: under-financed, under-organised, genially yet resolutely philanthropic.

Lessons have been well taken from the American experience. There are buddy-systems here too, and they are needed: the personal complications are often drastic. AIDS, with its usual double thrust, attacks the brain and nervous system of the hugely stressed patient, bringing about violent personality changes. The epidemic has so far followed the American graph, though the curve is unlikely to be as steep. The bathhouses and sex clubs of Manhattan are simply illegal here; and our new generation of junkies tend to sniff the stuff rather than mainline it. Even so there could be 10,000 cases by the end of the decade. And the THT will itself be the size of a hospital.

The DHSS withstood a lot of criticism, here and in America, when it took on powers to detain and quarantine AIDS sufferers. John Patten, the junior Health Minister, was quick to dismiss any fears of official panic or overkill. 'Good God, the last thing we want to do is start rounding people up.' The new ruling has been invoked only once: in Portsmouth, where a distracted AIDS patient was haemorrhaging in the street. Patten is addressing his task in discreet and avuncular fashion; he seemed quite unaware of gay sexual realities (believing, for instance, that 'fisting' was some form of spanking); but it is not the British way to look too closely at these matters, nor to sanitise them with the jargon of toleration. We shall all muddle through. One thing we do have (for the time being anyway): we have the National Health.

Meanwhile, everything has changed. *Being gay* – which Americans call a life-choice, and which we might perhaps call a destiny — is a different proposition now. But so is the other route, as AIDS becomes a part of the heterosexual experience. The liberation of coitus, the rutting revolution, has probably entered its last phase. When the danger is ultimate, then every risk is ultimate also. It is *over*.

Despite new genetic technologies, any cure or prevention is probably some way ahead. 'We have anti-virals which *seem* to inhibit the retrovirus which *seems* to have a linchpin role,' I was informed at the AIDS Medical Foundation in New York. 'Prospects are uncertain bordering on grim.' The vaccine for hepatitis B took seventeen years.

But some hope can be rescued from the mess, the human disaster of AIDS. The disease will probably obey Darwinian rules and seek an evolutionarily stable strategy, becoming less virulent, non-fatal. The cure, when and if it comes, will revolutionise medicine. Sexual relations of all kinds will soften, and the emphasis will shift from performance, from sexual muscle. Gay leaders prudently stress the need for trust, for confidentiality in the liaison between the various communities. In the short term, of course, they are absolutely right. But a better situation would clearly be one in which no confidentiality is necessary.

AIDS victims are in the forefront, at the very pinnacle of human suffering. Broadly speaking, they can do you no harm unless you elect to go to bed with them. We are in this together now. An opportunity presents itself. There is no good reason — only a lot of bad ones — why we shouldn't take it.

Observer 1985

*   *   *

Postscript This piece was written under unusual pressures. Early 1985 was the time when the British tabloids locked on to AIDS. Twice a week the headlines yelped of gay plagues and black deaths, blighted babies, panicking health workers, proposed quarantine, homosexual apartheid. I very much wanted not to add to the grief and vulnerability of the gay population, and I was greatly relieved when the piece went down well in that quarter, and also with the medical community.

Here is a minor, and personal, illustration of the ease with which one can get 'politicised' by such sensitive matters. A week after the

AIDS piece appeared I was proudly reading a short story of mine, newly published though written months earlier. To my horror (and the shock was physical, dizzying, armpit-igniting) I saw that I − or my Jewish-American narrator − had used the word 'faggots'! The locution was right for the narrator and right for the story; but I shouldn't have used it. Not *now*, I thought. Already, after a few months, I have relapsed somewhat and would probably defend the original phrase (the story, after all, was set in 1980: pre-AIDS); but I won't forget the seizure of remorse when my eye fell on *faggots*. I also began to understand the American tendency to euphemise with jargon, and its misplaced homage to the power of the word.

Looking into AIDS taught me other things too. I had never read any medical literature before; and I am here to tell you, if you don't already know, that with or without AIDS there is a dictionary ten feet wide full of stuff that is just raring to screw you up. Secondly, I discovered I knew nothing whatever about homosexuality. Having learned a bit, I now find the condition, the fate, the destiny much more interesting, much more sympathetic − and much, much stranger. I had never registered the *otherness*. Nor, it seemed, had anyone else. The article caused a certain amount of unease and hesitation at the *Observer*, which, with the *Guardian*, is the most liberal and humanistic newspaper in Britain. Those traditions quickly prevailed and the piece appeared as planned, though with one or two changes and in an atmosphere of worry. I was obliged to amend 'fucking queer' to 'filthy queer' in the first paragraph; and I had to bowdlerise the description of how the rectum deals with bodily fluids. The first change was routine but the second change puzzled me at the time. Agreed, the rectum's job is not a particularly glamorous one; yet someone has to do it. Why this resistance to corporeal truth? Even in a near-impeccably enlightened institution like the *Observer* I glimpsed a measure of the intransigence, the reluctance to know, felt by society at large.

Anyway, I thought I played the whole thing down. AIDS is more frightening and catastrophic than I chose − or was able − to suggest. But I have enough imagination, and enough health anxieties of my own, to guess at the feelings of the sufferer, lying in the sawdust of his defences, with nothing between him and the wind and the rain. Also, I believe AIDS will emerge as an evolutionary trauma, a tactical defeat for the species. Sex and death have never before been linked in this way, except by the poets. The ancient venereal diseases were fatal but late-acting: plenty of things could kill you before syphilis did. Perhaps the only remote analogy is an exclusively feminine one: not cervical cancer, but childbirth. Now, with AIDS, the opportunities for human distrust are boundless.

As for 1985, it took more than non-yellow journalism to ease society through to the next stage in its understanding, its confrontation with AIDS. It took Rock Hudson, a figure with the necessary TV-and-tabloid constituency, someone whose face we had known all our lives. People are now infinitesimally more receptive to the truth, and this is a start. But it will be a long and wretched road.

Saul Bellow in Chicago

The room at the Quality Inn was large and cheap, with thermal drapes and barebacked plugs. All it lacked was quality. But I stood at the very centre of what Saul Bellow has called 'the contempt center of the USA'; and the view was enthralling.

From my window I could see a Christian Science church that looked like a hydroelectric plant, the corncobs of two vertical parking lots, a stilted Marina Bank and the limousine glass of IBM Plaza, the El train, a slow roller-coaster, churning round the bend. Just over the crest stood the abandoned University of Chicago building, a charred, black-stoned old scraper, its golden turret like the crown of a tooth. Just below lay Sheldon's, prominently offering 'Art Material – *for the artist in everyone*'. On the telephone I arranged to meet the Nobel Laureate in the Chicago Arts Club at one o'clock. He would be identifiable, he cheerfully informed me, 'by certain signs of decay'.

I felt more than averagely nervous at the prospect of tackling this particular Great American Writer. I wondered why. After all, I've done quite a few of these guys by now. I knew that Bellow was no manipulator, eccentric or vaudevillian. He wouldn't be poleaxed by a hangover, as was Truman Capote. He wouldn't open proceedings with a het-taunting joke, as did Gore Vidal ('Oh to be in England', drawled Gore, 'now that England's here'). He wouldn't be a model of diffidence and sweet reason, as Norman Mailer had been, then later denounce me as 'a wimp' on British TV. Joseph Heller was all brawny and jovial self-absorption. Kurt Vonnegut was delightfully dreamy – a natural man, but a natural crackpot too.

Saul Bellow, I suspected, would speak in the voice I knew from the novels: funny, fluent and profound. A bit worrying, that. This business of writing about writers is more ambivalent than the end-product normally admits. As a fan and a reader, you want your hero to be genuinely inspirational. As a journalist, you hope for lunacy, spite, deplorable indiscretions, a full-scale nervous break-down in mid-interview. And, as a human, you yearn for the birth of a flattering friendship. All very shaming, I thought, as I crossed the dun Chicago River, my eyes streaming in the mineral wind.

One final complication: whereas the claims of his contemporaries remain more or less unresolved, Saul Bellow really is a great American writer. I think that in a sense he is the writer that the twentieth century has been waiting for. The present phase of Western literature is inescapably one of 'higher autobiography', intensely self-inspecting. The phase began with the spittle of Con-fessionalism but has steadied and persisted. No more stories: the author is increasingly committed to the private being. With all sorts of awkwardnesses and rough edges and extraordinary expansions, supremely well-equipped, erudite and humorous, Bellow has made his own experience resonate more memorably than any living writer. And yet he is also the first to come out the other side of this process, hugely strengthened to contemplate the given world.

Our meeting took place in the fourth week of October 1983. The previous Sunday 230 US marines had died in the Beirut suicide bombing. The Grenadan intervention was in its second day. It was crisis week – but every week is crisis week. Arguing in wide concentric loops, Bellow needed no prompting.

The adventure in Grenada, he said, was an opportunist PR exercise, designed to atone for, or divert attention from, the disaster in Lebanon. Reagan was helplessly wedged between specialist advice and public opinion. 'Experts' simply act in accordance with the prevailing standards of their profession. You get no morality from them: 'all you get is – "But everyone else does it."' After settling post-war Europe, America was pleased with her new responsibilities and felt she had marvellously matured. 'Not global policeman so much as Little Mary Fixit.' The US shows a persistent determination to 'angelise' herself. No moral ideas; instead, a conviction of her own purity. Pro-good, anti-bad, and right by definition.

Public opinion is in the hands of the media-managers: in other words, it is in the hands of TV, which is 'ugly, ignorant, self-righteous and terrifyingly influential'. This week the television screen throngs with bereaved families, each granted (and fully embracing) its sixty seconds of prime-time crack-up. A mother weeps over a framed photograph: 'My baby. Where is my baby?' A father wrings his hands: 'I say to him, Louie — don't go! Don't go!' By the end of the week the news shows will feature the obliging hysterics of the 'rescued' medical students from Grenada. Meanwhile, the American CO explains: 'We were not micro-managing Grenada intelligencewise until about that time-frame.'

'Oh bad!' as one Bellow hero puts it — 'Very bad!' President Reagan, TV-tested, is the latest face in 'a long gallery of dumb-bells'. As another Bellow hero remarks: 'Today's psychiatrists would not be shocked. Asked whom they love best, their patients reply in increasing numbers, "My dog." At this rate, a dog in the White House becomes a real possibility.'

So far as Bellow is concerned, however, the 'crisis' is general and omnipresent. 'For the first time in history', he wrote in his analytical memoir *To Jerusalem and Back*, 'the human species as a whole has gone into politics . . . What is going on will not let us alone. Neither the facts nor the deformations.' The result is interminable 'event-glamour', 'crisis-chatter'. That word *crisis* is part of the crisis. The crises are part of the crisis. And you can't see the crisis for the crises.

Mr Bellow was identifiable, in the anteroom of the Arts Club, not by certain signs of decay but by his dapper, compact figure and by his expression — one of courteous vigilance. I clutched a copy of *The Dean's December*, Bellow's latest novel, which I was re-rereading. 'As you see,' he said, when we filed into the dining-room, 'it's not an arts club at all.' Indeed, this snazzy private restaurant was one of the many examples I encountered of Chicago's flirtatious or parodic attitude to high culture. 'There's a Braque, a de Kooning, a Matisse drawing. But it's just a lunch club for elegant housewives.'

Bellow is sixty-eight. His hair is white and peripheral but the eyes are still the colour of expensive snuff. Generous yet combative, the mouth is low-slung, combining with the arched brows to give his face an animated roundness. In repose the face is squarer, harder. He looks like an omniscient tortoise. According to *Humboldt's Gift*, America is proud of what it does to its writers, the way it breaks and bedevils them, rendering them deluded or drunken or dead by their own hands. To overpower its tender spirits makes America feel tough. Careers are generally short. Over here, writers aren't meant to be as sane as Bellow persists in being, or as determined to have his say, in full.

He once told a prospective biographer (who wrote a whole book on his failure to write a book on Bellow): 'What can you reveal about me that I haven't already revealed about myself?' In the novels Bellow's surrogates have their vanities and blind spots (Herzog is 'not kind', Sammler was 'never especially kind'), their brainstorms and dizzy spells. Sanity, like freedom, like American democracy — he suggests — is a fragile and perhaps temporary condition. It is clear from his books, his history, his face, that Bellow has weathered considerable turbulence. As soon as you start scrutinising a writer's life (however monumental or exemplary its achievements may be), that life quickly takes on a human shape — only human, all too human.

Apart from the ingratiation, the danger of becoming a cultural functionary, the extra mail ('suddenly even more people think that what I want to do is read their manuscripts'), Bellow is appalled by the 'micro-inspection' to which Nobel Prizewinners are subject. 'One is asked to bare one's scars to the crowd, like Coriolanus.' Well, it is all in the novels, at one remove or another, for the not-so-idly curious. There you will find a moral autodidact, slowly crystallised and moving steadily now to 'the completion of his reality'.

Which is? 'Ignorance of death is destroying us,' Bellow has said. 'Death is the dark backing a mirror needs if we are to see anything.' A well-lived life leaves you on 'sober decent terms with death'; if you are a writer, though, it leaves you more than that. *The Dean's December* inaugurates Bellow's 'late' period but *Mr Sammler's Planet* prefigured it — old Sammler, with his 'farewell detachment', his 'earth-departure-objectivity': 'the luxury of non-intimidation by doom'. Bellow looks set to enjoy a Yeatsian old age. Just let him finish.

Chicago — 'huge, filthy, brilliant and mean' — is hardly a hermit's cot, yet in a sense Bellow belongs to the reclusive or spectral tradition of Frost, Salinger and Pynchon. The philistinism, the 'hardboiled-dom' of the place provides the sort of insulation which an American writer sheds at his peril. 'The main thing about Chicago is that it's not New York. There are no writers to talk to in

New York, only celebrities on exhibit.' His determination to stand aloof (especially from the youth-worshipping campus-fever of the Sixties) has moved certain pundits to label him as a reactionary. Was it fastidiousness or vocational sense that had kept him out of public debate?

'I now think I was probably wrong,' he said. 'Things are going down so fast, I think maybe I should have been involved all along. As for Vietnam, I went on record. But the war could be identified as an evil by Americans because it was packaged by television and was therefore comprehensible to an entertainment society. Other evils, money-mania, corruption, urban vileness — these are not package-able.' Out there in Chicago, as Bellow has written, lie 'many, many square miles of civil Passchendaele or Somme'.

What is the content of these data?

1. In Cabrini Green, the black housing project, a man butchers a hog in his apartment, and then throws the guts on the stairs. A woman slips and breaks her arm. In the ambulance 'she was smeared with pig's blood and shriller than the siren'.

2. In 'ratshit Woodlawn' old people scavenge for food behind the supermarkets. The store guards try to keep them off lest they poison themselves with spoiled fish, and then sue.

3. A black youth leaves his car in the parking lot of the courthouse, where he attends a hearing on a rape charge. In the boot of his Pontiac lies a young housewife, kidnapped at gun-point. Every few hours he takes her out and rapes her. Two days later he shoots her in a vacant lot and covers her body with trash.

These horror stories, and many more, appear in *The Dean's December*, in which Bellow contrasts the super-licensed rat-jungle of Chicago with the 'penitentiary society' of Bucharest. Citing Rilke's wartime letters, the Dean observes that there is no effective language for the large-scale terrors; during such times 'the heart must hang in the dark', and wait. But there is a countervailing urge 'to send the soul out into society', 'to see at first hand the big manifestations of disorder and take a fresh reading from them'. The result is head-spin, heart-fever. And the conclusion he reaches is that America now has an 'underclass', lost populations expected, even encouraged, to dispose of themselves with junk, poison and Saturday-night specials.

I asked Bellow how he had assembled his litany of depradation. Did he trudge round the jails, the hospitals, the projects? The process is largely an imaginative one, but it is a process much simplified in classless, dollar-driven, magimixed Chicago. 'The corruption is everywhere. You can say this for Chicago — there's no hypocrisy problem here. There's no *need* for hypocrisy. Everyone's *proud* of being a bastard . . . You just meet all these guys. You went to school with them. I used to play basketball with a Machine executioner. He lives out in Miami now. Quietly.'

Rather than dig up some of Bellow's more reliable academic pals, I went to see an old schoolfriend of his, a criminal lawyer whom I had better call Iggy. He was friendly. We were soon on first-name terms. 'You come all the way from *London* to talk with Saul?' he asked. Yes, it takes all sorts. Pushing seventy, pouchy, paunchy, yet still ignited with the American vigour, Iggy elegantly explained that there might be the odd 'telephonic interruption' from his clients — the fuddled rapists, bail-jumpers and drug-dealers he represented. At once there was a telephonic interruption. I looked round the file-heaped office. Lawyers Make It Stand Up In Court, said a sign. 'Will you *shut up* and listen?' said Iggy to his client.

Iggy and Saul studied at Tuley High. 'Ninety per cent of us came from illiterate immigrant families. They had a wonderful faculty corps there. At the last reunion dinner we had Saul come along. And you know? Of that 90 per cent, 90 per cent of them — no, 98 per cent — had made it. We'd all made it.'

Bellow had also told me about Tuley High. Fleeing the pogroms, his parents had left St Petersburg (he calls it 'Pettersburg') for Montreal in 1913. Bellow himself arrived two years later, the only child of four to be born on the far side of the Atlantic. (His writing, one reflects, has much of the candour, the adultness of the Russian voice.) In 1924 they moved to Chicago, to the slums of the Northwest Side. Bellow's father was an onion-dealer and part-time bootlegger.

'There was something oppressive', said Bellow, 'about being an alien, a hybrid — but then everyone was. You knew you were always going to have dirt under your fingernails, but this is a natural twentieth-century feeling. There was no bar to learning. And I wondered — by what right or title was I reading great books, while also discovering America: pool halls, ball parks. It was one of the worst slums in Chicago. By the time I was twelve, I had seen *everything*.' During the Depression the likes of Saul and Iggy lived off welfare hand-outs and municipal IOUs. 'But we came through,' Iggy affirmed. 'Even during that bad time we were full of energy and hope. We made it.'

I asked Iggy what he thought of Bellow's portrayal of Chicago chicanery. 'When it comes to corruption in Chicago', he said with deep satisfaction, 'Saul is a child. It's much *much* worse than he says.' Iggy ought to know. He was disbarred and jailed, after a lucrative misunderstanding, many years ago. 'In my opinion', he said, 'the best of Saul's titles is *The Dangling Man* [sic]. I have the first edition. Someone told me it's worth $400! When he dies it'll be worth even more. So I say to Saul, I say, "When you gonna die!"'

Has Iggy made it? His generation was among the most amibitious and resilient that America has ever produced. The slums of the Northwest Side still exist, but there aren't many bookish Russians and Czechs and Poles queueing on the library steps. They watch TV these days. And they're all just Americans now.

The next evening I met up with Bellow at the Cultural Center in the Old Library Building. 'Today's Activities', said the billboard wistfully: 'Chicago as a Literary City'. I had spent the day strolling round Chicago and wondering what literature or art or culture could seriously be expected to do about the place.

'The Dorm That Dripped Blood' announced the cinema sign. 'The Hounds of Hell DOGS LEAPING UP AT YOU IN 3D'. In the beanery thin old ladies in tracksuits serve enormous meals to the working people of Chicago, tribally gruff, hoarse, one-lining. 'I switched from Ultrason to Coherent,' booms a diner. Does he mean corporations or cigarette brands? At the next table a young couple discuss a portly paperback. 'I'm getting into Kate now,' says the girl. 'Kate's gonna marry Greg. That's what I think. Or David. She's pregnint but she won't make a commitmint.'

I went to see the Impressionist collection at the Art Institute. It rivals that of the Jeu de Paume — but there is a tangible air of donation, patronage, social power, all the tax-exempt American money that goes into religion, opera, academic quangos, writing fellowships. A highschool teacher was telling her class about

Seurat's *La Grande Jette*. 'It's set on a hot afternoon in Paris a century ago, long before air-conditioning. So what people used to do was, they . . . ' A businessman stared at a Monet. 'First class,' he decided, before moving on.

At the Cultural Center we sat and listened to Karl Schapiro as he read from his uncompleted autobiography. It was the same story: the young poet, working in a department store all day, reading and dreaming all night. When he grew up, he edited *Poetry Chicago*. Later there was a reception, with wine ('compliments of *Nit & Wit* magazine') and snacks ('supplied by Orange Products'). In his rusty checked suit Bellow resembled an appropriate cross between a distinguished man of letters and a retired gangster. I hung back as he greeted Schapiro, an old friend.

'Saul Bellow's here,' said a lady behind me. 'Where?' asked her companion. 'You're looking right at him . . . Mm, give me a Sidney Sheldon or a Harold Robbins. I don't want to be taxed too much.' 'Me neither. Give me a Ken Follett.' 'Give me a Herman Wouk.'

Bellow came over. He talked about the library, how its stack had been relocated, how the Byzantine splendours of its staircase and dome were now no more than a sentimental husk. He used to come here daily as a boy, for his Aristotle, Shakespeare, Spinoza, Tolstoy. Then I said, 'I think I know how I want to end my piece — with the question, "What then must you do?" But there's no real answer, is there?'

The previous day Bellow had filled me in on what he called 'the American search for personal form'. Whitman said that poets would one day tell Americans how to be adults. 'But this is not an art society. It is a money society, a pleasure society.' Most Americans — 'in an amorphous state, demanding forms for themselves' — now regard novels as how-to books about life, or about life-style. The writer is no curer of souls; he is on the level of the etiquette page and advice to the lovelorn. The busiest sections of the Chicago bookstores, I noticed, were those marked 'Personal Growth'.

'One must go on. No. One must go further.' Aware of all the prescriptive dangers, Bellow nonetheless believes that the time has come for serious (i.e. talented) writers to be serious, without losing lyricism or laughter. 'No more novels about adolescence, career problems, sexual adventure, wounded ethnicity.' Why not address 'the mysterious circumstance of being', and say what it's like to be alive at this time, on this planet? Then you depend on a process of seepage. That is all you can really hope for.

'We are usually waiting', writes Bellow, 'for somebody to clear out and let us go on with the business of life (to cultivate the little obsessional garden).'

And I was relieved, in a way, to be off his case. I survived a vast and inedible fish platter and a near-mugging under the El as I walked back to the Quality Inn. Actually it was more like an aggressive demand for charity, only slightly sharper than its London equivalent. The black youth waved a train timetable in front of me and did a spiel about missing his stop. 'So are you gonna help me out? Have you got a dollar?' 'That depends,' I wanted to say. 'Have you got a gun?' But I walked past his tough stare, without paying my dues.

In the hotel lobby a small black boy sat waiting for his mother to come off shift. He read out loud from his book: 'Help. Help. I axed . . . I axed the man to help me out. I'm stuck in the mud. Help me out. I'd help *you*.' Some days your life feels like a short story — or is it just the travel, and the preoccupation? This morning, even the black, bent, bald shoeshiner who slicked my boots with his fingers (he had his name on his breast, in capitals) was called ART.

In my room I looked out *The Dean's December* and re-read the passage about Toby Winthrop. Based on a real Chicagoan, Winthrop is a black ex-junkie and reformed Mob murderer who now runs a detoxification centre on the South Side. The Dean goes to see him:

A dirty snow brocade over the empty lots, and black men keeping warm at oil-drum bonfires. He parked and got out of the car feeling the lack of almost everything you needed, humanly. Christ, the human curve had sunk down to base level, had gone beneath it . . . Winthrop's office window was heavily covered in flowered drapes of pink and green. The body of this powerful man was significantly composed in the executive leather chair. If you had met him in the days when he was a paid executioner, if he had been waiting for you on a staircase, in an alley, you would never have escaped him. He would have killed you, easy . . . Until now Winthrop had sat immobile, but now he turned and began to lower himself towards the floor. What was he doing? He was on his knees, his big arm stretched toward the floor, his fingers hooked upwards. 'You see what we have to do? Those people are down in the cesspool. We reach for them and try to get a hold. Hang on — hang on! They'll drown in the shit if we can't pull 'em out ... they're marked out to be destroyed. Those are people meant to die, sir. That's what we are looking at.'

Many times in Bellow's novels we are reminded that 'being human' isn't the automatic condition of every human being. Like freedom or sanity, it is not a given but a gift, a talent, an accomplishment, an objective. In achieving it, some will need more time or thought or help. And, put that way, it doesn't sound too hard a lesson to learn.

Observer 1983